9P07
c2
11561
B10
46485

SOLO PRACTICE

BOOKS BY ELIZABETH MORGAN, M.D.

The Making of a Woman Surgeon
Solo Practice: A Woman Surgeon's Story

SOLO PRACTICE

A Woman Surgeon's Story

Elizabeth Morgan, M.D.

LITTLE, BROWN AND COMPANY
BOSTON · TORONTO

FIRST EDITION

LIBRARY OF CONGRESS CATALOGING IN PUBLICATION DATA

Morgan, Elizabeth, 1947–
  Solo practice.

  1. Morgan, Elizabeth, 1947–   . 2. Plastic
surgeons—United States—Biography. 3. Women
surgeons—United States—Biography. 4. Surgeons—
United States—Biography. I. Title.
RD27.35.M65A37   617′.95′00924 [B]   81–20713
ISBN 0-316-58298-0   AACR2

MV
Designed by Dale Cotton
*Published simultaneously in Canada
by Little, Brown & Company (Canada) Limited*

PRINTED IN THE UNITED STATES OF AMERICA

*This book is dedicated
to my brothers, Jim and Rob*

Contents

Acknowledgments

I would like to thank Clare Ring for helping me make my practice possible; my mother for standing by; Jacqueline Hoff for typing the manuscript; Molly Friedrich, my literary agent, and Genevieve Young, my editor, for their advice, encouragement, and criticism. I would also like to thank all the doctors and nurses who have helped me get started in my practice. Finally, I would like to thank my patients, who had confidence in me when I was just starting out.

The names of all people except my family and Mrs. Ring have been disguised in this book, as have the names of all hospitals. Any resemblance of a name to that of a real person or hospital is entirely accidental.

SOLO PRACTICE

1

I Am a
Plastic Surgeon

IT was nine o'clock on a Thursday morning. I am a plastic surgeon in solo practice and as usual I would be spending all day Thursday in the office, seeing patients. Today I was a few minutes early as I drove up to the back entrance of my brick townhouse office. It had rained during the night and my feet squelched in the wet grass between the parking lot and the back door. For the hundredth time, I made a mental note to get someone to build a short brick path to the back entrance so I wouldn't constantly ruin my shoes. By the time I had opened the door — balancing my camera and my surgical instruments under one arm, turning the key with the other hand, and clenching a paper cup with coffee from McDonald's between my teeth — I had forgotten the brick walkway once again.

A year before, I had hated my plastic-surgery practice. Back then I was really too busy to think — too busy to care about my patients, much too busy for any life of my own. I did seventeen to twenty operations a week, saw thirty patients on an afternoon; my office regularly ran two hours or more late, and while my patients waited in despair to see me, I began to wonder why I had gone through seven grueling

3

years of surgical training with sleepless nights, low pay, and a ceaseless barrage of criticism in order to spend the rest of my life doing what I didn't want to do — be an overworked, irritable surgeon, too busy to be a good doctor and with no time to be a real person. At last I had a flash of common sense and abruptly reordered my practice and my life. Feeling guilty, and afraid I would never earn enough to pay the overhead, I restricted my operating time, limited my emergency duty, and doubled the time I set aside for each patient.

It worked, though I still feel a jolt when I walk into the office and think back. But now I'm happy to be there, anxious to see my patients, knowing I will enjoy it. Once people seemed to ask too many questions. Now I have time to talk with them. I have time to explain the pros and cons. Virtually no question a patient asks before surgery is foolish.

By the time I got upstairs this Thursday morning, my first patient had arrived. Alexis was a young woman with the air of a scarlet tanager — gentle with a dash of the exotic. She had small hands and a delicate face, large and trusting eyes, and she wore a bright orange and black dress with a swirling skirt.

"Won't you come in?" I said, ushering her into my consulting room. Surreptitiously, I studied her face. My heart sank when I saw her nose. Alexis had come to see me about her nose. It was a small, well-shaped nose, slightly curved to one side. As she sat down, I studied her profile. It was perfect. This was terrible. The hardest thing in plastic surgery is to try to perfect the nearly perfect nose. There is a surgical axiom: "Perfection is the enemy of good." A good nose can be disfigured by overzealous surgery in pursuit of an elusive ideal. Alexis sat down in the blue velvet chair opposite my desk, arranged her skirt, and leaned back.

"I want to see you about my nose," she began nervously.

"I know. Why don't you tell me everything first and I'll

4

ask questions as we go along." I sat down behind my desk and pulled up a pad to make notes.

"Five years ago I had a nose surgeon do my nose. It was too big and I didn't like it, so he operated. Maybe he butchered it. I don't know, but about three years later it began to curve. He wasn't a plastic surgeon. He was an ear-nose-and-throat surgeon. Was that a mistake?"

"No. He did a good job on your nose. It is by no means butchered. Both plastic surgeons and ENT surgeons can do nose operations. None of us gets perfect results all the time."

"That's good. Anyhow, my nose started to curve about two years ago and it stayed curved. Is there anything you can do about it?"

I got up from my desk and sat beside her to study her nose closely, and then handed her a mirror.

"You look into it so we know we're talking about the same thing. The top is curved, here."

"Yes." She studied herself. "My profile is all right. It's the front view."

"Your profile is excellent. The dorsum — that is, the top of your nose — is certainly slightly curved, though not enough to consider it deformed."

I studied her nose again, and we both said almost in unison, "The tip is a little too long and a little too high."

We laughed and I returned to my desk.

"Good. Now we know the problem. Tell me, did your nose really curve suddenly after three years?"

"My sister-in-law said it was curved ever since the operation," admitted Alexis, "but it only started to bother me later."

"That makes sense. Usually it is curved a bit. Then the curve becomes more noticeable. Have you seen your original surgeon about it?"

"Yes," admitted Alexis. "That's why I came to you. He

said it would be very, very easy to fix and he would guarantee it would be straight."

"Absolutely not. Nothing can be guaranteed."

"I know, so I went to a plastic surgeon, and he really depressed me. He said my nose was ruined, that he'd have to break the bones and start over again and it might end up looking even worse."

I took Alexis to the examining room and examined inside her nose carefully. The inside was blocked and, not surprisingly, she said she had trouble breathing. That bothered her as much as the curve.

"All right," I said, "now I'll tell you what I think. I fall halfway between what the other two surgeons have told you. There is no way it would be easy to make your nose straight. At the same time, your nose is much too good to try anything radical." She nodded. "Your trouble breathing will probably be much improved by removing the deformed cartilage inside your nose. Working on the inside cartilage may help to correct the curve. During the same operation, I can also do a bit of carving at the tip to improve it a tiny bit. I will not do much because it looks good already, but it may make the difference you want. Now, to give you the best chance of a straight nose means putting a graft of cartilage inside to straighten it, but that may make your nose look less delicate and broader. What I suggest is that you let me work on the inside to correct your breathing and try to straighten it, but I'll save a piece of cartilage in case someday you want to take the risk of a cartilage graft to straighten your nose. I can store that cartilage under your skin, behind your ear."

"Whew." She held up her hands in protest. "Let me get this straight. You remove some of the inside cartilage to help my breathing, and try at the same time to straighten the nose and tip from the inside?" I nodded, and she went on. "What you take out you put under the skin of my ear in case my nose doesn't straighten out and I want to try a graft in it later?"

"Correct. It's the only way I can think of to improve your breathing and give you the chance of a straight nose without the risk of trying to rebuild your nose, which, seriously, may really ruin it."

"It may straighten my nose a bit, but there isn't the risk of ruining it? Maybe I should do that."

"I won't let you make up your mind right now," I warned her. "Number one" — I ticked the items off on my fingers — "I want you to go home and think about it, because I can't promise anything. Your nose may be as curved as ever or improved so little that only you can tell. Number two, talk about it with someone else — your parents, your best friend, anyone you want. Number three, come back and talk a second time. You'll have questions I haven't answered, and also I want to go over the possible complications again and do a physical exam before the operation, if you decide to have it done. I'd rather have you decide against the surgery than make a snap decision that you regret after the operation."

She hesitated for a moment. "Okay. That's good. Can my mother call you if she has questions? You know what mothers are like."

"She can call anytime."

As it turned out, a month later Alexis did have the surgery, and her nose, while still not completely straight, improved enough to please her — and me. I loved my restructured practice. I loved my patients and the problems they posed — from the delicacy of Alexis's nose to the bloody challenge of putting together the hand of an impatient man who forgetfully shoved it into a running lawnmower. I had time for my patients and enough time for myself.

"I can't believe how happy I am," I said one evening to Clare, my secretary, as I leaned back in a chair in the waiting room and put my feet up at the end of a long day. "I'm so damned lucky I can't stand it. I have everything. I'm even a fellow of the American College of Surgeons. I got the notice in the mail today."

"You had a rough time getting here," said Clare with a smile. A very pretty woman in her fifties, with a soft voice and a soft smile to match, Clare had been with me ever since I had started my solo practice three years before. "Don't forget about Dr. Tewkesbury. Until this year, it's been a constant battle."

She was right. It had been hard.

In a sense my private practice began the day I finished my seven years of surgical residency in the Midwest. I felt like a slave set free. But I had no income and almost no savings. I knew virtually none of the Washington area doctors — no one to look to for help or advice in getting started there. Worst of all, I was a plastic surgeon about to go into private practice, and the message from the local plastic surgeons was already clear: I wasn't needed. I wasn't wanted. There were too many plastic surgeons in Washington already.

A lot of people think, rather patronizingly, that plastic surgery is "a good field for a woman" — as though plastic surgeons are overpriced beauticians. Some believe I "escaped" into plastic surgery because the demands are few and money comes easily. Actually, plastic surgery is not an easy field for a woman or for a man. It appeals to me because of its scope. It doesn't confine me to children, as in pediatrics, or to women, as in gynecology, or even to one part of the body, as in heart surgery. Plastic surgery involves reconstruction — fixing the body, putting it back together again — in children with birth defects, teenagers with maimed legs from motorcycle accidents, workers with fractured hands, housewives who have lost a breast in cancer surgery. Plastic surgery is a fascinating, diverse field, and results, good or bad, are visible. I can know when I do things wrong — or right.

I started my surgical training in 1971, a month after I graduated from medical school. I was by no means the only woman who wanted to be a surgeon. Nora and Heather, classmates from medical school, became surgeons too.

As a surgical intern, I first thought I wanted to be an orthopedic surgeon. An orthopod needs a lot of strength to work with the "big bones" — knees, hips, backs. I discovered I wasn't strong enough, and I was surprised to find bones bored me. After putting on a cast or fixing bones with glue and metal and nails, you then have to wait for months to see if they heal. I am too impatient. Orthopedics was not the field for me. I liked heart surgery, but you can't be close to your patients if you're a heart surgeon. You're too busy. As a heart surgeon, you sew new valves or blood vessels into the quivering heart as it sloshes about in iced salt water after you've split the chest with a saw and held it open with metal retractors. If the heart starts up again at the end of surgery, you've done a good job and you are happy. But it's your team of cardiologists, residents, and nurses who keep the patient alive after surgery. I decided the specialty was too remote to suit me for the rest of my life. Hearts alone were not enough.

One morning in my second year of surgical training, I operated with a plastic surgeon, Dr. Owen, for the first time. Using a scalpel and a saw, he took off half a patient's cancerous tongue and lower jaw.

"Don't get sick," he warned me as he passed the jawbone with the tongue dangling from it to a nurse. "There's more to come."

I was looking directly into the patient's throat. Half of his face was gone — the skin sagged inward where the jaw and cheek had once been — and I was appalled that such mutilating surgery was allowed in a modern hospital. At first I wanted to walk away in protest. But Dr. Owen then reconstructed the hideous defect with a two-foot slab of skin he lifted from the shoulder — a swatch still attached temporarily to the lower chest, which supplied enough blood to prevent gangrene. It was miraculous. The patient now had a face again, and he was eating a few days later.

A few days after that operation, I assisted while Dr. Owen repaired the cleft palate of a year-old child. Then he fixed the cut tendon in a housewife's hand; she had severed it by holding a bread knife the wrong way while slicing a bagel. The same day, he operated on a garage mechanic whose legs had been burned when his gasoline-soaked jeans caught fire. The variety was fascinating. Even more important, Dr. Owen, like me, was interested in his patients as people. Plastic surgery makes a visible difference — and it helps psychologically, as well as physically.

I decided to try to become a plastic surgeon. The training is one of the longest of all the medical specialties. First, I had to have five years training in general surgery. I was tired after one week and stayed tired for all five years. After that, I had two years of plastic-surgery training — learning how to operate under a microscope, how to move skin and muscle, how to cover wounds from car accidents or cancer surgery, how to put faces and hands back together, and how to make wounds heal. Plastic surgeons are the only doctors trained to understand the healing of human tissues.

What about cosmetic surgery? My plastic-surgery training took place at first-rate university hospitals where the attitude about cosmetic surgery was a rather scornful one. The plastic surgeons I worked with did occasional cosmetic surgery, but reluctantly. I was in training with Dr. Forbes, a distinguished professor, when I saw my first cosmetic patient, a cocktail waitress who had waited three months to see him for a consultation.

"You want bigger breasts?" Dr. Forbes asked, somewhat disapprovingly, after examining her. She was a 36-C.

"Yes." It was her turn to look surprised.

"Why?"

"I want to be a magazine centerfold, and I think it would help if my boobs were bigger than this." She caressed her right breast casually, as if checking it for size.

A look of distaste came over Dr. Forbes's puritanical face. "It's expensive."

"I can pay."

"Someone else might be less expensive."

"That's okay."

"I won't be able to do it for six months."

"Whenever you can fit me in," she said cheerfully. "I'll wait."

After she left, he turned to me. "Cosmetic surgery is part of plastic surgery, but it glorifies the surgeon too much. I don't enjoy doing it. I like the challenge of reconstructing a real deformity."

My professors did so few face-lifts that I had to wait a year before I saw my first. Some of them claimed they were not interested in the money that cosmetic surgery might bring them.

I was naive when I began my plastic-surgery training. I thought good plastic surgeons did not do much cosmetic surgery. Two years later — in June, a month before I opened my own solo practice in plastic surgery — several professors who had taught me to disdain "cosmetics" left their teaching jobs for private practice, openly proclaiming their intention of becoming rich. I wondered if plastic surgery was the right field for me — if I would soon be doing cosmetic surgery for profit alone. But it was too late to change.

Actually, I almost didn't get to start my practice that year. My two years of plastic-surgery training were almost stretched into three years, partly through my own folly. When my first year of plastic-surgery training began, I was assigned to work at Midwestern University Hospital with a well-known plastic surgeon named Arnold Tewkesbury. Working with him was the worst three months of my life. Dr. Tewkesbury, a tall, dark Englishman bored with surgery and cynical about his practice, was witty, intelligent, and accustomed to adoration from his patients and his residents.

"You're going to see the greatest triumph of plastic surgery," he whispered to me one morning in the hospital hallway. His attention wandered briefly as his eyes tracked a passing nurse in a tight blouse; he sighed and turned back to me. "Before the operation my patient looked fifty. How old does she look now? How old?"

I shook my head. He snorted. "Forty-nine." He pushed open the door to her room, and without another word, cut the bandages off the face of his startled patient. Her face was badly swollen, black-and-blue from the surgery.

"How do I look, Dr. Tewkesbury?" she asked anxiously.

"You look gorgeous!"

She laughed, gratefully.

"She looks like hell," he said as we walked down the hall away from her room, "but she is happy." He shrugged.

Arnold Tewkesbury's female patients fell in love with him. I learned to resent him. I was the only resident assigned to him and another group of busy plastic surgeons. I had had almost no sleep for three months — only eight hours a week. I was exhausted, irritable, and much too tired to learn. My brain was a fog. I couldn't walk in a straight line. If I sat down, I fell asleep. I usually worked alone, without instruction from Tewkesbury or the other surgeons who were supposed to teach me. I became disillusioned and bitter. I was a doctor — a surgeon — and I wanted to learn plastic surgery. Instead, I was being used as cheap labor.

If I hated Tewkesbury, he hated me. I was insubordinate, rude, a typical outspoken, overworked surgical resident. I stumbled around grumpily in a rumpled gray operating dress, my skin green from lack of sleep, my eyes hollow and cadaverous. I ended my three months with Tewkesbury on terms of cordial animosity. He would not try to hurt my career. I would keep my opinion of him to myself. It was an unspoken truce.

Six weeks later, at an American College of Surgeons meeting, I had recovered from the fatigue of my Tewkesbury rotation. I was now assigned to a cancer hospital, where I was learning facial reconstruction. I was much happier and my good spirits had returned. At the ACS convention, the evenings began with reunions. The second night of the convention, one of my medical-school professors, Dr. French, offered to escort me to the University Hospital reunion, a formal affair. Dr. French was a gentle, slightly stooped, silver-haired professor of pediatric surgery, who usually came to the conventions with his wife.

"Let me take you in, Elizabeth. Let's start a rumor," he said, gallantly offering his arm. "You're single and I've been married forty years. Susan hasn't missed a meeting before, but grandchildren get born at inconvenient times." He patted my arm affectionately. "I know I'm short, but you have to stand up straight. We're going to wake up the entire room."

We did. I was in three-inch gold heels and a floor-length

bright orange silk dress, slit up one side. For the first time in months, I didn't look like a limp, sexless resident. There was a lull for about three minutes, until the residents who knew me reassured horrified professors that I was only a surgical resident, and that Dr. French had not left his wife and got a girlfriend. Dr. Tewkesbury gave me a curt nod over his double scotch.

The next morning I sat studying the convention program in an almost empty auditorium before the scientific session started. I heard footsteps and looked around. It was Tewkesbury. He walked firmly down the aisle, nodded to me, winked, and sat down in front of me, turning around to stare.

"You don't know what you did to me last night, Elizabeth." He put his hand out, squeezed my knee suggestively, and gave me a seductive smile. "You don't know what you did to me," he repeated, massaging my knee. Confidently, he moved his hand up my leg.

I was appalled. "I don't know what you mean," I floundered. Surgical residency doesn't train you for awkward social situations. I felt hopelessly gauche. He repelled me and my face said it for me.

He got the message, removed his hand, and strode out of the auditorium, humiliated and insulted.

Dr. Tewkesbury had never thought of me as a woman when I worked with him, but, dressed up for a cocktail party, I had caught his eye. The trouble was that during my years of surgical residency, I too had forgotten how to behave and had almost forgotten that I was a woman.

Tewkesbury was very angry. He was an important man, and a short time later he wrote to the American Board of Plastic Surgery, which supervises residency training, saying that my work with him was unsatisfactory and that I had agreed with him to repeat the year. It was not true, but approval of my first year's training was suspended. The Board members knew and trusted Tewkesbury. They did not know me. The Board does not want to certify unqualified surgeons.

I had to face beginning again, all for a personal grudge. I complained bitterly to my mother, but I knew it was partly my own stupid fault. My father urged me to resign. My brother Jim wanted to hire a hit man. Rob, my younger brother, then in law school, suggested I sue all two thousand Board-certified plastic surgeons. The only obstacle was money for legal fees.

"No," my mother agreed, "all you can do is live with it. After all, worse things have happened."

"I can't think of any right now."

"You could have leukemia, to name one," replied my mother crisply. It was a tone in her voice that meant she was anxious.

"Mother, I won't get sick. I can take it," I said soothingly.

"And don't use your bedside manner, either," she laughed. "I wish things could be easier for you, Elizabeth. It's fine to be a surgeon, but first of all, I want you to be happy."

That December I was working with Dr. Villiers, the plastic surgeon in charge of my training program. One afternoon after his patients had gone, he ran his fingers through his straw-colored hair, straightened his tie, and looked at me in embarrassment.

"It's hard having to do an extra year, isn't it?"

"Yes, it is," I admitted. I was thirty. I felt ancient. I wanted to be a woman and a person again, not a resident. I was ready to quit. I knew only four other women surgeons — we were all friends — Nora and Heather in general surgery, Joanna and Sylvia in plastic surgery. But none of them was even in the same city and I rarely saw them. I almost never met eligible men. My professors were older and married, and my co-residents by now were mostly younger than I was. I had known surgery would be hard, but it was ruining my life.

Dr. Villiers rubbed his chin thoughtfully. He had a daughter himself and he knew I wasn't happy. "Want to give it a try?" he suggested. "I think we can mount a Tet offensive for the spring thaw. You get Forbes and Thierry and Flint to write to the Board, petitioning approval for your residency to end this July. I'll write for you as your Chief. We could blow Tewkesbury off the map. You don't need a third year. You want to get out of the trenches." He straightened his cuffs. "Keep it under your hat. Tewkesbury is a powerful man."

Four weeks later, Dr. Forbes and his colleagues Dr. Thierry and Dr. Flint had all recommended to the Board that my first year of training be approved. They were friends of mine and had taught me and encouraged me, and they were all eminent surgeons — but none had the political pull of Dr. Tewkesbury.

"Don't talk about it," Dr. Villiers said, waving his hands like an orchestra conductor silencing the brass, when I asked him what my chances were. "You've got to sneak in like the enemy at night. It's an ambush. A surprise attack at dawn. If Tewkesbury knows, he can line up his team and crush us. Don't tell anyone!"

The Board met in late winter. Dr. Villiers grabbed me by the elbow in the hospital lobby the next morning and looked around suspiciously. "My spies have been giving me information," he whispered. "Don't believe it till you see it in writing, but rumor has it that we won." He looked around again, but there was only an orderly getting off the elevator pushing a breakfast cart. "You had those letters lined up on your side, one-two-three. Tewkesbury didn't have anything good to say for you, but we caught him completely off guard. Did what he could to stop us, but too little too late, like Napoleon at

Waterloo. The Board came down on your side, but don't count on anything till you see it in writing." He shook my elbow encouragingly and hurried away.

The Board sent me a letter on May 15, six weeks before my eighth year of surgical training was due to begin. The Board had reviewed my appeal and was granting me permission to end my residency after two years after all. My residency would end in six weeks! Ma Bell made a lot of money on my phone calls to my family.

But it was all very sudden. I had no plans. I now had to decide if I would take a teaching position at Midwestern University or go into private practice on my own. My friends Nora and Heather had taken salaried teaching jobs and were happy. I like to teach, and having a regular salary would avoid the problems of running an office and collecting bills, but I had to admit to my own failings. An academic surgeon should be able to do laboratory research and should enjoy committee meetings. My research talent is nil, and I get restless on committees. Above all, I didn't want to settle in the Midwest. I decided to go into practice at home, in Washington, D.C., and I flew back for interviews with four established plastic surgeons, hoping one of them would want me as a junior associate. My first interview was with Dr. Randolph. His waiting room was a vast expanse of beige carpeting, decorated with black-and-orange plastic chairs. When the last patient left, a white-uniformed nurse led me down a narrow corridor to the consulting room. Dr. Randolph was a rather reserved, older man.

"You are coming to Washington to practice on your own? Why?"

"It's my hometown."

"We have too many plastic surgeons in this area, Dr. Morgan. I'm not looking for an associate. I don't know anyone who is."

Solo Practice

It was the same story at every interview. I also applied at the local medical schools. They did not need another academic plastic surgeon. No one wanted me, so I had no choice. I had to open my own office — solo practice, something I had never considered. I flew back and told Dr. Villiers my decision. The next day, John Napier, another professor, called me into his office.

"I want to talk to you. You can't make it on your own." He fixed his piercing gray eyes on me like a snake staring down a mesmerized mouse and pushed me into a chair. "You'd be crazy to try solo practice. Life is tough out there, you turkey. It's hard enough for a man. You won't make it. You don't like cosmetic surgery much, and that's all there is in private practice."

"You're trying to talk me out of it." I folded my arms and glared at him. He didn't understand: I had no choice.

"You're crazy." He glared at me. "Of course, Elizabeth, you always have been obstinate." We both laughed.

Dr. Villiers was less pessimistic. "You'll do fine, but no home runs," he said after thinking it over for a few days. "That's all I have to tell you. You can't do in private practice what you can do with a team of twelve in a university hospital. No muscle-bone free flaps on hundred-year-old alcoholics your first year. Don't be fancy. Be a good solid surgeon. I did it. You can do it." He meticulously adjusted his cuff links. "It's fun being on your own. It's like growing up."

One of my problems was that I wasn't sure I approved of cosmetic surgery. I had never had to think about it much. I knew how to do a face-lift. But I didn't know when to advise a patient that it was a good idea. It's easy to talk people into cosmetic surgery, but cosmetic surgery done for the wrong reasons may not help a patient at all. I was afraid I might fall into doing cosmetic surgery for the money. That's a common temptation, but surgery is not like a haircut. Patients have bled to death during face-lifts. A doctor shouldn't blithely do whatever a patient asks without giving advice about what is best. As a resident, I didn't have such responsibility. And now my overworked, harassed, but ultimately carefree days of residency were about to end.

The last face-lift I did with Dr. Villiers was a good example of the surgeon's dilemma. The patient, Mrs. Schmidt, was an elderly woman. Pamela, Dr. Villiers's secretary, came into the office with Mrs. Schmidt's chart and closed the door.

"Mrs. Schmidt says she's here for a face-lift, Dr. Villiers. Don't get mad at me for saying so, but she doesn't look as though there's a *thing* you can do for her."

Pamela stepped out and returned in a moment, ushering in Mrs. Schmidt. Dr. Villiers rose courteously and Pamela made her exit, winking at me. Mrs. Schmidt was a frumpy, sixtyish widow. Her face was pale, her hair gray, unkempt, and unwashed. It straggled around her face. She wore no makeup; her eyebrows were colorless, but her mouth was tight and determined. She clutched a dirty-beige plastic handbag with one strap frayed off. She wore dirty, flat laced suede shoes, baggy red cotton trousers too short for her, and a velour sweater in a conflicting shade of red. Unless she overhauled her looks completely, a face-lift would make little difference.

"And what can I do for you, Mrs. Schmidt?" asked Dr. Villiers with a smile. He gestured her into a chair.

"A face-lift," said Mrs. Schmidt, clutching her purse nervously on her lap. "I want you to do a face-lift. I need to know how much, and what's involved."

"The face-lift tightens the lower face and the jaw. It does not remove wrinkles," said Dr. Villiers emphatically, "and it won't do much for this." He drew his hand along the natural fold that goes along the corner of the mouth. "It works best on the jawline and upper neck. It leaves scars in front of and behind the ear, but they don't usually show."

"Is it dangerous?" She gazed at him intently, concentrating on every word.

"Bleeding and infection can occur. Sometimes a nerve is damaged and you get a weak nerve in the face, but it usually goes away by itself. Stitches are out by ten days. You can go out in public, with makeup, in two weeks."

"How much?" She tightened her grip on her purse.

"My fee is fifteen hundred dollars. The operating room costs about three hundred. You pay it all in advance. You'll be sedated, comfortable but not asleep. That way you bleed less."

"When can you do me?"

"Within a couple of weeks." Dr. Villiers fidgeted with the fountain pen on his desk, turning it in the holder. "I don't want to sound impertinent, but why do you want a face-lift?"

"I don't like the way my face droops." Mrs. Schmidt ran her hand vaguely over her jaw and lower face.

"Do you go out much? Friends? Social life?"

"No. What does it matter to you? I have the money, if that's what you're wondering. I don't dress up, but I can pay you. Now if you want." She fumbled for her wallet. Dr. Villiers waved it away unhappily. "No, no. That's not what I meant. Let my secretary fix up a time and go over the operation permission and all that. Don't part with your money too quickly." After she'd gone, he said, "Kind of a nut, isn't she?"

"A nut? She doesn't need a face-lift. She needs new clothes, a haircut, and some makeup. I wouldn't operate on her."

Dr. Villiers sighed. "Patients don't come perfect, you dreamer. She wants a face-lift. I can do a face-lift better than anyone in town. Sure, many patients have personal problems — but what of it? I'm not a psychiatrist. They want a face-lift and, in my experience, it makes them happy." He stood up. "You'll learn, kid, when you're on your own."

We did Mrs. Schmidt's face-lift two weeks later.

"Is there someone with you?" I asked when she arrived in the operating room.

"No. I didn't tell my son."

"Someone has to take you home."

"I have a friend. I'll call her when I'm ready to go."

She changed into the white operating-room shift, which made her look more pathetic but less down-at-heel. I started to pull her hair into little ponytails to keep it out of the way during the operation. I had found that women often wanted to talk about personal problems just before cosmetic surgery, especially if they hadn't been asked about them earlier. It was odd that she hadn't told her son about the face-lift.

"So you didn't tell your son," I remarked conversationally. "He'll have a nice surprise."

"I certainly hope so. He's going to be mad as a hatter. Sick as mud." She smiled to herself, looking down at her hands.

"Do you have other children?"

"No, thank God. He's the only one. And what a one. No mother should have a son like him." She lay down on the stretcher and I marked for the face-lift incision with blue surgical marking ink.

I walked to the other side of the stretcher to mark the left side of her face. "Is he married?"

"Is, was. I don't know and I don't care. He may be divorced, but he'd never bother to tell me. Just moved back into my apartment five years ago. Said his wife didn't understand him. She's got the baby, but he doesn't care. What a father he is. Just lives off me. Momma, give me this, give me that. That's all he cares about. Is everything going to be all right? Dr. Villiers does a lot of face-lifts, doesn't he?"

"Sometimes three a day."

"Is he any good?"

"Excellent." It was true.

In the operating room, the nurse anesthetist who would be with Mrs. Schmidt during the surgery injected intravenous Demerol, but Mrs. Schmidt was detached and calm even before the sedation, as though she had resigned herself to a necessary punishment. I injected novocaine into the skin where I had marked for the incisions. Once we were ready to operate, Dr. Villiers started on the right side, cutting through the skin above, in front of, and behind the ear. Epinephrine, a hormone in the novocaine, closes the small blood vessels, so there was little bleeding. Once he had cut through the skin he carefully used scissors to lift it off the face and upper neck. After thirty minutes, you could put your hand right into the face and run it under the skin of the cheek, neck, and behind the ear.

"Not much bleeding," grunted Dr. Villiers. His surgical gown had been tied too tightly and he shifted his shoulders uncomfortably. He packed a bulky moistened gauze pad under the skin, which made Mrs. Schmidt's face look as though she had the mumps.

"Turn your face to the right, my dear," said Dr. Villiers, turning her head for her.

"Is everything all right, doctor?" Mrs. Schmidt asked with the indifference of a waitress inquiring about someone's meal.

"All right?" repeated Dr. Villiers cheerfully. "My dear, I am ze maestro. You have come to the very best. It had better go fine, otherwise I'll leave town. My excellent resident, Dr. Morgan, is going to do some work on this side."

"She's a very nice doctor," murmured Mrs. Schmidt drowsily.

"Sure, just like Ivan the Terrible," whispered Dr. Villiers out of Mrs. Schmidt's hearing range. "No one would believe how my residents make me suffer. Now don't cut her ear off, for God's sake."

I cut through the skin and peeled it off the left side of the face, just as Dr. Villiers had done on the other side. He followed my scissors with watchful eyes, squeezing first one eye and then the other in painful anticipation that I might do something wrong.

"Looking good," muttered Dr. Villiers. "Good progress."

At that point, the lights went out. There was shocked silence, but before Dr. Villiers could explode in rage, the emergency generator at the end of the operating-room hallway whirred loudly and the emergency overhead lights came on, dimmer than full lights, but plenty to work by. The chief of anesthesia came in — a short, anxious man with thick bifocals.

"Listen, Jacques, is this going to take long? The whole city has had a blackout. Where do you stand with this case?" He bobbed up and down trying to glimpse over my shoulder to see how far along the operation was.

"I can finish in twenty minutes," Dr. Villiers said, taking the scissors out of my hand.

"And do everything you need to do?" asked the chief of anesthesia. "I don't want to hurry you, but I want you to hurry. We're running on the emergency generator."

"Absolutely. Who do you think I am? I could do this operation blindfolded, with one arm." The chief of anesthesia scurried out.

"Is everything all right?" asked Mrs. Schmidt sleepily.

"Apart from the fact that we're under enemy attack and

the Russians have landed," said Dr. Villiers, "things are fine. Some idiot in city hall overloaded the electric system and the lights went out. For this we pay taxes. Fortunately, the hospital has an emergency generator."

Mrs. Schmidt nodded sleepily and the emergency lights went out.

"What the hell is going on?" spluttered Dr. Villiers in a whisper, his eyes wide with fury and his surgical mask slipping off his nose. "What sort of a show is this? I'm doing an operation and the place is falling apart. What about my patient? Does no one think about my patient? What am I going to tell her? She is maimed for life because I was operating in the dark? Who the hell is running this operating room today? I want the hospital administrator in here, and I want him now."

There was a rush of footsteps out in the hall and a bobbing flashlight came into our room, held by the chief of anesthesia.

"Listen, Jacques, the emergency generator isn't working."

"I noticed."

"Can you finish with a flashlight?"

'What choice do I have? It's either that or join a jazz combo. Who's paying you to do this to me? With friends like you, I don't need enemies."

"I didn't turn the lights off."

"Who the hell did? Don't tell me. The world is falling apart. I can't even operate in peace anymore. Disaster is sweeping the globe. If you'd shine that damned light into the wound, we could do this operation."

Hurriedly he finished off my dissection in the neck, sweating, muttering, and squinting to see better in the dark. The circulating nurse hovered behind him with a sponge to wipe his brow when he turned to her, so sweat wouldn't drip into the wound. We turned Mrs. Schmidt's head back so she faced the ceiling, and the nurse anesthetist gave her some more sedative. Dr. Villiers put in a few key sutures to direct the pull of the face-lift. We trimmed the excess skin — there is never much — and sewed the incisions closed. The chief of anesthesia and our circulating nurse each held an unsteady flashlight, one on my side, one on Dr. Villiers's, so we could see. It was like operating in a coal mine — a flare of light surrounded by pitch black. We wrapped the dressing on, and the operation was over. I accompanied Mrs. Schmidt's stretcher to the recovery room and I was surprised by the sunlight coming in through the windows, a pleasant change from the darkened corridor. There was no electricity yet, and one patient, still too much asleep to breathe, was being "bagged" by a nurse — she was pumping oxygen into and out of his lungs by hand. None of the respirators were working, since they were all powered by electricity.

Mrs. Schmidt went home that afternoon. The next week, I took her stitches out.

"You look good," I said, unwrapping the gauze dressing.

"Yes, I am feeling pretty good. My son is really angry. I think I got to him this time."

"Because of the face-lift?"

"Yes, because of the money I spent on it. I know he's waiting for me to die so he can get my money. If I have my way, he won't get a penny. I'll spend it all so he can't touch it. It makes him mad to see me spend my money. And with a face-lift, there's no way he can get it back. It's not like jewelry or a house or furs. He's been shouting at me all week, except when he is so mad he can't speak. I don't know what I'll do next to get him." She shuffled out, smiling furtively, still grubby, ill-dressed, unattractive. The face-lift made her face look tighter, but it had not really helped her. She was a lonely, bitter, neglected woman and she didn't know what a close escape she had had. If the anesthetist had accidentally oversedated Mrs. Schmidt as sometimes happens and she had stopped breathing during the blackout, it would have been difficult to detect the problem and perhaps impossible to resuscitate her in the dark.

A blackout was unlikely, but it had happened. It was also unlikely that Mrs. Schmidt would simultaneously stop breathing. Fortunately, that had not happened. But was the face-lift we did going to help her so much that the risk to her life was justified? I didn't know. I felt rather lost, and I was frightened at the prospect of having to take responsibility for such momentous decisions if I went into solo practice. I wanted to be a good doctor and to help people, but I was not sure I could do it on my own.

2

Starting Out

WHEN I got off the plane in Washington, eleven years of medical school and surgical training behind me, I was met by my mother and my brother Jim. My mother looked more than ever as though a gust of wind would blow her away. She has wide blue-gray eyes, silvery hair, and a gentle but humorous look around her mouth — she is beautiful, always smiling — and extremely thin.

"Did you have a tiring flight?" she asked me protectively.

"These your bags?" interrupted Jim, extending his long, powerful arms through the crowd and pulling two red suitcases off the conveyor belt. "Let's get the hell out of here. The Fourth of July traffic is already building up out on the roads." Jim has my mother's eyes, but has black, straight eyebrows and a broad, determined jaw. He looks quite intimidating, although that's misleading: he has never started a fight in his life.

My father had stayed behind "to hold the fort," a favorite expression of his from his army days in World War II. He and my mother, though in their middle sixties, were still working — five days a week, evenings, and some weekends — as consulting psychologists who did educational testing, marriage counseling, and child guidance. Their office was in their home, and had been ever since we were children. They worked together with most patients, but my mother did all the guidance for children under twelve, as well as providing a lot of counseling to career women running into conflicts with their husbands or at their jobs. My father's specialty was teenage boys and young men who weren't succeeding in school or at work. The family living room was their clients' waiting room, the dining room was for their secretary, the first-floor bedrooms had become consulting and testing rooms long ago.

Jim and Mother and I drove home and went inside, talking happily. There was the clatter of the typewriter, and the familiar sound of my father's consulting-room door opening. He walked softly into the waiting room — a broad, stocky man, bald, bounding with energy, looking much younger than his age. He has a thick, smooth skin, creased deeply at the edge of the mouth, but otherwise without a wrinkle.

"Hello, hello, Elizabeth." He gave me a hug. "Good to have you home. Take care of her bags, Jim, and don't make so much noise. I'm testing in the front room." He bounded away.

"Welcome home," I said sarcastically, "but please don't talk."

"Don't get bitter, Elizabeth," said Jim. "You know how Dad is."

"Let's have coffee on the back porch," said my mother, who is the calming influence that has kept her temperamental family together. On the back porch we talked over my plans.

My parents had generously lent me one of their consulting rooms to use as a temporary office. An office address and a county business license would mean I was legally in private practice, though no one knew I existed. I was going to live in a small house down the road with Jim. My parents had bought the house twenty years before, as an investment, but were lending it to us, rent free, until Jim finished his training as a stockbroker and until I had a thriving practice. I urgently needed a proper office, not one room in my parents' house, but it would get me started. I could see a few patients there while I found and equipped my own office. Few doctors start out with a free stopgap office and home. I was not married. I had no family to support. Almost all the men I had worked with had had to take out huge loans to support families (or to pay for alimony and child support) as well as fund a new office, unless their wives supported them and the children. For the moment, with the work and debt of my new practice ahead, I was glad to be thirty, single, and free.

I had to take out an initial loan of $38,000, a staggering amount. Dr. Villiers had told me I would need at least $50,000, but I didn't want to be that much in debt. As a seventh-year resident, I had earned $18,000 a year. I had tried to save money, but the amount I needed was far more than I had earned in two years. I sat down and worked out my minimum: $5,000 for equipment, like examining tables (at $900 each), stools, shelves, filing cabinets, and furniture; $12,000 for a secretary's salary; $10,000 for rent; another $5,000 for telephone installation, electric bills, a typewriter, stationery, folders, bandages, postage stamps — all the miscellany of any office. That plus a new car came to nearly $40,000.

Jim helped me do the calculations. I didn't want an accountant after seeing what had happened to Dr. Villiers. His accountant had gotten him deeply in debt, and came around every month to tell him how many face-lifts he had to do to pay the bills. I wanted to keep things simple, or as simple as I could, since I had no idea what I was doing. The car was a must, because my '68 Dodge had just died. I needed a secretary too, and my mother suggested I call the secretarial agency she had always used.

The first person they sent was Clare Ring — a charming

woman, very pretty, with violet eyes, a flawless pink skin, and a quiet, demure manner. She had a wonderful sense of humor, and to my astonishment she not only did everything I knew needed to be done, but told me of things I had overlooked. She had been an executive secretary for years, and was efficient without ever appearing to hurry. There was an amazing amount for her to do. I didn't even know what licenses I needed, but Clare found out. It took her three days, and hours on the telephone tracking down county officials, but she never lost her patience. I tried unsuccessfully to follow her example.

My biggest project was arranging for hospital privileges, so I could operate. Being a doctor does not automatically give you the right to use a hospital. You must apply to each hospital's medical staff for permission and have your credentials reviewed. Privileges may or may not be granted. Some private hospitals already have enough doctors and have a "closed staff." New doctors are not accepted. Or you might be denied privileges because other doctors don't want your competition. I had grown up in Elwin County at a time when there were few doctors and no hospitals there. It was all farms then. Now it was a crowded suburb with hundreds of doctors and a large hospital half a mile from my home. I called Dr. Bassano, an ophthalmologist and friend of my father's

"Put in your application to the Metropolitan Medical Center, by all means, Elizabeth, but I can't be too encouraging. The ophthalmology staff is way too big and may be closed. I'm not sure about plastic surgery."

"So I may not get privileges at all?"

"Elizabeth, things have changed while you've been away. There are physical limits to how many doctors can use a hospital. You'd better speak to Ronald Meade first. He's the chief of Plastics."

I smiled, thinking of how Dr. Tewkesbury hated the word *plastics.*

"It's not plastics like a petroleum product. It's *plastic surgery*, from the Greek word, 'to mold,' " he would snarl. I could smile about Tewkesbury, now that I was free.

On July 9 I turned thirty-one, and I started my birthday with a call to Dr. Meade's office to ask if I could talk to him about joining the plastic-surgery staff at Metropolitan.

"Sure, honey," cooed his secretary with a southern drawl. "He knows you're going to apply. Now you drive over here tomorrow about noon and he'll see you. Can you come then?"

I could make it anytime. Clare wrote in "Dr. Meade" in my appointment book. It was my only appointment for that day.

Dr. Meade's office occupied the eighth floor of an exclusive medical office building, and had been tastefully if unimaginatively decorated by a commercial decorator in practical shades of brown and beige, except for the waiting-room chairs, which were black-and-orange plastic (like a petroleum product). Black-and-orange plastic chairs are found in almost every Washington doctor's waiting room. A scowling young man in a leg cast self-consciously lifted his leg aside so I could sit down, and for half an hour I waited for Dr. Meade, flipping through year-old issues of *Parents'* magazine. "No orange plastic. No old magazines," I told myself, making mental notes for my own office.

The cast-legged man was the last patient. Dr. Meade's secretary motioned me over to her desk and led me to a cheerful room with a huge picture window, a leather-topped desk, and built-in bookcases. A handsome, solemn man in a dark suit was talking on the telephone. He slowly stretched his arm over the desk to shake hands with me, the phone still held to his ear, and pointed with a distracted smile to a comfortable green-velvet armchair. I sat down.

"Okay, dear," he said slowly into the mouthpiece. "You can take the car, but I want you and it back home by dinner." He hung up. "Kids! You have to be a firm. I'm Ronald Meade." He spoke with a noticeable pause between each word, choosing his words carefully, "Pleased to meet you, Elizabeth." He hesitated. "I hear through the grapevine you're thinking about opening an office around here."

"Yes."

He gazed out the window at the lake below. "Looked anywhere else?" Dr. Meade said after a while.

"How do you mean?"

"Are you sure you want to settle here? I don't want to discourage you, but we have a lot of plastic surgeons at Metropolitan. An awful lot." He studied the ashtray on his desk with care. "It's hard starting a practice." He looked up at me and shook his head gloomily. "Anywhere. This area?" He shrugged. "It'll take you a long time to break even. Years maybe. We're pretty saturated with plastic surgeons. What are you interested in?"

"General reconstructive surgery, not purely cosmetic surgery."

"That's good." He sighed. "I had a young man here the other day. Says he's just interested in money. I hate to hear that." He shook his head. "That won't work here. California, sure. New York, yes, but Washington is a conservative town. Plastic surgeons here aren't rich. As a resident you hear a lot of stories, but none of us are quarter-of-a-million-dollar boys. We work hard. We get by. We support our families, make a living." He stopped talking and inspected the red dots on his gray tie. "What makes you choose this area?" he asked, still consulting his tie.

"My family lives here."

He nodded to his tie. "For how long?"

"Oh, the past thirty years."

He looked up, startled. "Thirty years? That's a long time."

"I know. We're almost the original settlers."

"Any family still living?" he asked sadly, as though, after thirty years, they must be dead.

"Yes. All of us and we're all in Washington. I'm the last to come back." There was a long pause.

"You really plan to open your office in this area, then," he observed in a matter-of-fact tone.

"Yes."

He leaned back in his chair. "You want privileges at Metropolitan, I guess."

"Yes, I do. I've sent in my preliminary application."

He nodded. "I know," he said. "I've seen it." He shook his head doubtfully. "You'll find there's a lot of emergency work."

"I don't mind. I've done a lot as a resident."

"Night call?"

"Yes."

"Weekends?"

"Yes."

"And I expect you to be available."

"Of course."

"No vanishing acts when it's your call. We take our call schedule pretty seriously."

"Of course." I had been a resident ten days ago. The idea of skipping out on my night call was appalling, but also novel. Dr. Meade stared at his folded hands for a while and then at his empty memo pad, frowning in thought. I sat tensely awaiting his verdict.

He looked up at last, smiling. "There won't be any problem with privileges, Elizabeth. We'll give you temporary privileges, if you need them, until the paperwork is done," he said slowly, "but I won't be able to put you on the emergency-call schedule for a few months. Happy to have you." He reached over to shake my hand.

I was in! I never thought it could happen so easily. "I don't care about emergencies, Dr. Meade. I only came home ten days ago, and besides opening my office, I'm studying for the Board exam. I don't want emergency cases now."

"Part One of Boards?"

"Yes."

"I remember." Dr. Meade smiled. "They were bad enough, but for Part Two, one of my examiners was Converse. He was mean. He liked to fail people. The best day of your life is passing Part Two of the Boards."

The door flung open and an energetic stocky older man stood in the doorway gesticulating.

"Ronald, I'm leaving town for the weekend. No patients. No problems." He grinned at me. "You must be Elizabeth Morgan, I'm Peter Wallace, Ronald's associate. There are a couple of other new plastic surgeons in town. Have you met Robert Fletcher? He's one of the other ones. Don't be like Robert. He sent out an awful flashy announcement. Commercial. Don't be commercial. Has Ronald here been the voice of doom? Don't listen to Ronald. He's a pessimist. You'll do fine. It takes time, that's all." He walked over and shook my hand with enthusiasm. I automatically stood up. Peter raised his eyebrows and pushed me back down onto the chair. "Those days are over, kid. Don't stand up for me. I'm not a professor. Remember, you're a woman now, not a resident. See you on Monday in the OR, Ronald."

"Just a minute, pardner." Dr. Meade slowly pulled out his diary from his breast pocket and put on his glasses. "Mrs. Connors," he read deliberately. "Face and eyes. Monday. Eight A.M. Saint Barnabas outpatient. That's where you're planning to be Monday?"

"Right on." Dr. Wallace gave a mock salute.

"Have a good weekend," said Ronald slowly, but his associate was gone. Ronald sighed. "Have you been through the hospital yet?"

"No, I haven't, Dr. Meade."

"Come and make rounds with me. I'll show you around." We walked out of the parking lot and he helped me into his car. "Listen," he said as he backed up, "we're all on a first-name basis here. I call you Elizabeth. You call me Ronald."

Clearly he didn't want new plastic surgeons in his territory, but since I wasn't going to go away, Ronald was going to be fair, kind, and friendly, and probably especially so to me because I was a woman. He may have spoken against me behind my back — dealing with Tewkesbury had made me paranoid — but Ronald was helpful whenever I asked for help. After the struggle of my residency and the Tewkesbury problem, when my being a woman had made my life so much harder, I realized with surprise that being a woman now probably made my life easier than it was for a man starting out on his own.

Dr. Robert Fletcher's announcement arrived in my mail the same day. Dr. Wallace had had a point — Robert Fletcher's mailing was not the traditional engraved office announcement, as formal as a wedding invitation. It was a snappy fold-over ivory card printed in blue ink. He called himself "Washington Reconstructive Associates," a big title for a surgeon in solo practice. Inside the announcement was a printed summary stating where he had trained, giving a rundown of his published papers, and listing the kinds of operations he wanted to do, including cosmetic surgery. My first instinct was to sneer because the announcement was different, but on second thought, it wasn't such a bad idea. It wasn't flashy or commercial after all. I wouldn't have chosen ivory paper and blue ink, but that was a matter of taste. I wouldn't have chosen the black-and-orange plastic chairs in Dr. Meade's office either. Robert Fletcher was not just another respectable surgeon — he was exceedingly well trained — and the announcement was the only proper way he could make this widely known. His credentials were at least as good as those of the established Washington plastic surgeons, and I wasn't surprised to learn later from a friend of his that he had been offered the chairmanship of a plastic-surgery department before he left the university for private practice. I called Dr. Fletcher's office to suggest I come by that afternoon to meet him.

"Good afternoon. Washington Reconstructive Associates. Dr. Fletcher's office. May I help you?" said a sweet womanly voice with a lilting foreign accent. She was rather breathless by the end. I introduced myself and was invited over to meet "the doctor" that afternoon. Robert's office, which opened a few weeks before mine, was in a modern brick office building and had a yellow striped sofa but no plastic chairs. Robert met me in his waiting room, and I knew his practice would be a success. He looked so stalwart and reliable. His face was strong, almost as though his features were carved in stone. He reminded me of a college friend, the son of a Polish prince — royal but ready to fight. No wonder Dr. Wallace wasn't happy with Robert — he wouldn't be easily managed. Robert's budget was even tighter than mine; he had a family to support and bigger debts to pay off. He proudly showed me his office furniture, all of which he had built himself. He was artistic and it showed in his furniture as well as his surgery. He had a small consulting room, a small examining room, and a large corner room that was a fully equipped operating room with picture windows on two sides.

Office operating rooms designed for major surgery were a must in 1978. Like everything else, medical offices have fashions, and major operating rooms were "in." It took several years before reports came out indicating that such facilities were expensive to run safely, time-consuming to supervise, and underused except in a large group practice. A major OR includes a standard operating table, which costs three to four thousand dollars, a large autoclave, heavy overhead lights, intravenous equipment, all the major drugs, and resuscitation equipment. To keep the OR stocked with supplies, such as bandages, drugs, and sutures, to look after the instruments, which cost thousands of dollars, and to look after the patients before and after surgery requires at least one full-time OR nurse. The main advantage for the surgeon who has his own operating room and is willing to run it at a loss is convenience: he can operate whenever he wants, instead of booking a hospital OR. Robert saw my doubtful look.

"They are expensive, but I've managed to keep my costs to a minimum. The biggest overhead is hiring a nurse to run the operating room, and so far I'm not busy, so I have time to run it myself."

"I haven't seen a patient yet. I'm still getting organized."

He smiled. "I've been there but I'm getting past that stage. Taking call at Metropolitan's emergency room will keep you busy and pay the bills. Most people in the county have some kind of insurance. You don't do too much work for free and it gets you known."

"Meade and Wallace have been helpful. They've given me advice on how to get started."

Robert looked at me curiously. "Don't be innocent. They're nice guys, but they're not thrilled to have you or me around. They'll do their best to help you, but once you start to operate you're competition."

"As long as I don't starve, I don't mind."

"You won't starve. This area needs plastic surgeons. You and I are the first new plastic surgeons in years, but don't expect favors from the established guys. They won't refer patients to me. They're not bad, but they're looking after their own practices. If you want, you can let them refer all their welfare patients to you, the ones who can't pay. You can't blame them. No one likes to work for free, and if you're gullible enough to take anyone's free cases, they'll be happy to send them over. This isn't residency, this is life! Any questions I can answer?"

I hesitated. "Actually, there is one. Everyone is evasive about how much to charge. They tell me their cosmetic prices, but what do you charge for reconstructive surgery?"

"Sven Ohlsen has been in practice for years and he really helped me. Here's his rough guideline: Four hundred dollars for every hour in the operating room. Two hundred dollars for every hour in the emergency room."

"What?" I was shocked.

"It's not as much as it sounds, if you give good medical care. The fee includes hospital and office visits, and they can take more time than the surgery. Plus you add in all the time you waste hanging around waiting for an operating room, the time your secretary spends on insurance forms, and the time you spend doing hospital paperwork."

"So I can make more money if I don't spend time looking after my patients after surgery."

"Right on." Robert patted me paternally on the shoulder. "Now you know why all the surgeons who trained you want to do the cutting themselves and make the residents see their patients after surgery — it's cost-effective. Only we're not residents anymore."

Money and medicine are inextricably bound up together. There are no rules, but I was beginning to see that the best doctors think about their patients first, and the others think about their money first. Robert and Dr. Meade and Peter Wallace were good colleagues, but I wondered about the quality of the other doctors I would be working with — and

I wondered about myself. Money changes people and I was afraid it would change me.

I invited Robert and his wife over for dinner, but he declined politely. Whatever his reasons, we were to be close and friendly colleagues but never friends. I was puzzled until it dawned on me that I did the same thing myself. I had never mixed my private life with surgery when I was a resident, and it was probably a good idea to keep it that way now that I was out on my own, at least in the beginning. My sole objection to Robert was that when I wanted to reach him by phone I could never get in my name first before his imperturbable secretary had finished her greeting: "Good morning. Washington Reconstructive Associates. Dr. Fletcher's office. May I help you?"

After meeting Robert I went back to my office and called Dr. Villiers to ask if he would write a letter of recommendation to Dr. Meade in my behalf. I wanted to get my Metropolitan application completed as soon as I could.

"How many hospitals are you applying to?" Dr. Villiers grunted.

"Just Metropolitan for now."

"Apply to them all, kid. Apply to every hospital in the area. Once you've got privileges, you can pick and choose. After you're established it's hard to get in, but right now they'll be out to help you. Did this Dr. Meade give you the usual sob story — we have too many doctors, we're all starving, we don't need you, you'll never make it?"

"Yes, he said Washington is a hard area in which to start a practice. I hope I made the right decision."

"We all do it, kid. Don't let it get you. I don't like competition moving in any better than the next guy, but it doesn't mean anything. He sounds like a good guy. By the way, I hope you're not putting Tewkesbury's name on any of these applications."

"I did for Metropolitan. It said to list every plastic surgeon I had worked with."

"Hopeless!" cried Dr. Villiers despairingly over the phone, so loud that Clare jumped. "Hopeless! After everything I taught you, you ought to be smart. Do me a favor."

"Yes?"

"Put your hands around your neck and strangle yourself. Okay, okay, let it go. Now don't be dumb. Don't put his name down on your applications. I'm trying to keep this in words of one syllable so you understand. He told me he wouldn't do anything to hurt you, but this isn't Girl Scouts. This is life, kid. You can't trust anyone. I think he'd love to kill your practice before you even start. If you're lucky, Metropolitan won't write to him. If you're not lucky, he may stop you from getting privileges. Are you studying hard for Part One of Boards? If you fail, I'll strangle you myself. I keep telling Horace to study, but you're not here, so I can't beat on you. I want you both to do well."

That was incentive enough. Horace and I had been residents under Dr. Villiers at the same time. Self-confident, aggressive, and smart, Horace was also balding, bulgy-eyed, and often nasty and disagreeable. He had often got me to do his emergency call as well as mine. Horace had joined a group practice as a junior associate. My revenge so far had been to show him I could make it on my own. I wanted to tweak him again by doing better than he would on the Board exam. It helped to keep me studying for Boards — reading thousands of pages of ill-written, verbose plastic-surgery texts, taking notes, cursing, and trying to remember which hillocks in the embryo become the adult human ear.

Two days later, I was studying the biochemistry of anesthetics while lying on the battered sofa in our living room. Jim was in the kitchen, in a passionate tête-à-tête with a computerized workbook on stockbroking. His licensing exam was coming up. We were sympathetic to each other but irritable. The phone rang. Jim said, "Oh, crackers!" and threw his book on the floor. I answered the phone.

"Hello, Liz? This is Ronald Meade. If you have a moment, I'd like to ask you something." His voice got slower and slower, as though he hadn't been wound up for the day. I knew he wasn't calling with good news.

"Certainly," I said. Jim picked up his book and shut the kitchen door in an aggrieved manner.

"I'm calling you from, uh, home. Yes," said Dr. Meade, "I'm at home." He seemed reluctant to continue.

"Good," I said lamely.

"Are you at home?"

"Yes, I am."

"Not interrupting anything, am I? I certainly wouldn't want to call at a bad time."

"Not at all." I heard Jim open the refrigerator door in search of a snack.

"I'm calling about a very difficult question." There was a long pause. "I don't think I've ever come up against anything quite like it." Pause. "Nothing like it ever before." Pause. "Are you with me?"

"Yes, I'm right here."

"Good." He sighed heavily over the telephone. "I have here in front of me a letter. It's a letter from a man who signs himself Tewkesbury. There's a well-known man in plastic surgery called Tewkesbury. This seems to be the same one." Sigh. "Have you ever met him?"

"Yes. I spent some of my plastic-surgery training working with him."

"You did? That's interesting. That's what he says. Have you got a copy of this letter?"

"No."

"No? Well, maybe he wouldn't send you a copy of it. He

says in this letter that you don't know how to operate. In fact, he says he couldn't trust you to look after a patient properly, even if you did know how to operate. Strong words. Strange letter. Very strange. In fact, he says he doesn't think you should be allowed to practice. Not in this area." Dr. Meade took a rest and stopped talking. After a while he said, "Anything you'd like to add?"

"What can I say? I am a safe surgeon. I do look after my patients."

"Yes . . . give me some background, dear."

"I only worked with Dr. Tewkesbury for a short time. He hasn't seen me operate for almost two years."

"Oh? That's interesting." There was a rustle of paper. "He doesn't say anything about that in this very strange letter. He doesn't seem to care for you."

"No, I don't think he does."

"Have any ideas why?"

"I didn't think he was a good teacher, and I wasn't tactful about it. That upset him." How could I explain? It was too complicated.

"Yes. Anything else? Anything personal? Give me some background."

"I only knew him professionally."

"Do you think he's a good judge of your surgical ability, dear?"

"No."

"What makes you say that?"

"It's been several years since I worked with him and he seemed to have a lot of personal problems then."

"So he had some problems?" Ronald said cheerfully, as though he saw his way now. There was a long pause. I thought for a moment that the line had gone dead, but it was just Ronald thinking and giving me time to talk. He was an intelligent man, and his slowness was either a habit or intentional, to relax people. Nothing could make me relax. I waited and twirled my hair nervously, a fidget I've had since grade school. "You know, I not only got this letter, I got a phone call today," he continued. "A very powerful man, a surgeon in this area and a friend of Tewkesbury's. I won't tell you his name. He told me that Tewkesbury didn't want you going into practice and had asked him to stop you from getting your hospital privileges." Again a rustle of paper. "He said he didn't know you personally, but that he'd trust Tewkesbury's judgment. Said he was a very fair man." There was a rumble as Dr. Meade cleared his throat. I wondered to myself whether they needed plastic surgeons in Saudi Arabia. With my luck, Tewkesbury would be a consultant to King Khalid. I drew a black cloud with falling rain in my textbook and waited for Dr. Meade to tell me I wouldn't get privileges.

"So what do you want?" he asked abruptly.

"Me? I would like to have hospital privileges." It was what I wanted, not what I expected to get.

"Yes. That seems a good idea," said Dr. Meade, as though it hadn't occurred to him before. "Maybe I'll drop in to check on you when you operate. You wouldn't mind that? Just to see how you're doing?"

"You mean you're still going to give me privileges?"

"Frankly, I don't like big shots trying to control my hospital and push me around. Starting out is hard enough without this nonsense. Whom I give privileges to is my business, and to me your application looks acceptable. These big boys are too big for their britches. If that's all, I'll go and watch television with my kids."

"Dr. Meade, I don't know how to thank you," I started to say.

"That's another thing. We're a friendly group in this area. Call me Ronald." He hung up.

It was impossible to tell him how grateful I was, but he may have guessed. He had started out alone too. Thank God for private practice. I was independent, being given a fair chance to prove myself by men who had gone into private practice to stay independent. I tried to study the double carbon chains of novocaine, but Jim opened the kitchen door, shaking a jar of orange juice.

"I heard the whole conversation. It's something about the Tarantula, isn't it?" Tarantula was Jim's nickname for Tewkesbury.

"Yes, but everything's all right."

"Fantastic. Have some orange juice and tell me what's going on, and then I'll tell you the difference between notes and bonds. Maybe I could call up the Tarantula and get him to invest in sugar futures. I could sell him short when the market is long and put him a million in the hole."

"You don't need to, Jim. He tried to keep me off the Metropolitan staff, but darling Ronald doesn't like outside interference."

We toasted Ronald Meade with orange juice. I turned to the chapter on the life cycle of the epidermal cell.

An hour later I had had enough studying. I couldn't concentrate. All my mind was doing was adding up my loan and adding on monthly interest and calculating how fast it would all be spent by the time I had paid Clare's salary and the phone bill and malpractice insurance. I can't do arithmetic in my head, so it kept coming out wrong, and I started to worry that all this worrying would bring back the ulcerative colitis that had plagued me for a few months as a resident. I saw myself with huge hospital bills and going deeper and deeper in debt.

"It can't be that bad," said Jim, coming out of the kitchen. "Let's go to the Mayfield Mall and catch a movie. Once when I was there I saw Elizabeth Taylor and John Warner strolling along. No one else recognized them. She has beautiful eyes. That's all you notice when you meet her."

"Did you talk to them?"

"Sure. They're used to it. He's a farmer, and I wanted to catch his ideas on soybeans."

There were no movies worth seeing so we had coffee instead.

"How does mother look to you?" Jim asked abruptly.

"Tired," I said, after thinking about it. "Very tired."

"You haven't been home much. Life can be pretty tough when Dad's in a mood."

That was no surprise. My father's Latin temperament showed itself in warmth, generosity, openness, and unpredictable depressions and tempers.

"I don't think Dad likes growing old," added Jim, "and he's spending a lot more time in the country, chopping down trees to prove he's as strong as he ever was. That leaves a lot more work for Mother to do in the practice. She doesn't look as though she has cancer, does she?"

"People with cancer don't look like anything in particular, Jim, but it's a horrible thought. Maybe she'll come on a vacation with me after Boards. Can you convince Daddy to retire so they can both slow down?"

"Fat chance. You tell him. You're the doctor."

"He'd get angry with me."

"He'd ignore me."

Dad had taken a dozen yeast pills a day for two years to prevent cataracts, and nothing I could tell him made any difference. His daughter, the doctor, was all very fine but he believed in magic, and he didn't like advice from anyone.

"Maybe Rob can do it."

Not even calm, logical Rob, my younger brother who could reason with anyone, could convince my father to retire,

45

or semiretire, and if Dad wouldn't, my mother wouldn't either. I didn't know which to worry about more — my father's moody silences or my mother's fading color. Between her own patients, running the business side of the psychology practice, and running the house, she was working twelve hours a day or more, with no end in sight. She was sixty-four and it couldn't go on like this.

"Mother, you have to slow down or you'll get ill."

"Elizabeth, I'm perfectly fine. I won't get ill."

"You will get ill if you keep working so hard. You told me the same thing two years ago and you were right."

"I can't possibly afford to get ill until I'm sixty-five. I don't have health insurance. It's too expensive and I get medicare when I'm sixty-five."

She spoke jokingly, but she was absolutely serious. She would not get ill till she could afford it, and it was only a year away.

3
A Little
Business Discussion

I took Dr. Villiers's advice and applied to every hospital in Washington for privileges. Besides Metropolitan, I applied to Highcliff, Mattaponai, Radnor, St. Barnabas, Glamorgan, Memorial Hospital, Kruger Hospital, Holyrood, Cromarty Clinic, Friendship Affiliated, and even Tallis General Hospital, seventy miles away and in the foothills of the Blue Ridge Mountains.

Tallis General replied that they were happy to receive my request for an application because there were no plastic surgeons in their area but asked me if, realistically, I planned to drive seventy miles to operate when my office was five miles from half a dozen other hospitals.

It was a sensible question, and I withdrew my request, to Clare's relief. She hates filling out forms, and each application was eight or nine pages long.

"Why don't these hospitals get together and make one form?" she asked in despair, but she struggled on. "And why don't they make the blanks long enough to fill in the information they want? Holyrood gives me one line for your training and your training takes up half a page. It's absurd!" She finished them at last, but it took her weeks. Her hardest job was making me telephone other doctors to ask for letters of reference. I have never liked making phone calls, but Clare was firm. I finally did the telephoning and the applications were mailed.

While I waited for the hospitals to reply, a matter of months, I struggled with the question of where to open my office. The room my parents lent me had no sink, and an examining table was out of the question because the hallway proved too narrow. The lighting was not bright enough and there was no room to store bandages or patient files, nor was there adequate wiring for a cast cutter or a small sterilizing autoclave. I urgently needed a real office of my own.

I also needed malpractice insurance, because doctors cannot serve on a hospital staff without it. Ronald Meade gave me the name of his insurance agent, Judith Kosinski. She was a short, dark-haired woman of forty with a brisk, businesslike manner and a forbidding pine-paneled office. I knew immediately that she would be good with numbers, and I was intimidated. I needn't have been.

"Most doctors can't do math," Ms. Kosinski said pityingly, "and I don't ask them to. That's my job." She fussed with her calculator for a few seconds. "Roughly, here's what you can expect. You can choose one of two kinds of malpractice insurance. If you practice only in Virginia the premium will be two thousand."

I concentrated, trying to take it all in.

"Just a moment. What is the premium?"

"The premium is what you have to pay," said Ms. Kosinski.

"You mean the fee? The cost of the policy?"

"Yes." She poised her index finger for more calculations. "Ready?"

"Two thousand dollars is a lot of money."

Ms. Kosinski smiled. "Just wait till you hear the D.C. premium!" She punched more numbers into the calculator.

"If you practice in D.C., the policy will cover you for any surgery, regardless of where it is done. It is a better policy, but you must have a D.C. office. The premium will cost you ten thousand dollars." She looked up at me. "That is what you pay," she explained again, taking care to speak slowly, in words of one syllable. She resumed her normal tone. "In advance. Of course, the premium will be adjusted next January."

"So it might be less then?" I asked hopefully.

"Dr. Morgan, 'adjust' is a word we use in the insurance business. I don't remember in fifteen years any time that premiums have been adjusted down." She leaned back in her leather armchair. "It will cost you more next year," she said slowly, to be sure I understood.

"I can practice either in D.C. and Virginia for ten thousand dollars, or in Virginia alone for two thousand." I hadn't expected such a difference. "Let me see if I can afford a D.C. office. I'll call you back."

I went home and made myself miserable trying to estimate the cost of a D.C. office. After filling a wastepaper basket with crumpled yellow sheets of scribbled numbers, in which my arithmetic and that of my calculator never added up, I decided I could — just — afford to rent a home in D.C. and use it for my office, as permitted by D.C. zoning regulations. I could easily afford an office in Virginia. Or I could rent an office in D.C. and commute from Virginia. I could not afford a separate house and office in D.C. The D.C. office was important to me, because all the medical-school hospitals were in D.C. Though I was in solo practice, I still wanted to teach at one of the medical schools. But to teach, I had to be on the staff of one of those hospitals. For that I needed D.C. malpractice insurance. And for that, I had to have a D.C. office. The $10,000 for D.C. malpractice insurance was a high price to pay for the privilege of teaching at a medical school, which

I would have to do for free. Apart from salaried professors, all doctors in private practice who teach at medical schools do so without pay.

"It's not a bargain for you, it's baloney," said Jim cynically. "You are kindly allowed to pay through the nose in order that a medical school will kindly allow you to give away hours of your time for free. That's no deal, that's a rip-off, but if you want a house in D.C., call Rupes. He can help you if anyone can."

Rupes was Rupert Spencer-Neville, a friend of Jim's — a tall, lean English aristocrat with an intellectual look. He was a business real estate investor. That same afternoon, he introduced me to Mrs. Perez, the real estate agent who had found him his first apartment building. She enthusiastically described a "perfect" home-office for rent at a reasonable price in fashionable Georgetown, and drove us in to see it.

"All the chic Washington doctors have offices in their homes, dear," said Mrs. Perez, smoothing her pink cotton dress as we climbed out of her car. She was a plump, agreeable divorcée from Alabama, in her fifties. Her hair was tinted a shade of gray that was almost blue, and her hair and mine were limp with the humidity. It was late August, the heat was fierce, and we were in fashionable Georgetown, a former swamp.

"I can see you living here already. You'll be the rage. I'll let you lift my eyes!" She led me around the corner to High Street. "This is it!" she announced triumphantly, pointing to a massive four-story Victorian mansion with a wrought-iron gate, a turret, bay windows, and a carriagehouse at the back. She led me up the steep wrought-iron steps, with Rupert following. His hands were clasped behind his back and he looked at the house with a frown.

"The original owner was a fabulously wealthy eccentric

lady and a dear, dear friend of mine," said Mrs. Perez. "When she died I sold it for a song — a mere quarter of a million — to a darling lady, Mrs. Wald, who lives in Palm Beach. She renovated it and wants a reliable tenant. Like you, dear." She patted my hand. "A plastic surgeon can afford this house."

Rupert inspected the garden dispassionately. The boxwood shrubs were untrimmed and the roses unpruned. "The value of this house when you sold it to Mrs. Wald, given the market rate, was at most a hundred and eighty thousand," he said. "Her quarter of a million offer was an overbid. The garden needs a lot of work. Elizabeth would have to deduct from her rent the cost of a gardener once a week."

"It wouldn't be much work. She could do it herself. You like gardening, don't you, dear?"

"Of course," I said. The last gardening I had done was planting tulips for a Girl Scout badge and my mother had done most of it, but it was a cozy childhood memory. I desperately wanted to get out of the heat, and wished that Mrs. Perez would open the door.

"Ridiculous," snapped Rupert. "She's a plastic surgeon, not a gardener. She wouldn't have time."

Mrs. Perez made a sour face at him behind his back, winked at me, and threw open the twelve-foot-high double front doors. It was like opening the gates to a castle. She took my hand and led me inside. The mansion was quiet, dark, and cool. The vast entrance hall, complete with chandelier, led on the right through a graceful arch to a ballroom with french windows leading out to the neglected garden at the back. The moldings around the high ceiling were elaborately carved leaves and fruit. To the left of the central hall were two huge rooms, like the formal salons at Versailles. The kitchen was at the back of the house, long, narrow, impractical, and unimportant — for the maids, not the rich owner, to struggle in. Mrs. Perez led me up the wide, graceful spiral stairway as though she had me on a leash. She ran her hand along the balustrade.

"Beautiful, isn't it? You'll give lovely parties here."

Rupert sauntered slowly behind, his hands now shoved into his jacket pockets. "Cheap renovation, Mrs. Perez," he said. "Wald can't have put more than twenty-five thousand into it. What does she hope to sell for now? Half a million? She won't get it, except for an embassy, and it's too small for an embassy."

Mrs. Perez gave him a withering glance and ignored him. I followed her in a daze. The second floor had another central hall, leading to mirrored marble-tiled bathrooms at either end and four gigantic bedrooms with interconnecting folding doors.

"Your bedroom," said Mrs. Perez, gliding gracefully into the first bedroom. "And a study." She moved to the second. "Now across the hall, you'll use this room for perhaps a sitting room. The fourth is a guest room." She stopped in the fourth bedroom. "Downstairs, you'll use the ballroom for your waiting room, the two salons as consulting and examining rooms. It's perfect for you." She clapped her hands enthusiastically.

I agreed completely. My romantic soul had me moved in already, only I wasn't sure if my role was as a working Washington surgeon, a society hostess, or a fairy princess.

"Bees," said Rupert, popping out from the bathroom at the back. "Did you mention the bees, Mrs. Perez? There is a giant colony of bees on the back wall of the house. They won't be bad now, but in the spring they'll invade the entire house. Why doesn't the owner get an exterminator?"

"She had an exterminator come twice," said Mrs. Perez weakly.

"Bees are still here," persisted Rupert. He turned to me. "A good negotiating point. Ought to take twenty-five percent off the rental value."

The top floor had three bedrooms, a bath, and kitchen.

"Maids' quarters," said Mrs. Perez. Then she led me to the "basement." It was only partly underground, and had a bathroom, a kitchen, and four rooms, each the size of a large hotel room.

"What's this?" Rupert pulled open a heavy door. "A meat locker?"

"No, a wall safe, dear boy. The former owner had it built because she lived entirely on this floor. The upkeep of such a large house was too expensive for her." She gave a little gasp and covered her mouth. "Not really too expensive," she explained hastily, "but too much bother."

"How much are utilities?" demanded Rupert. "Fifteen hundred a month?"

Mrs. Perez nodded.

"More in winter, of course," Rupert went on. "It will cost a fortune to heat. You're asking two and a half thousand?"

Mrs. Perez nodded again. He looked at me.

"That's too high. If you're interested, Elizabeth, I'd offer twelve hundred a month rent, which will be close to three thou a month, after utilities, phone, et cetera. You can rent out this basement apartment at six hundred, and rent two of the top-floor rooms at two hundred each to some college girls. It's illegal because it's not zoned for rental, but you could probably get away with it. You'll only pay out two thousand."

I came to earth with a bump. "Not to mention a full-time maid to keep it clean, the gardener, and supervising three tenants. I can't afford it, but it's a lovely house."

"I agree, dear," said Mrs. Perez sadly. "No one can afford

this house. Those who can want something more modern, but I loved showing it to you." She patted my hand, this time to console me.

The three of us went to La Ruche for ice cream, and even Mrs. Perez decided I had to live in the suburbs and rent an office in town.

The next day I started my office search by reading the classified ads for office real estate. The date for Board exams was coming close, but I needed a break from studying. "Medical office in Burden Building, deluxe new high-rise building in downtown D.C." sounded perfect. I called the number.

"Hello, Burden Real Estate," barked a man's voice.

"Hello. I'm Dr. Morgan. I saw your ad in the *Morning News* for the medical office in the Burden Building."

"You saw it where?"

"In the *Morning News*."

"We don't have an ad for an office in that building. We don't need to advertise that building. It's one hundred percent leased."

"But —"

He hung up. I found another ad in the *Morning News* for a medical office in another building. I dialed another number.

"Hello, Burden Real Estate." It was the same man.

"Hello. I'm calling about the office space you advertised in the Malden Medical Building."

"What agent?"

I consulted the ad, my fingers smudged with ink. "Mr. Sorbi."

"He's on the other line. Hold on," barked the voice, and he disconnected me.

I called back. "You disconnected me. I was waiting for Mr. Sorbi."

"Yeah." I was put on hold.

"Hello. Mr. Sorbi speaking," said a syrupy man's voice five minutes later. "You're interested in our little seven-hundred-sixty-square-foot office in the Malden Building? How many square feet do you need, doctor?" he asked respectfully.

"Between seven hundred and a thousand." I wasn't sure. Will Van Tromp, a medical-school classmate who had opened his practice on the Gulf Coast had told me to get 1,000 square feet, but I felt cautious now, after Mrs. Perez. I couldn't afford too big an office.

"Do you have a specialty, doctor? Obstetrics? General practice?" asked Mr. Sorbi.

"I'm a plastic surgeon."

Pause. "I see! You're a plastic surgeon! Well, well." There was a bright and cheerful sound to Mr. Sorbi's voice. "I'd be happy to show you our seven-sixty office, but let me show you another one that has become available in the same building. It's a tad bigger at fourteen hundred feet and comes with many nice extras, like special wallpaper, track lighting. It won't hurt to look at it."

We made an appointment to meet the next day at nine. Mr. Sorbi was in his thirties and looked prosperous with his dark blue business suit, black brief case, his sleek black hair, and his round tummy that bulged slightly over his belt. He beamed at me with such enthusiasm that my heart sank. I look like a sucker, and the trouble is, I can act like one too. I knew that without Rupert I would have signed my name to a year's lease on Mrs. Perez's mansion and would have regretted it later. Today I was alone.

"You will not sign, Elizabeth," I told myself. "Don't sign anything. Jim would kill you."

Mr. Sorbi courteously held the door and ushered me into the glass high-rise office building. Inside, the gray linoleum declared that this was a medical building. The foyer was dim and stuffy. He pressed the elevator UP button and we waited five minutes.

"I'll show you the tiny office first," said Mr. Sorbi when the elevator came, "and let you take a peek at the nice one afterwards. I'm not trying to sell you anything." We got out at the third floor and he breezed into an office labeled J.P. SMITH. PODIATRIST.

"Hello, hello," said Mr. Sorbi to the secretary who looked up from behind a glass wall. "Showing a possible tenant around so we can rent the space." He pulled papers out from his briefcase. "You're moving out on the sixteenth. We want to rent without delay. Dr. Smith's moving to a bigger office," Mr. Sorbi explained to me. "Got too successful." He gave me a big smile and showed me around the office. The tiny waiting room had gray walls. There were three poky gray rooms off a small corridor where an elderly lady was soaking her bunioned feet in a stainless-steel vat. She jerked with surprise when we appeared. Mr. Sorbi gave her a friendly nod, and kept talking.

"You might manage here," he said after we looked around. "But frankly, as a plastic surgeon, you need something bigger." He whisked me to the elevator and we rose to the eleventh floor, where we got out into another windowless, stuffy corridor with gray linoleum tile. I was depressed. It reminded me too much of being seven years old and going to Dr. Harris's office for my tetanus shot. I would be depressed coming to work in this building, and my patients would be depressed coming to see me. Mr. Sorbi pushed me through the door of an office marked HENDERSON LARKINS. OPHTHALMOLOGY. APPOINTMENT ONLY.

"A prospective tenant!" Mr. Sorbi announced loudly as we entered. The white-uniformed secretary behind the glass screen glared at him over her glasses. This waiting room was larger, with yellow burlap wallpaper and bright track lights around the wall.

"A nice extra," said Mr. Sorbi, running his hand over the wallpaper. "It has a nice texture. Feel it, doctor."

The waiting-room chairs were black-and-orange plastic.

"The track lights and the wallpaper you get free. The tenant put them in at his expense. We don't charge you, but it upgrades the office, doesn't it?" Mr. Sorbi pushed me into a corridor. "A nice little work space." He nodded to a cubbyhole where a nurse sat at a table filling in forms. "The bookcases look built in." Mr. Sorbi squeezed behind the nurse with difficulty and edged under the table on his knees to check. "Yes, built in." He climbed out and dusted off his trousers. "Another extra you get free." He smiled triumphantly. "Frankly, this is a superb rental property. I didn't realize what a lot you get thrown in. This office will move fast." He opened the door to a consulting room. "Here's your consulting office. A magnificent window. You don't often get a corner window!"

The window was opaque with dirt and the view was an alley and a blank brick wall.

"Quite impressive. You'll have three nice examining rooms." Mr. Sorbi threw open the doors to each. In the third, Dr. Larkins was examining a patient's eyes in the dark.

"Shut that door!" he shouted without turning around.

"Showing a new tenant," called Mr. Sorbi. "Walk in and take a look," he urged me.

"No, I don't need to," I said uneasily, lowering my voice. "It looks like the others."

"You're the boss," said Mr. Sorbi and he guided me by the elbow out of the office and back to the elevator.

"How much is the office?" I asked, once we were in the lobby. The grimness of the building was wearing off. I was dazzled by how much I would get for free in the large office.

"Around twelve something a square foot," said Mr. Sorbi in an offhand manner. "I could check."

"How much rent would I pay a month?" Square feet meant nothing to me.

"Fourteen hundred dollars a month? Something like that. The going rate for commercial rents is rising all the time." He opened his briefcase and pulled out a handful of paper. "It seems to be twenty-four hundred dollars a month. More than I expected, but such high-class rental property, doctor. It's not much to pay for prime real estate in the city." He nodded wisely, and I did too. The shock was over. Money suddenly seemed irrelevant: I needed this office.

"You can move in in six weeks," said Mr. Sorbi. "Gosh, you're lucky to find any medical office. There's no turnover in medical real estate." He dangled a printed sheet in front of me. "If you're interested, here's the contract. Take it home. Read it. Sign it. Get it back to me . . ." He sighed. "I have to be honest, doctor. There is a serious interest in this office from another doctor. I like you. I'd hate for you to be disappointed." He put the contract in my hand. "If you need the office, you should sign now." I opened my purse and hunted for a pen. "I'll also need a deposit for twenty-four hundred dollars, and the office is yours."

Suddenly, I was a sober, sensible woman, not a sucker. I didn't have that kind of money.

"I'll take it home and think about it."

Mr. Sorbi shook his head. "Someone else may get in before you."

"I want to read the contract first."

"Whatever you want, doctor," said Mr. Sorbi, peeved.

I staggered out of the building into daylight. I hadn't signed. The haze cleared rapidly, followed by disbelief. How could I consider signing a contract, without reading it, for a nondescript office in a horrid building? I didn't need yellow burlap wallpaper and track lighting in downtown Washington. I needed something affordable, and I could find it in the suburbs. The medical schools would have to live without me.

I went back to the office and while I was there read the contract I had not signed. Among other provisions, it held me liable for any injuries to patients of mine, regardless of whether they were hurt in my office or elsewhere in the building — and "regardless of management neglect."

"I'm well out of this," I said with a sigh of relief to Clare.

"Well out of what?" asked my father, coming into the room.

"The office in town."

"You don't want to rent an office. The rent will ruin you. You can't afford it. Stay here."

"Daddy, an examining table won't fit. It's nice of you, but it won't do as an office."

"I wish I were you," said my father with sudden fierceness. "I wish I were your age with your training. I'd make a million bucks."

"Daddy, I'm not a doctor to get rich. I want to do well, but I'm not out to get rich off my patients."

"If I were you, I'd make a million bucks. A million bucks, if I were young again."

He said it to tease me, and I knew he didn't mean it. My father had always been generous and he had never gotten rich off his own patients or in any other way. But I was irritated, despite myself.

My mother had a practical suggestion — that I call Admiral Cuthbert, a family friend, who was a successful speculator in suburban office real estate. The admiral was happy to help.

"If you need an office, my dear, call the Friedman Agency. Tell them to show you the new townhouse offices going up in Twickenham. You could go into one of my buildings at Mayfield but they are not convenient yet. In a few years you move there."

He also explained to me that in commercial real estate, the rent includes commission for the agent of the lessor *and* commission for the agent of the lessee. I didn't know which I was, but I did understand that the commission was included, and I had nothing to lose and a lot of advice to gain by using an agency.

Clare was listening and had looked up the Friedman Agency phone number for me before I hung up.

"You might want to call them now," she said gently, emphasizing "now." I dialed again.

"Hazelton here," said a man with a deep southern voice.

"Hello, I'm interested in seeing the new townhouse office buildings in Twickenham. I'm a doctor."

"Yup" — he said it slowly, like "yu-up" — "I could be your agent for that."

"When is a good time to see the offices?"

Long pause. "Anytime."

"Tomorrow at nine?" I suggested.

"Yup." He cleared his throat. "They're still building."

"Yes, Admiral Cuthbert told me."

"Wear boots. The place is under mud."

"Oh. Weren't they scheduled to be finished this September?"

The southern voice sighed faintly. "To a builder, September means January for sure."

"Oh."

Long pause. "Don't let it get you down. It's a good property. Brick and copper."

"Brick and copper?" It meant nothing to me. "Very nice."

He chuckled. "Brick for the buildings. Brick is expensive, thirty cents a brick. Copper for the drains. Most buildings use tin."

"That sounds excellent."

"No building is worth getting excited about, but you're not wasting your time."

The next morning was pouring with rain and at nine, in boots, I waited for Mr. Hazelton in a drugstore next to the building site. A handsome man of about thirty-five sauntered up.

"I'm Hazelton." Pause. "Mr. Hazelton." Pause. "Rick Hazelton." He turned around to survey the pouring rain, then added, "It sure is raining." He looked down at my boots and nodded approvingly. "Today, you look at the property." He handed me a printed contract. "I don't like some things in this contract, but it's negotiable. You look at the building, but let me talk. Builders don't want to talk to women." He led me across the parking lot, through an opening in a brick wall, and the mud began. The office building was a brick shell with open spaces for windows. Parts of a brick walk had been laid down and we jumped from brick to brick across the mud.

"Brick," said Mr. Hazelton approvingly. He smiled at me briefly and led me into the building. Wires dangled from the ceilings. Two workmen were hammering on the walls, and muddy water lay in puddles on the cement floor.

A short, friendly man of about fifty in a red plaid coat and jeans came up. "I'm Dougall, the foreman. Looks great, don't it?"

"You got a long way to go," said Mr. Hazelton.

Dougall's face fell. "No, we're almost done." He turned to me. "Ma'am, it's a beautiful property we're building. First rate."

Mr. Hazelton grunted. "I don't see your plumbing."

Dougall turned back to him. "Yeah, yeah, it's right here." He led us to an empty area at the far side of the building.

"Will be," said Mr. Hazelton. There was a silence, broken by a gust of warm wind and rain that swept across us.

"Where's O'Donnell?" said Mr. Hazelton.

"Around," said Dougall.

"Yeah," said Mr. Hazelton. Nothing happened and the three of us stood there. Mr. Hazelton looked critically at the wires, the workmen, and the mud puddles.

"I'll get him," said Dougall after a few minutes.

He left us, and Mr. Hazelton walked slowly around the building kicking the walls, counting electrical outlets. Dougall returned.

"He'll meet you at the trailer."

We followed him across the muddy compound, and, halfway, Mr. O'Donnell, the builder, a blond, broad-shouldered man also in a red plaid jacket and jeans, joined us. The four of us approached the trailer in silence. Mr. O'Donnell went up the steps first. Dougall and Rick Hazelton waited for me. Dougall gave me a friendly smile. "It's going to look very pretty, miss," he said happily.

Once we were inside, Dougall unrolled a map lying on a wooden bench. "Let me show you the landscaping. Nice trees here . . ." His voice trailed away and he looked at Mr. O'Donnell. Negotiations were about to begin.

"Well," said Mr. O'Donnell.

Mr. Hazelton said nothing, but slowly opened his jacket and pulled out a copy of the rental contract. He unfolded it on top of a metal desk and ran his finger slowly down items one through seven. His finger stopped at seven. He held it there and said nothing. Mr. O'Donnell held out for a while and then he spoke again.

"Well," said Mr. O'Donnell.

"CPI," said Mr. Hazelton.

"Yeah."

Mr. Hazelton shook his head and ran his finger down to item eight, which listed the price per square foot of office space. "First floor, front," he said slowly.

Mr. O'Donnell looked over Mr. Hazelton's shoulder at the contract and scowled. "Eight-ninety-five," he said at last. "What is she?" He jerked his head in my direction.

Mr. Hazelton looked at him coldly. "Doctor's office."

Mr. O'Donnell turned to examine me. He had icy blue eyes. He turned back to Mr. Hazelton. "We're not looking for doctors. This is commercial."

"Would you like some coffee?" Dougall asked me anxiously.

"No, thank you." Rick Hazelton had told me not to talk and I was following orders. Dougall looked unhappy and touched the sleeve of my coat. "They're having a little business discussion," he explained apologetically. I smiled and nodded. I was learning why most doctors are poor at business matters. We talk too much.

"Trash," said Mr. Hazelton.

"Included," said Mr. O'Donnell. Mr. Hazelton took out a pencil and wrote down on the contract, "Trash included." "*Your* agent ought to put that in the contract," Mr. Hazelton added severely, and then, "Heat."

"Oil," said Mr. O'Donnell.

"Oil?" said Mr. Hazelton in shocked tones.

"Oil." Then, reluctantly, "Oil heat pump."

"Better." Long silence. "Units?" asked Mr. Hazelton.

Mr. O'Donnell unrolled a blueprint and pointed to the front building. "September."

"No," said Mr. Hazelton. It started to rain again and the raindrops clattered on the trailer's metal roof.

"We hoped," said Mr. O'Donnell a few minutes later in an aggrieved tone, as though he had been interrupted. There was a long pause. "We've signed half the first-floor front."

Silence.

"Maybe December," said Mr. O'Donnell.

More silence from Mr. Hazelton.

"You can't find good help nowadays," said Mr. O'Donnell.

"Nope," said Mr. Hazelton. He rocked back and forth on his heels a few times and turned to me. "Questions?"

"No, thank you," I said meekly.

He and Mr. O'Donnell nodded to one another, and Mr. Hazelton led me out of the trailer. Once we were beyond the brick walls, he relaxed. "It's a good property, but here's what we learned. They're not selling fast, because of the CPI, which ties the yearly rent increase to the Consumer Price Index, which is higher than inflation. It favors the builder, but we'll try to beat them down. They don't want doctors because it means a lot of plumbing work and O'Donnell is a brick man. He started in brick. The heating is the best and cheapest available. O'Donnell's a multimillionaire from his buildings, and he didn't get that way by giving property away. Still, the price is lower by four dollars a square foot than comparable prime space, so he is building for tax protection, not for big profit." He gave me a copy of the contract. "Read this. If you like the building, we'll discuss the contract, take a second look, and talk with O'Donnell's agent. If you still like it, we'll have a lawyer work on the contract. Then you'll be ready to sign. If you don't have a lawyer, I'll introduce you to Catherine Bennett. She's excellent."

"I don't have to sign a contract today?"

Rick Hazelton clutched his hair. "This is business, Dr. Morgan. You don't do that in business. O'Donnell is not a crook, but if you sign the contract the way he wrote it, you're giving him money." He looked at me pityingly. "You do understand that though I'm your agent you don't pay me? My commission is taken out of the rent you pay, and paid to me directly."

"Yes," I said. "I do understand that much."

Jimmy was amused when I told him how I spent my morning.

"You've been in the Midwest too long. Now you see why slick businessmen get creamed when they come to the South. They are sharp and they talk fast and they think the southerners are dumb because they talk slow. A talker gives away information. A quiet man can drive a harder bargain."

Catherine Bennett, the lawyer referred by Rick Hazelton, was a southerner, from Kentucky. She talked openly with me — but then, I was her client. She was a beautiful blond woman, slightly older than me, with a ready laugh, happily married. She soon became a good friend. I was impressed by her. She had started her own law firm, invested successfully in real estate, managed her own office building, and still had time for her husband and children.

Two months later, Rick Hazelton met with Catherine Bennett and me so I could sign the office contract, the final result of Hazelton's negotiations on my behalf with O'Donnell's agent. I had read the contract before, but I read it carefully again before I signed. Rick watched me read it in amazement.

"She's learned a lot about business in two months," Catherine told him proudly. "She'll do fine."

Medicine is not business, but there was a lot of business to opening my office, for which I was quite unprepared. I knew a lot about plastic surgery but I was an innocent in the real world, after my seven years of isolation during training. Without my family and friends, I would have quickly been over my head in debt. I was very grateful, and still am.

4

If You Can't Fix Copiers, Try Doctors

BY the end of September I had been in practice three months, but I had not yet seen a single patient. I had hospital privileges at Metropolitan, thanks to Ronald Meade, and privileges at the other hospitals promised or pending. My loan had bought me the new car and paid the deposit on the Twickenham office, but no one knew I existed. No one would know I existed until I sent out office announcements, and I couldn't send out announcements with my telephone and address until I had my permanent office, which had yet to be built.

"October," said Mr. O'Donnell when Clare called him.

"Nope," said Rick Hazelton when she called to ask if this could possibly be true. "Ask him about the inspections. When they're done, you're about a month from move-in."

"Inspections?" said Mr. O'Donnell, aghast when Clare called him again. "We're not even thinking inspections yet."

I didn't have time for patients anyway. I was studying for Part One of the Plastic Surgery Boards, and making lists of what I needed in my new office, and sleeping. I cannot believe how much I slept. I yawned by nine at night, and slept until ten the next day. Jim, a late sleeper in his days of free-lance writing, coughed in loud disapproval when he left the house for his brokerage office at seven-thirty in the morning. (He was working while he studied — the firm paid for his training and the exam fees.) He always woke me up and I promptly went back to sleep. My body had survived seven years of sleep-starved nights during my surgical training and it was catching up at last. The irony of a doctor's training is that residents are taught to restore patients to health by a system that ruins their own. I had seven years of little sleep, no exercise, and junk food. In June, as a resident, I had looked askance at private doctors who wouldn't get out of bed to see a patient at night. Now, I too was reluctant to take night call. I wondered if I would be too tired to cope with a busy medical practice, but Ronald Meade, Peter Wallace, Robert Fletcher, Sven Ohlsen managed. If they could, so could I. Except for an office, office equipment, and patients, my practice was ready. I wanted to order the equipment before I left for the dreaded Board exam because it might take weeks to arrive.

"Why are you up so early?" Jim asked me one morning when I climbed out of bed at seven. He made himself a breakfast of a large glass of Coke and a dish of fudge-ripple ice cream. Some people's bodies like to be insulted. Jim's teeth were in perfect condition, he stayed fit without exercise, and suffered no apparent vitamin deficiencies. Also, he didn't smoke and rarely drank.

"Dr. Devereux has offered to introduce me to the man who set up his office for him."

"Who is Dr. Devereux?"

"Someone Rupert knows."

"Why do you need someone to set up your office? Can't you make a list of things you need and go out to a medical-supply store and buy them?"

"Jimmy, you know me. If I could consider renting that

Georgetown mansion, I don't have business sense, and it's easier and better to have someone do it for me. Every doctor hires a professional to set up his office."

Jimmy stirred the fudge ripple and frowned. "In the business," he said, meaning stockbroking, "doctors are well known to be fools. What about that plastic-surgeon friend of yours who bought underwater Florida real estate and phony mail-order diamonds from Chad? Did he have a professional set up his office for him?"

"Yes."

"Enough said. Think carefully before you make an agreement. These professionals are in the business for their health, not yours. By the way, I've decided to go to New York and do commodities. The stock market is dead. Real estate is dead. Commodities are the big money. Soybeans and pork bellies. That is action." He ate the ice cream dreamily. "There's a client at the office who buys pork bellies for his own account. He makes millions a month. Would you be interested in a sixty-five-year-old pork-belly millionaire? No, I take that back. I just remembered that he's married."

I left Jim studying hog-futures listings in the *Wall Street Journal* and set out to see Dr. Devereux, whose office was on the sixteenth floor of a downtown office building. I walked down a wide corridor decorated with modern art and into his waiting room, a bright area with a friendly atmosphere. Comfortable upholstered chairs and small sofas beckoned me, and blue-and-green flowered wallpaper gave the room a cheerful look. On the far side of a glass partition sat a receptionist, surrounded by ivory file cabinets and a mass of paper forms.

"Elizabeth?" asked Dr. Devereux, coming into the waiting room. "Rupert tells me you have come to Washington after fifteen years of training. Welcome back. Let me show you around." We walked together down a short corridor. "I'm a cardiologist and for me this is a great office. Fred did it all for me. I don't want to sell you anything, but Fred truly helped me. I couldn't have opened this office without him. I've been in practice awhile. It's my second office. He gave me four examining rooms. Each one has an examining table, a built-in desk, a hook for clothes, a mirror, and a dictating machine. It's a thoughtful office. There are a lot of things to think about when you design an office." He looked at his watch. "I hope Fred comes. He said he might have time. He's really in demand. See if he can work you into his schedule. He can help you." I followed Dr. Devereux into the secretary's area to meet a charming woman with lovely green eyes who was the doctor's business manager. She made Fred sound like the mastermind I needed for my office.

"Fred convinced us to try a new computer billing system," the business manager explained to me. "It should make things easier, but the computer has been programmed wrong and all our bills are being rejected by the insurance companies. I hope Fred remembers to bring in some more forms. I've asked him twice."

"Hello, hello, folks! A good day all!" A scrawny man in a blue-jean jacket pushed his way through the door into the secretary's area. A fashionable gold chain glittered on his neck, and his face was deeply tanned, with a bright smile.

"Fred," said Dr. Devereux, "meet Dr. Morgan. She's starting an office of her own."

Fred looked hurriedly at his slim gold wristwatch. "I think I have a few spare minutes." He grinned at me. "Be glad to give you a few pointers." He spread out the fingers of his right hand in a gesture of beneficence. "Free advice from a pro, no strings attached. If what I say seems good to you, we could be a team, but you're under no obligation. No obligation at all." He nodded emphatically. The business manager cleared her throat.

"Fred, did you forget those computer billing forms? The end of the month is coming and we need to send out the bills. Remember, no bills out, no money in."

"Next week!" He held up his index finger admonishingly. "I told them we need those forms next week, or we take your business elsewhere. You have to set limits."

"Precisely. I want them this week!" the business manager said firmly. Fred nodded and turned to me, steering me into the hallway.

"Let me show you the layout of Dr. Devereux's office, as an example. You aren't in cardiology are you?" He turned to look at me and guessed the usual women's specialties: "Gynecology? General Practice? Pediatrics?"

"No, I'm a plastic surgeon."

"A plastic surgeon! I'm the person you need. I opened a beautiful office for two new plastic surgeons in Ross. You don't have to worry about money, my dear. I had those boys in their office on July first and they made a thousand dollars each their first week. They were busy. Don't worry about money." He guided me into an examining room.

"Let me show you . . ." He lowered his voice, "Now with all due respect to Dr. Devereux, this office of his, good as it is, is not what you want or need as a plastic surgeon. You need an entirely different style. Something a bit, well . . . you can't do it on a shoestring, not in plastic surgery. You have to create an image." He waved a hand at the examining table. "This is strictly functional office furniture. You need an electric table, and for you . . ." He looked at me meditatively. "I would say you need a yellow examining room, a blue one, and a green one — different colors, different feelings. Something bright, cheerful but pastel. Now!" He pointed his finger at me. "As a plastic surgeon, has it ever occurred to you what kind of office desk you need?"

"No," I said, "it hasn't. I have a desk, already."

"No! No! No!" He clutched his head. "My dear Dr. Morgan, can I call you Elizabeth? I think we'll be good friends. Your attitude is the way terrible mistakes get made. You have a patient across the desk from you — you are sitting opposite him and you have to show him his preoperative photographs. You must have an L-shaped desk, so you can turn the slide viewer — you need a big-screen model — to him and away, without wasted motion. Don't waste motion. Wasted motion is wasted time, and time is money."

"Where do I get an L-shaped desk?" I asked.

Fred thought for a moment, arms folded, leaning against the wall. "Not easy to say. It has to be custom-made. I know a very good man who could make you one on a special order, but it takes several months. When do you want your office open?"

"I have a temporary office, but my permanent one may be ready as early as November." I could hear Rick Hazelton saying "Nope," but I was optimistic.

Fred shook his head thoughtfully. "I hate to rush you, but if you want your office open in November you have to order your desk in the next week or two."

"How much would it cost?"

"Not much more than a regular office desk, maybe fifteen hundred dollars, maybe two thousand. He's reasonable."

"Two thousand dollars for a desk?"

"Opening an office is expensive, but you can't worry about money. Money is not a problem. Dr. Devereux didn't believe me, but I told him — get a big loan. No rinky-dink business. A good doctor needs a big loan. He couldn't get ten thousand from his local bank, and I said forget it. I took him to the biggest bank in the state — I have a lot of useful business connections — and in ten minutes they gave him fifty thousand dollars. *You* need more than that, at least seventy-five thou, but you can't let that bother you. You have to do it right —

money is quality. You don't want your patients to think you're no good. You're young. You're a woman. You need authority. Quality gives you authority. Another thing!" He put his hands behind his back, and jutted out his chin. "Has it occurred to you that you need a quick, easy-to-remember number? I can get you — with my business contacts — a special business number. A phone number is a seven-digit number — and so is *plastic*. Get your phone number P-L-A-S-T-I-C. You couldn't swing it, but I have punch at the phone company, and I could arrange it for you. There are a thousand things to think of and that's what I'm here for. I think of everything and I arrange it. You can't do it. You don't get taught useful things in medical schools. Doctors don't know zilch about starting a practice. You need someone. You need me."

"If you do set up my office for me, how do I pay you? What is your fee?"

"No fee," Fred shook his head firmly. "A percentage. Only ten percent of the bill. It doesn't come to much. I make my money doing volume. For a thousand dollars, you only pay me a hundred, and that means I've done everything — called the company, found your best deal, gotten you a doctor's discount. On top of that, I get you my own business discount from my special contacts, plus delivery when you need it, and when you want it." He glanced at his watch. "I have to run. I have a business partner to meet for lunch. I don't want to push you. I'm not the hard-sell type. You do what you want, but I am going away next week for a two-week vacation, and if you are thinking of opening an office, start now! Don't let time get away from you." He glanced at the business card I had given him. "Morgan," he said. "I used to fix the copying machine for some Morgans, years ago. Well, nice talking with you. Bye!" He gave me his card and sailed out of the office. I thanked the business manager and Dr. Devereux after Fred left. I was convinced I needed Fred.

"Elizabeth." The business manager stopped me. "Dr. Devereux and I like Fred, but we both want you to understand him. He helped us. He's a nice man, he's honest, but please don't feel you have to ask him to help you because of us. Dr. Devereux has been in practice quite a while. He knows exactly where to draw the line, and so do I. If you do use Fred, have a budget and make him stick to it. You have to control him. Supervise him. You must keep him to a budget," she said urgently.

I thanked her, but my decision was made. My office was going to be expensive. Fred thought a $50,000 loan was not enough. I had hoped not to need a second loan after the one for $38,000. I drove home in the pouring rain, trying to accustom myself to the strange new world in which $75,000 was "not much money." I narrowly missed driving my new car into a truck with a flat tire that had stopped on the freeway. I swerved, the truck driver jumped back in surprise, cursing me, and I went on musing. Fred was right that women lacked authority as surgeons. I found myself thinking of the "good old days" when I was a resident. But that was nonsense. I gripped the steering wheel and decided to keep my budget firmly in mind and immediately to ask Fred to do my office for me. I missed my exit, took a detour home, and was disconsolately eating a cheese sandwich when my parents dropped by.

"Where have you been, Elizabeth?" My father's gaze strayed to the trash bin. My father throws nothing away and considers Jim and me extravagant. He has a collection of old towels, note pads, and broken china that he has salvaged from my discarded possessions. It is amazing how often they prove useful, to my chagrin.

"I was over at Dr. Devereux's — he's a friend of Rupert's, Jim's real estate friend. He introduced me to a man. I'm going to ask him to do my office for me."

Solo Practice

"You don't need someone to do your office," said my father scornfully. "You're not throwing this away, are you?" He extracted from the trash my college physics notebook, which I had finally discarded. "This could be useful. May I have it? All this man will do is spend your money. You have a brain. Do it yourself at half the cost."

"Daddy, I can't. It's too complicated." I went back to my bread and cheese.

My mother came in behind my father with a bunch of roses from her garden and studied Fred's business card. "It's a common name. But I don't suppose he likes to be called Fred, does he?"

"Yes."

"A thin, energetic man who likes jewelry."

"Yes."

"He used to fix our copying machine for us many years ago. Now he's a doctor's business advisor, is he?"

"Yes."

"I hope he's better at that than he was at fixing copiers. He was a nice young man, but the machines always broke down as soon as he left."

My bread and cheese were tasteless. I had expected sympathy from my mother. But how else could I get all the equipment I needed? I didn't even know how to order office stationery. Then Jim came in.

"Big trouble at work today," he reported. "Three brokers left for Forrester, taking a million dollars in accounts with them. Too much excitement to get any work done, so I came home. Did you find someone to open your office?"

I patiently explained to my attentive but doubting family my need for an L-shaped desk and color-coordinated examining rooms, and that Fred would only charge me ten percent, which would be more than made up for by the business dis-

74

counts he could get me. My mother nodded encouragingly. My father inspected the trash while he listened, shaking his head from time to time. He came up with an empty jam jar, which he kept, and a torn manila folder, which he replaced in the trash.

Jim listened politely for a while and then broke out laughing. "Sure," he said, "the desk is two thousand dollars, a special for you, plus tax, plus delivery, plus ten percent of the gross for him. Elizabeth! You don't need a special-order L-shaped desk to be a plastic surgeon. The guy's a con artist."

"He is not."

"It's nothing personal, Elizabeth. If doctors were good at business, they'd be businessmen, not doctors. He may help a hardheaded man like Devereux, but this Fred hears you're a plastic surgeon, sees you're a woman, and he knows he's found a soft touch. The glitter in his eyes is the dollar sign. He'll spend a hundred thousand dollars of your money, charge you ten thousand dollars for the honor, and get a ten percent kickback from his business contacts. Some deal, for him. Why don't you make a list of what you need and go to a medical-supply house and buy it? The rest you can get from an office-furniture store and a printer."

"I can't do it," I protested. "I walk into a medical-supply place and say I'm a woman doctor, and before I know it, four salesmen will swoop in for the kill and I'll buy three electric examining tables and an operating microscope. I can't think clearly when salesmen are hounding me to buy. No one can."

"Milk, anyone?" Jim poured himself a glass and drank it down. "You have a point. That's what makes them good salesmen. Tell you what. I'll come with you."

"Jim, it won't help. I'm the doctor."

"Sure, you're the doctor" — he poured himself some more milk — "but that's none of their business, right? I'll be the doctor. I won't say I am, but unless we tell them, they'll assume you're a nurse or something. You look around, choose what you want while they work on me. It's a great scam."

"Terrific," said my father with hearty approval, fishing up a mildewed kitchen sponge for inspection. He sniffed the sponge, drew back in distaste, and replaced it in the trash. "Jim is absolutely right. Do it now."

Two hours later Jim and I were in a medical-supply house and a salesman was trying to sell Jim a ten-thousand-dollar operating table. Jim folded his arms cross his chest thoughtfully.

"I agree it's a nice machine," Jim said as the salesman demonstrated the foot pedal and the table rose swiftly into the air, "but the price tag is high. It's for an established doctor, not one starting out."

"We can give it to you on the installment plan," said the salesman. He didn't pay the slightest attention to me, and I was pottering around the showroom happily testing drawers on the examining tables I could afford. "Works out as a tax benefit for you, sir, because you can deduct the interest and depreciate the table and pay us off over three years." He handed Jim a printed payment schedule.

Jim studied it. "Eighteen percent interest is no bargain."

"Beg pardon, sir?"

"This works out to eighteen percent interest." Jim handed back the payment schedule.

The salesman looked at it. "Yes, it does. I must say I never worked out the yearly interest rate. You're pretty sharp. Most doctors don't notice it either."

Jim caught my eye. I was ready to order my tables, and I nodded back.

"I'm not a doctor," said Jim innocently. "I'm sorry. It's my sister who is the surgeon. I don't need an examining table. I'm a stockbroker."

I ordered everything I needed that afternoon — five thousand dollars' worth: two tables, two stools, two metal carts, dressings.

"Wastebaskets," the salesman said at the end, convinced we weren't an easy touch and he'd do better helping me save money, not spend it. "You need two. Don't get these." He kicked the orange ones that were on display. "They're forty-two fifty. Rubbermaid sells the same thing for eighteen dollars in gray. Save you a couple of bucks. I'll order them." He made a note of it, walked us to the door, and shook hands. "I must say, you two had me fooled. I have to remember your technique. That's really smart." He waved good-bye as we drove off.

"He enjoyed that," said Jim on the way home. "Good salesmen don't like selling to suckers. It's too easy. Now listen, what do you think of my getting a job with the Chicago Board of Trade — can't you see me running around, going long on corn, short on hogs?"

"You'd be great," I said, and Jim would be. He has many talents and thrives on excitement. "But you said yesterday you hated Chicago and you could never stand to live there."

"Yes, I remember that. It is Midwest. I prefer New York, and I guess Chicago is not New York, is it? I'll have to think about it."

A few days later, Jim decided against the Chicago Board of Trade and I had to leave to take Part One of the Board exam.

"I'll say this, Elizabeth," said Jim the night I left, after I had moaned for five minutes about my inability to memorize the name of the blood supply to the groin flap. "You'd better pass Boards because I don't think I could stand it again. Just to take your mind off the exam, I'm going to explain buying stock on margin."

"Jim, thank you, but it won't help, and anyhow, you explained it last night."

"So tell me about buying on margin."

"I don't remember, but I have to pack."

"I'll keep you company." He sat down at the top of the stairs with a Coke. "Buying on margin is borrowing half the money from the brokerage house . . ."

He drove me to the airport, and by the time I boarded the plane, I not only knew about margin calls, but I remembered the blood supply to the groin flap.

The exam was to be given in the Paris Inn at the end of a five-day review course, which everyone — including me — attended, taking notes furiously. A central computer had supposedly arranged a hotel room for each examinee, but, as computers do, it forgot to reserve a room for me. The hotel clerk shook his head firmly, unmoved by my plight. "We don't have a room, ma'am. I know for a fact that there is not one hotel room left in town this week. It's convention time. There's nothing we can do to help you. Why don't you share a room with someone else?" he suggested.

I gave him a sour smile. All the plastic surgeons I knew were men. Yes, I could see myself suggesting to John Stilwell that I share his room.

"Hey, Liz," said a familiar voice behind me. "There's no problem. Share my room." It was Sylvia Train. We had been plastic-surgery residents together, and friends ever since. Sylvia — tall, tawny-haired, cool — was one of the few women who were mothers, wives, and full-time surgeons. She managed it with apparent ease.

"It would be fantastic," I said.

"For me, too. You have no idea how nervous I am about this exam. I know absolutely nothing. I haven't studied. I am a nervous wreck. Complete ignorance. You can imagine how easy it was for me to study. Ann is learning to walk and Vicky won't budge without Mommy. I'll fail for sure."

We spent the next five days sitting on our beds in the Paris

Inn, cross-legged, quizzing each other. It was like college again.

"Okay, Sylvia, what's the embryologic origin of the ear?"

"Six hillocks, mandibular and maxillary arch."

"Which is which?"

"I think it's the tragus from the maxillary and the rest of the mandibular."

"Right, your turn."

"Name me the nerve that causes Frey's syndrome."

"Glossopharyngeal through the pterygoid plexus. Why in the name of God do we have to learn all this nonsense? We're doctors, aren't we? We're surgeons? Have you ever needed to use this information? Has anyone ever taught you this information? What is the point?"

"Don't argue, Elizabeth. There is no point. It's a little game to amuse a group of aging plastic surgeons who call themselves the Examining Board. Give me the nerve and blood supply to the rectus femoris flap."

The night before the exam, at six-fifteen, Sylvia suddenly threw her study notes in the air and screamed, "I can't take it. I can't take it. What will I do if I fail? I know nothing."

"Let's have dinner."

"Don't be so reasonable."

"I'm not being reasonable. I'm petrified."

"It's too awful for words. Let's have dinner."

The hotel had been built around a huge courtyard. Our room was in an annex, but from the fifth-floor balcony, as we awaited the elevator, we could look down on a pianist and a singer in the bar below. As the music drifted up through a loudspeaker system, a man charged out of his room, slammed the door, and collided with Sylvia. It was her friend Tom Blotnick, another plastic surgeon studying for the exam.

"My God!" he shouted, staggering back. "Can you believe this hotel? This is the rottenest hole I've ever been in. I could hear that goddamned singer all afternoon. I called the management a hundred times and told them to stuff a potato in her mouth, but no — sing, sing, sing. Why is this exam being given here?"

"It's all right, Tom," said Sylvia soothingly. "You'll be just fine." She patted his curly head maternally. "Come to dinner with us — that's a good boy. Don't worry."

We sat down to dinner, and were joined by two surgeon friends of Tom's — Greg York and Louis Zaccaro.

"Where are you from?" said Greg, a tall, bony, black-haired man. "Be sure to order seafood. This is oyster city."

"I'm Elizabeth Morgan. I'm starting my practice in D.C."

"Listen, if anyone wants to open your office for you, tell him to go to hell."

"What do you mean? Someone did offer to open my office for me, but I decided to try it on my own."

"Smart girl. Let me tell you what happened to us." He nudged Louis, who was short and red-haired. "This is Louis. Louis and I are partners. Did we ever get taken to the cleaners! A friend introduced us to this guy six months before we finished our residency. We wanted to open an office and did he seem like a heaven-sent angel. The deals he could get for us sounded golden. He promised our office would open on June fifth, and he would have it ready. All we had to do was to walk in."

"For a mere ten percent commission. A deal," said Louis bleakly. He stopped our waitress. "Make that scotch a double, miss. June fifth I arrived, and not only was the office not quite ready — it was empty! Empty! No furniture. He had some buddy lined up to make our furniture for us — did your guy try the L-shaped desk on you? Now we have to wait until November! The desks came and the 'L' is on the wrong side — we're both left-handed, and his carpenter friend put the 'L' on the right. Had we told him? A thousand times!" He tossed down the double scotch as though to obliterate painful memories and Greg York continued the saga.

"Our stationery was wrong the first time — he spelled our names wrong. Not just the last names — even Louis was printed wrong. The second time *plastic surgery* was spelled wrong, and the third time the address was wrong. We had to go out and buy folding plastic garden chairs for the waiting room so we could see patients, because we were on call at an emergency room that first week. It was bloody hell. A monkey would have done it better. And every time we'd tell him we needed something, it was tomorrow, tomorrow. See this coffee?" continued Greg, stirring in milk. "I never used to take milk in coffee, but honest to God, the man gave me an ulcer. He spent money we didn't have. His 'deals' are higher-than-market prices from dealers who give him a kickback. Half the stuff he bought for us is junk. The stationery, even when he got it right, is tacky. All you need is a secretary, chairs in the waiting room, an examining table, and some bandages. We were two honest boys from the Midwest and we got taken to the cleaners!"

"You should have done what I did," said Tom. "An academic job with a salary and no headaches."

"Perpetual adolescence," said Greg impatiently. "I don't want someone telling me what to do the rest of my life."

The rest of the dinner was spent in gloomy predictions that we would all fail Boards. The exam, given once a year, is multiple-choice and computer-scored. If you pass, you then take Part Two, the oral part, in which you describe operations you have performed. Part Two is also given once a year, and you have three chances to pass. If you fail all three times, you can practice without Board certification or go back and do part of your residency over again. A lot of plastic surgeons fail. In 1980 almost a third failed the written exam, and another third failed the oral exam. We were nervous with good reason.

"Have you seen Tewkesbury?" Sylvia asked me after dinner. "He's in town for some meeting. I saw him in the lounge last night. He'll be surprised to see you. In fact, I was surprised to see you. He told me you had decided to take an extra year of residency because you thought you weren't good enough. Such a friend. He seems to have settled down a lot. He's looking much happier."

The next morning the exam proved difficult, but not impossible. Sylvia and I sat far apart, so as not to distract one another. Our studying had been worthwhile. We had lunch together in the coffee shop before the afternoon session began. In the restroom after lunch I was surprised to find a middle-aged lady sobbing loudly.

"Are you all right?" I asked foolishly. She was obviously not.

"No, there's nothing you can do," she moaned. "Go away, please." She looked up at me. "I recognize you. You took the exam today too."

"Yes. Are you a plastic surgeon?"

"In Houston."

"Are you sick?"

"No. I'm sure I failed the exam today."

"No, you didn't," I said, patting her on the shoulder. "I'm sure you did fine."

"You don't know. I didn't have time to study. I'm in private practice. How could I study?" she demanded bitterly. "I've been in practice twenty years. I can't stop and take a month off to study."

"You can take it next year then."

"No!" She was almost angry. "You don't understand. I already failed twice." She took a deep breath, shook my hand away, and wiped her face. "I studied with Blau. I was his resident, and later, his associate. I never took Boards because it wasn't necessary back then. Blau died. I went into practice and three years ago my hospital changed its rules. I lose my privileges if I don't pass the exam. They gave me until this year to pass." She glanced at her watch. "It's time to go back for the rest of the exam."

"Perhaps you'll do better in the afternoon session," I said to cheer her up.

"No, I know this is the hardest part for me." She pursed her lips. "I don't know what I will do now."

Will Van Tromp, my plastic surgeon friend from Louisiana who had advised me on how many square feet I needed, had a seat near mine and I found him stretching.

"How is it going, Liz?" he was asking when someone came up from behind me.

"Hey there, Will. How's it going?" It was Tewkesbury's familiar voice. I almost screamed. We both turned to face each other, and the Tarantula looked at me in shock. "You're here?" he said angrily, and walked away. Will laughed.

"You're not his favorite female, are you? You must have done something to burn him. He's not a guy to forget a grudge. Don't let him throw you, kid."

All the same, I was thrown. My concentration was gone and bitter memories came back, edging out all the information I had stored for the exam. I knew that I would fail if I let this panic control me. An acid-faced proctor tapped on the microphone.

"Ladies and gentlemen, please take your seats. The slides will begin in five minutes. Write your answer on the answer sheet we pass out. It's self-explanatory. Any of you who don't understand the printed instructions are welcome to leave and come back next year when you can read." Will gave the V-for-victory sign, and we settled down in our seats.

The exam began with slides, projected on a screen, showing microscopic sections of diseases of the hand, face, and skin. We had thirty seconds to identify each one, sixty slides in all. The first five went by me. I saw them but they made no impression. I was imagining the Tarantula's glee — and Jacques Villiers's and Ronald Meade's dismay — if I failed the exam. It was a disgrace to fail. The sixth slide was easy for me. It was a melanoma, and I knew skin diseases well. I had to flashback to the first slide — that must have been verrucous nevus; and I remembered the third, that was a basal cell. I was back in the groove. Seven was a fibrous xanthoma. The Tarantula faded away. The exam lasted till 5:00 but I finished at 4:30.

Sylvia had gone by that time and I went to the hotel lobby in search of my suitcase.

"All right, don't speak to me," said a voice. I saw nothing till I looked into a deep, plush lobby sofa. It was Grant, an old friend. Surely Grant had passed Boards years ago? He laughed.

"No, dummy, I'm not taking the exam. I'm here for a conference. Did you pass?"

"I think so. If I didn't, there's no hope, because I studied like mad. How are you?"

"Bored. You can't be a doctor these days without spending most of your time in conference. You'll find out about CME soon enough. This was on birth defects. I didn't pay any attention. I've heard it all before. I got in late last night, and I slept through most of the meeting. I have to leave today to do a transsexual tomorrow morning."

"A what?"

"A transsexual. A male-to-female change, on a guy as crazy as a loon. Why he wants me to hunk off his dingus and give him boobs I don't know, but I'll do anything for two thousand dollars."

"Grant, you can't do that kind of surgery. Those sex-change people are crazy. A scalpel won't make them normal, will it?"

Grant laughed. He liked to see me get indignant, and I could never tell when he was serious. "Don't get worked up. I'm going to stop. They are not only crazy, they cause trouble after the surgery. The guys fall in love with me and my wife gets jealous. I don't like having weirdos chase me around, but apart from that, Liz, what are your objections? Surgery is business. They have the money and want an operation. I can do the operation and want the money. The psychiatrists clear them ahead of time. Hell, if it hadn't been for transsexuals, I wouldn't have been able to build up a plastic-surgery collection for the hospital library — operations bring in money and you need money for everything — academic practice, private practice, health plans, it makes no difference." He groaned. "I'm exhausted. I hate travel. Listen, do you know a Dr. Tewkesbury?"

I looked at him steadily. "Yes, I know him."

"I met him briefly. He's not signing up for your fan club. He might try to torpedo you on Part Two." Grant winked suggestively. "Want me to give him your love? That might make him change his mind."

"No, but if you see him tell him how much I appreciate his helping me get hospital privileges."

Grant laughed. "What a determined guy! Did he really try to stop you?" I nodded.

"I've got an idea," said Grant. "I'll tell him you're in private practice, making barrels of cash. He'll have a seizure, he'll be so mad. Seriously, Liz, if you have a problem case and need an older surgeon's advice, you can give me a call. Some of us are nice guys and we like to help people get started."

I thanked him. It was comforting to know there were good surgeons willing to stand behind me.

Sylvia and I sat together on the flight to D.C.

"Please don't talk about the exam," she begged me.

"Never." It was the last thing I wanted. We were silent for a while. Then we looked at each other.

"What about the last slide?" she ventured.

"I'm pretty sure it was a sarcoma," I said. Sylvia winced.

"What about the tenth?" I asked.

"That was a malignant mixed." It was my turn to look pained. We talked about the exam the whole trip — the more we talked, the more I knew that my answers were wrong and I had failed. Sylvia transferred to another flight when my trip ended in D.C. My mother and Jim met me at the airport.

"I failed," I told them immediately. It was best to get it over.

"Elizabeth, are you sure?" asked my mother, looking closely at me.

"Now, Mother, don't pay any attention," said Jim, deftly picking my suitcase off the conveyor belt through a barrier of other passengers. "She always says that. Don't encourage her. She'll feel tragic."

We laughed and went out to the car, but I didn't change my mind. I knew I had failed. If being a secretary didn't suit me — and I knew I wasn't tidy enough to be a good one — I would try for a job as a food store checkout clerk.

5
John Lennon

I thought about Boards as little as possible. My hurdle now was to make my practice work and have a social life too. I wanted to meet lots of people, make friends, and do all the things I had missed in my twenties.

Robert Fletcher had told me months before that my "lifeline" would be emergency-room work. In the Washington area most people work, and most of them have medical insurance. This did not mean, as I found out, that they would pay my bills, but emergency work meant I could count on some money coming directly to me from insurance.

"Be sure to get people to sign the damned insurance forms," Robert instructed me, "in the emergency room, if you can. Half the people I see don't keep follow-up office appointments, and if you don't get that form signed, you're out of luck. Once their faces are sewn up, they don't care if you get paid or not."

Robert was right about the emergency-room work, but I had to wait weeks to get my name on the Metropolitan call schedule. I didn't have to wait for emergency calls to get my first patients though. Back when I first came home from my residency, a man named Ray Patterson had called. He wanted to see a woman plastic surgeon, not a man, and I was the only woman plastic surgeon in the area. Clare explained to him that I wasn't ready to take patients. I didn't even have malpractice insurance, although she didn't mention that. He called again shortly after I took Part One of the Boards, and Clare gave him an appointment for the next day.

"He sounds peculiar," Clare said, hanging up the phone. "Brusque, almost rude. I asked him why he was coming to see you, but he wouldn't say." She folded her hands on top of the typewriter. "I'm running out of things to do, Elizabeth, now that all your forms and licenses and applications and medical papers are done. It's time for people to start calling."

I saw two patients that first day — Ray Patterson and Leslie O'Connor, who was referred to me by Odette de Blanchaud, an internist I had met by chance at a hospital conference. Odette was working in the Metropolitan emergency room while her husband, an oncologist, started his practice. She was going to start one of her own after that. She was the opposite of the sturdy-shoe, tweed-suit woman-doctor stereotype. She was thin and graceful, with a beautiful face — high cheekbones, intelligent gray eyes, and masses of blond hair. "It's too much for our little boy to worry about both his parents. He's only four, but he can tell when we're anxious — and starting a practice is an anxious time, as you know." Odette did her medical training in America, but grew up in France, and she spoke with a slight accent. Suddenly she interrupted her personal history — "You don't do noses, do you? Of course you do cosmetic work, but are you interested in reconstruction?"

"Yes," I said emphatically.

"I know a girl who needs you desperately. Leslie O'Connor. I'll tell her parents to call."

Clare was thrilled when Leslie called, and she scheduled

an appointment for her after Ray's. I was still using my parents' office — Mr. O'Donnell's new office building, true to Rick Hazelton's prediction, was far from finished. When I called, I was told I could move in "sometime soon." When Clare called, she was told to call back in the morning.

"Don't worry," Hazelton told me. "You'll move in on January first, believe me. No matter what they promise you, you won't be able to move in earlier. Even reliable builders are always four months late."

Using my parents' consulting room was awkward, because it obviously was not a doctor's office. It was a small room with two big windows, painted a cheerful sunflower yellow and furnished with a sturdy, thirty-year-old Army-surplus oak desk and two comfortable armchairs — suitable for a psychologist, not quite as useful for a physician. I longed for the security and reassurance of a "proper" office as I awaited my first patients.

Clare poked her head through the door. "Mr. Patterson is here." She handed me the registration form he had filled out. For occupation he had put *Disabled from foot injury.*

"What is he like?"

She thought for a moment. "A handsome young man, but he doesn't look disabled. All I can say is, he's odd."

I put on my white coat and headed down the narrow hall to the waiting room. Clare's description made me realize for the first time how vulnerable we were. The office was empty except for us. My parents had turned it over to me for the day. My father was spending the day in the country, while my mother was doing the weekly food shopping. Their secretary only worked in the mornings. On the right side of the house was parking space for another building, on the left was an empty house, and behind us there was an empty lot on which a real estate speculator was planning to build a warehouse. The country road was quickly becoming a suburban commercial and industrial strip, but we were isolated. I wished I had taken karate classes in medical school.

I opened the door to the waiting room. Mr. Patterson was a rather pathetic, droopy young man with longish, unkempt hair and dirty sandals. His shoulders slouched. He followed me into the hall but dashed back to the waiting room and returned clutching a green plastic bag. We went into the consulting room and I closed the door and sat down behind the old oak desk. "Please have a seat, Mr. Patterson." I pointed to the two armchairs opposite me. Mr. Patterson did not sit down, but leaned across the desk staring at me, pushing his face close to mine. I leaned back, feeling threatened.

"Please sit down, Mr. Patterson. Tell me what I can do to help you."

"The hospital sent me. I wanted a woman plastic surgeon and you're the only one." He smirked and slapped the plastic bag onto the top of the desk. "I've been thrown out of doctors' offices for this before." He watched me intently and slowly opened the bag.

Still smiling at me, he slid his hand slowly into the plastic bag. I tensed. He whipped something large and hard out of the bag and slammed it onto the desk. It was the cardboard jacket to a record album — *Meet the Beatles*. Mr. Patterson pointed to the photograph of John Lennon.

"Make me like him," he said. "And I also want you to remove this scar on my face." He touched his sideburns.

Through the window I saw an old blue pickup truck turn into our driveway. My father was back from the country. I relaxed. "Mr. Patterson, plastic surgery cannot make one person look exactly like another." He had a round, bland face and brown eyes. "No one could make you look like John Lennon."

He kept his eyes fixed on me and continued to smile. "You

are the woman to operate on me. I went to another plastic surgeon. He refused. He threw me out of the office and said I was nuts, but I am prepared to pay. You see my nose?" He pointed to his well-shaped straight nose. "I want you to make my nose turn up like Lennon's." I looked down at Lennon's face on the record album. His nose did not turn up.

"Then I want you to work on my eyes."

"What's wrong with your eyes?"

"There is something wrong with the way my eyes are set in my face. I want you to work on that." He tugged at his untrimmed sideburns and laughed.

"I'm not sure what you have in mind," I protested.

He ignored me. "I also want you to remove this scar." He pointed to his sideburns. "I got this scar when I was young. If I didn't have this scar, I would not need to wear the sideburns so long to hide it. If I shave off my sideburns, people will notice my scar." I stood up and meticulously examined the skin in front of his ear. Giggling, he pulled his hair away to show me the scar. There was no scar.

"I don't see a scar," I said.

"There isn't one. It's not a real scar, but when I was young, the skin got bruised because a neighbor hit me."

"If there is no scar, I can't operate on it, can I?"

"You can try."

I shook my head. "Surgery can improve a scar," I explained slowly, "but it can't erase it, and besides that, I can't operate on a scar that doesn't exist. Do you understand?"

"No." Ray Patterson kept smiling, but abruptly turned to the left and looked over his shoulder as though someone had come up behind him.

He shifted his eyes sideways so he could see me. "I am going to make it big, doctor. I was in India, studying yoga for a long, long time. I've had visions. I am a prophet. I could have thousands of followers. Will you operate on me?"

"Mr. Patterson, I can't possibly operate. I could never make you look like Lennon. No one could, and you don't have a scar." I glanced at his registration form. "When did you hurt your foot?" I wondered to myself if he had suffered a brain injury at the same time. He turned to look at me, and suddenly whirled around to look behind again.

"I never hurt my foot. I'm on total disability. I didn't have any injury, but I need a lot of narcotics for the pain." He looked back to me. "The pain is unbearable. Would you write me a narcotic prescription? My regular doctor is on vacation."

"No."

"I really would like you to operate," he whispered.

"Mr. Patterson, I'm sorry. Surgery won't help you."

"I could do with a prescription for the pain, doctor."

I stood up, opened the door, and guided him back to the waiting room. He walked into the middle of the room, stopped dead, looked over his left shoulder, bolted out the front door and ran to his car, gunned the engine frantically, and raced out of the driveway in a shower of gravel. Clare looked at me in astonishment, and just then Leslie O'Connor walked in with her mother. "He was in a hurry to get away," remarked Mrs. O'Connor.

"He's late for another appointment," said Clare smoothly, as she handed Leslie a registration form.

I was fascinated by Leslie's nose. Normal noses come in various shapes and sizes. The nose is useful but rarely an object of great beauty. Most people want nose surgery to remove a bump in the middle that they have been teased about. Plastic surgery can modify such a nose but it doesn't make a vast difference.

Leslie's nose was another matter. She was a slim college freshman, with a friendly smile and bright blue eyes. Except for her nose, she was pretty. Her nose deformed her whole face. It was flattened in the middle, squashed at the tip, and bent to one side. The nose bones between her eyes were pushed to the right, so her eyes seemed to squint, when in fact they did not. When I examined her, she could barely breathe through her nose because the inside was as crooked as the outside. Leslie's mother came with her to my consulting room.

"That way Mom can ask the questions. I'm too scared to do it," explained Leslie shyly.

"Leslie is a good girl, Dr. Morgan," began Mrs. O'Connor somewhat belligerently. "She wants her nose fixed, and I agree. Frankly, I don't care if you think Leslie is vain or being foolish. She's doing fine in college. She has lots of friends, but she wants the surgery. She's a great kid and I'm behind her all the way."

I was surprised by her argumentive approach. "There's no question she needs corrective surgery on her nose," I offered.

"Oh." Mrs. O'Connor thought for a moment and then smiled at me, her belligerence gone. "That's good. I hear a lot of people saying beauty surgery is silly, but I think they're dead wrong."

"This is not beauty surgery, Mrs. O'Connor. Leslie's nose must have been badly broken sometime long ago, perhaps even as a child."

"Yes, our pediatrician told us he thought she'd broken it a couple of times. She was hit by a swing in school in first grade," said Mrs. O'Connor. "Could that make her nose look like this? It never grew right after that."

"Definitely. 'Cosmetic surgery' improves what is normal," I explained. "Leslie's nose is not normal, so we call the surgery 'reconstructive.' Her nose may not be perfect after surgery, but it will be much improved."

I examined Leslie's nose and took photographs of her face for my records. Such a severely deformed nose is uncommon. During my residency, Dr. Villiers had taught me that before surgery such a patient should be sent to an ear-nose-and-throat specialist for a second opinion, because surgery might have to be performed in two stages — one to correct the inside of the nose, one to correct the outside. If too much is done at one time, instead of improving the appearance, the surgery worsens it. The nose may collapse and look squashed flat like a boxer's. I thought Leslie's nose needed only one operation and I didn't want to get a second opinion, but I could hear Dr. Villiers growling: "No home runs, kid. No razzle-dazzle surgery when you start out. Good punches but no fancy footwork." I discussed the surgical risks with the O'Connors, tentatively scheduled the surgery, and arranged for Leslie to see Dr. Henry Klein, an excellent ear-nose-and-throat surgeon, for a second opinion. He was a sharp, rather intense man, but he would be kind to Leslie, and would be honest with Leslie and with me. He wouldn't "steal" my patient. Cosmetic and reconstructive nose surgery is done well by both plastic and ENT surgeons. Some ENT surgeons, when consulted for a second opinion, will slight the plastic surgeon who referred the patient.

"You certainly need a nose operation [sigh], but are you sure you want a plastic surgeon to work on you?"

"What's wrong with a plastic surgeon?"

"There's nothing wrong with a plastic surgeon. I wouldn't want one operating on me, that's all."

"Why not?" The patient is now alarmed.

"Plastic surgeons don't know how to do nose surgery properly. Of course, medical ethics prevent me from saying anything about it."

The patient is desperate. "Will you do my surgery?"

The doctor hesitates.

"Please, doctor. I don't want a butcher working on my face."

The doctor is gracious. "If you insist."

I know plastic surgeons who undermine their ENT colleagues in the same way. Wherever specialties overlap, some doctors seem more concerned about their competition than about their patients. Dr. Klein was not like that.

Two patients do not make a busy afternoon, but when Leslie and her mother left, I was tired. For the first time in my professional life I had had the final word. There was no Dr. Villiers — or Dr. Tewkesbury — to ask me what I had done or order me to change my surgical plans. I flopped onto the floor by Clare's desk.

"My first day!"

"Okay, okay, get to work, you two." It was Jim, coming in the front door of the office. "The ten-billion-dollar mastermind computer at King, Mills, and Jacobi died today, so we couldn't do any work. I came by to waste your time, as well as mine. Do you realize Dow Jones could be hitting a thousand, but there's not a thing I could do about it? Did you see any patients today, Elizabeth, or are you collecting unemployment?" He opened the refrigerator in the office kitchen and studied its contents.

"I saw my first patients today."

"Great!" He handed Clare an apple, tossed one at me, and took one for himself. "Anything interesting? What did your very-first-ever patient in private practice want?"

"He wanted Elizabeth to make him look like John Lennon," said Clare primly.

Jim choked on a wedge of apple core. "Seriously, Elizabeth?"

"Yes."

After I told him about Ray Patterson, Jim shook his head. "Don't tell that story to anyone else outside the immediate family till you're well established. You have problems enough with credibility as a woman. With that Beatles story, people will think you're really a joke."

He had a point. Often when I told people that I was a

doctor — a plastic surgeon with my own office — they would say: "You don't operate, do you? I can't imagine a nice girl like you doing a real operation. All that blood!"

Plastic surgery usually is not bloody. The epinephrine we inject stops the bleeding so we can see what to do. Surgery, except in an emergency, should be an orderly series of steps, planned in advance — not a bloody muddle with instruments flying amid confused shouts. The talent needed to be a surgeon is not unlike that needed to be a good cook, and women are certainly capable of both. But some people, even patients, won't call me "Doctor," because they want to be polite: it is a "man's title" and they think it is a rude way to address a woman. So Jim was right about my credibility. If I told people my first patient wanted me to make him look like John Lennon, a lot of them would conclude I was merely a make-up artist, regardless of how often I explained that I was a surgeon.

"You had two phone calls," Clare told me later that week. "Ray Patterson called to beg me to make you operate on him. I said you didn't often change your mind."

"No, he doesn't need surgery. He needs a psychiatrist."

"Good point. And a Dr. Morton Jones called about Leslie O'Connor. There's his number."

"Henry Klein's on vacation," barked Dr. Jones when I returned his call. "In fact, he may decide to retire to Florida. His office sends me some of his patients. I've seen Leslie. Cute kid. So you're just opening your office. Good luck! It's hard enough starting alone, but do you honestly think you can make it as a woman?"

"Yes," I snapped. It was none of his business. I didn't like his voice.

"Maybe I shouldn't ask that question." He sounded taken aback. "I'm sure you'll do fine."

"Thank you."

"Listen, about this girl you sent over to Klein. I do a lot of nasal-obstruction work. Leslie has a bad nose. It really makes her kind of plain. I'm glad you sent her to me."

"I am planning to operate on Leslie, but I referred her to Henry Klein for a second opinion. I wasn't referring her for surgery." I wanted to make that clear.

"Of course not. I agree with you that all the work can be done during one operation. I suggest though that I come in for the operation and maybe do some of the inside work. Nasal obstruction is my specialty. I've done a lot of research on nasal function. Anyhow, I'd like to take a look at her turbinates and the septum in the OR. I'd appreciate the chance to join you in the OR, operate with you, and get to meet you. I need a good plastic surgeon for my patients."

I hesitated. I like operating solo and I didn't like Dr. Jones's manner. At the same time, it was Leslie's nose. I could do the septal surgery too, but it seemed wrong not to accept Morton Jones's offer to help me reconstruct the inside of Leslie's nose. It was his specialty as well as mine. Cooperation between doctors is the mark of good medicine.

"All right," I said slowly, thinking it through. "My secretary has booked Leslie's surgery at Mattaponai. I'll give you the day . . . it's the twenty-third."

"I want to do her at Meadows. I don't go to Mattaponai," objected Dr. Jones. Meadows was miles away from my office and I didn't have privileges there. "I don't go to Meadows," I countered.

"No problem. I'll get you permission to operate at Meadows that day," said Dr. Jones breezily.

"No, I prefer to operate at Mattaponai, and Leslie is my patient. I will arrange for you to have special operating privileges at Mattaponai for that day."

"Damn. Well, have it your way. I want to do it the twenty-fifth, not the twenty-third, so set it up and get back to us, will you? Great. Bye."

After he hung up I glared at the telephone and felt sorry for myself. I had looked forward to helping Leslie but I recognized that I would not enjoy this operation as much as I had hoped. I asked Clare to make the schedule changes, and I called Mrs. O'Connor to explain that Dr. Jones and I would be operating together.

Leslie was not my first operation in private practice, as it turned out. A few days later I was called by the emergency room at Glamorgan Hospital.

"Hi, Dr. Morgan? This is the secretary at GH. Can you come over for a case?"

"A case?" I had privileges at GH but I couldn't imagine what they wanted me for.

"A case."

"You'll have to explain."

"It's a boy from a car accident."

"I'm not on your emergency schedule yet, I'm sure."

"You're not? Let me check." Papers rustled.

"You are Dr. Elizabeth Morgan, aren't you?"

"Yes."

"You are a plastic surgeon?"

"Yes."

"The surgery department has your name down for emergency call for the rest of the month."

"Really?"

"Can't you come?"

"I'll come, but you'll have to tell me how to get there."

"I'm no good at giving instructions, doctor. I'll get you lost."

"I'll find my way."

The hospital was half an hour away, but I finally arrived. My patient was Jamie Willis, a beautifully behaved five-year-old black boy who had gone into the car windshield when a truck hit his mother's car from behind. When I got to the emergency room he was sitting on a stretcher with a bloody bandage over his forehead, listening to his mother tell him a story. He was an only child, and his father, a truck driver, was away in Pennsylvania when the accident happened. Jamie blinked but didn't cry when I injected the novocaine, and he lay so still that I was able to sew up all the many lacerations on his face in an hour and a half. He walked back with me to the waiting room, holding his cowboy hat in one hand and my hand in his other. His mother, who was anxiously biting her fingernails, rushed over to him. Simultaneously the door to the waiting room flew open and a huge, handsome man strode in.

"Oh, my boy!" He scooped Jamie up with a sigh of relief and tenderly adjusted his cowboy hat. "Man was I scared you were hurt bad."

"Are you Mr. Willis? They told me you were in Pennsylvania," I said.

"I was, doctor."

"Pennsylvania is over a hundred miles away. Jamie's accident happened two hours ago."

"That's right, doctor."

"You're sure you weren't in Maryland?"

Mr. Willis laughed. "Jamie's my son, doctor. I got it on the CB that he was hurt, my buddies up ahead cleared my way down the Penn Turnpike, and I hit the gas. I made good time, but then I was traveling empty."

Jamie healed beautifully. His was my first operation in solo practice and my first success — but lacerations on the forehead are not as challenging as a nose reconstruction. Leslie's surgery a few weeks later was my first scheduled, major operation, and I wanted everything to be perfect. The morning of her surgery I found Morton Jones sitting in the doctors' lounge, stirring sugar and powdered cream substitute into a cup of coffee.

"Hi. Hi." Morton jumped up and shook my hand vigorously. "Nice to meet you, Liz. You like to be called Liz, right?"

"I prefer Elizabeth."

"Good. Good." He opened a zipped leather instrument case. "I brought some of my specials." He produced from the case a thousand-dollar collection of instruments for nasal surgery, including a diamond rasp, special hooks, and retractors. "Here." He handed them to me. "Take them to the circulator nurse and have her get them ready for me."

I poured myself a cup of coffee and looked at Morton in mild surprise. I was his surgical colleague, not a resident or a medical student. He shook the instruments at me again, as though I were an inexperienced poodle in dog obedience class.

"The circulator is at the OR desk, Morton, if you'd like to give her your instruments."

"Sure. Yeah, I'll do that. Listen, I'll go ahead and do the turbinates first, okay? You're starting out and your time is free. I've got an office full of patients this afternoon. I'll do the turbinates, maybe take a look at the septum, and you can do the rest." He picked up his coffee and headed for the OR desk. I glanced down the hall before going into the nurses' locker room to change into scrub clothes. Morton was trying to drink coffee and talk to the circulating nurse at the same time.

Back when all doctors were men and all nurses women, there was no confusion about where to change clothes before surgery. Every OR has a lounge with coffee for the nurses next to the women's locker room, and another for the doctors next to the men's locker room. Mattaponai had an informal rule that barred doctors from using the nurses' lounge, and vice versa. Most nurses prefer the separation because they can complain indignantly about surgeons without being overheard. However, there are now males nurses as well as female doctors, and because we are the mavericks, the rules don't apply to us. I am free to have coffee in the nurses' lounge, because I'm a woman, or in the doctor's lounge, because I'm a surgeon.

The doctors' coffee was cold so I poured a cup in the nurses' lounge before I changed. "I'm so much in love with him," Julie was saying to Ginny about a doctor I knew. Julie and Ginny were circulating RNs. "Paul is the only man for me. I feel so lucky after everything I've been through since the divorce. I thought I would never feel again."

"You'd better be careful how you talk about it here, Julie," warned Ginny, "or you will be in big trouble." She looked at me suspiciously. "Don't tell."

"Tell whom?" I asked.

"Anyone. Don't mention Paul's name with mine," Julie pleaded.

"I wouldn't talk about it, but what's wrong with it?" I asked. "He's not married."

"No, but nurses aren't supposed to date doctors."

"That's absurd. They can't tell you whom to fall in love with."

"No, but I could get fired for it."

"No one would fire you for whom you date after work, Julie."

Julie laughed bitterly. "Tell that to Betty, the nurse in room five last month. She got fired for dating a single, widowed surgeon on the staff here. So I'm serious. If you talk about Paul and me, I could lose my job."

"That's out of the Dark Ages." I was shocked.

"That's nursing," said Ginny brightly. "Time to get to work."

I changed and went to the pre-op room, where Leslie O'Connor was awake. "Something to relax you," said the anesthetist, injecting Valium into her intravenous tubing. I walked beside the stretcher. Once inside the OR, Ginny and I helped Leslie climb across onto the operating table. The anesthetist injected a narcotic and Leslie fell asleep. I had turned to go to the scrub sinks in the hall outside, when Morton bustled in, his hands scrubbed. "Okay, I'm ready. Set her up for me, Liz. Then, you go wash." I was about to obey him when I stopped. I wasn't a resident. I was the surgeon in charge.

I had Leslie's surgery planned in my mind and I didn't need to make marks on her face to guide what I would do. On the other hand, I would never be in charge if I didn't assert myself now.

"If you have a marking pen," I said to Ginny, "I have some planning to do before the prep." I shaded on the outside of Leslie's nose the distorted cartilage under the skin that I would need to remove. Morton didn't get the point.

"Okay," said Morton, "that's enough. You go wash your hands so you can assist me with the important stuff."

"Morton, please be careful with how you prep. I don't want my marks washed off. You'll have to be gentle, and take your time."

Morton fidgeted uncomfortably with the novocaine syringe. "Where's that circulating nurse? Ginny? That's your name? Honey, you do the prep, I'll supervise."

I had staked out my position as another surgeon, but it spoiled the fun of operating. I had to fight back. Nose anatomy is complicated, and I had spent a lot of time analyzing what Leslie's nose needed. If too little was done, her nose would still be deformed; if too much, her nose would collapse. She would need cartilage taken from her ear to build up the top of her nose. Without it, she would look worse than before. Morton was a skilled surgeon, but he had not thought about Leslie's nose the way I had. He wasn't interested in how it looked, only the "inside" work, but what was done inside would affect how her nose looked in the end. I thought he was in too much of a rush, and I wanted Leslie's nose done my way. I went out and scrubbed, then rejoined Morton by the operating table. Leslie was still asleep, and Morton was examining the inside of her nose with a fiberoptic headlight attached to his forehead.

"I need a headlight, too," I said. Ginny had a second one ready and helped me fit the strap around my head.

"You don't need a headlight," said Morton. "I'll show you everything you need to see."

Ginny turned my headlight on.

"These are really bad," announced Morton, peering into Leslie's left nostril. "Take a look. Never seen anything like it!" The inside of the nose is a small area, and one head, close up, blocks the view. Morton's head completely hid the inside of Leslie's nose; despite frequent urgings from Morton to "take a look," I continued to see Morton's right ear. I looked at him, annoyed, and inadvertently shone the intensely bright fiberoptic light beam into his eyes. Morton yelped and jerked his head away. "Careful with that headlight!"

"Thank you, Morton." I examined the nasal septum. "You agree that you will work mainly where it's deformed in the middle? You'll leave enough support for a graft?" I asked.

"Right, Right," he said impatiently. "It won't take ten minutes. I'm going to start with the turbinates." Morton began, stripping the lining off the turbinates and delicately removing deformed bone and the tissue over it. It was not easy.

"Hope you're watching how I do it," he said as he went along. "This is my own special technique." I did watch.

"It looks like a standard turbinate submucosal resection," I observed.

"Yes, it's similar. Similar."

"What do you do differently?"

"It's the same really," he admitted. "But I'm careful."

"Aren't all surgeons careful?" asked Ginny.

When Morton finished the turbinates after an hour and a half he turned to me. "Liz, I know you want to do this nose, but you have to let me do the septum. I have a new way of doing the septum I want to show you. Morcelization."

"I'm planning to do that."

"You've never seen it done my way. It avoids the whole problem of nasal support." He had the scalpel in his hand, and without a physical fight, I could not stop him. The most disgraceful scene I could imagine would be two surgeons squabbling over who should cut into human flesh.

"You do it," I said, "but the septum is causing a lot of the deformity and you have to work on the septum until you get it straight, but you can't take so much that she loses her support."

"Of course. See how I'm doing this morcelization?" I watched closely.

In morcelization, the surgeon removes the deformed cartilage, which is then cut into fragments that are re-placed in the nose. Before this technique was invented, all the deformed cartilage was thrown away, leaving tissue inside the nose without support, so it tended to flap from side to side with each breath. While Morton took out the deformed cartilage, I chose the pieces that could be carved up and used to reconstruct the tip of Leslie's nose.

"How does that look?" asked Morton. "Pretty good?"

I studied Leslie's nose. "No. You'll have to take the septal base off the vomer groove and reposition it."

"Obviously. Just what I was going to do."

Twenty minutes later Morton had the base repositioned. "Fantastic," he said. Leslie's nose looked much better — but the tip was still on the left side.

I studied her profile and looked down from the top. "No.

She needs more work. You have to get that tip in the middle as much as you can."

Morton was not happy. He moved to the head of the table and studied Leslie's nose.

"Yeah," he grudgingly admitted. "It could look better." He removed more cartilage, going carefully.

"Better," I said from the head of the table. "I'd like to stop right there. We've taken a lot."

"I'm going to take more," said Morton.

"No. It will collapse. I'm going to reconstruct the dorsum with an ear cartilage graft."

"It's okay now," said Morton, stripping off his rubber gloves. "But suit yourself. I'll leave you to do the pretty stuff you plastic types do. I have patients to see. I'll dictate the operating note."

I was glad to see him go. I could have done just as well without him. He had no "special" techniques after all, and though the turbinates and septum were fixed, the operation was only half done. I had yet to reconstruct the outside of the nose.

I took cartilage from the ear, shaped it to rebuild the top of the nose, repositioned the nose bones, and reshaped the cartilage at the tip and side of the nose. The whole operation took four hours. For Leslie, everything had gone well. She could breathe through her nose for the first time in her life and her nose was straight and looked normal. She was grateful, and so was her mother.

At the end of the month, I billed Leslie's insurance company for $600, half the normal nasal reconstruction fee, since Morton and I had operated jointly. They rejected my claim and Clare called to ask why. The insurance company wrote me that it had received an earlier bill and paid the claim in full — to Dr. Morton Jones. The adjusters could not understand my claim for additional payment.

It took nine months and a bitter phone call to Morton to make him write to the insurance company on my behalf. Finally I was paid $300 as a "surgical assistant."

After seven years of salaried surgical training, protected from the money aspects of medicine, it seemed unbelievable to me that doctors would work against their colleagues to enrich themselves.

"Sure," said Robert Fletcher when I told him about it. "Same sort of thing happened to me, too. It doesn't sound as though you would have referred any patients to him. Am I right?"

"You're right."

"So naturally, he'll take you for what he can get while he has a chance."

"Robert, that's unbelievable."

"He's a good businessman."

"Well, I'm sick of businessmen."

"Join the crowd. Don't get paranoid. It's not because you're a woman. It goes on all the time."

I wasn't so sure. Morton would have been less sure of himself if he had had to deal with Robert Fletcher, who was physically intimidating, or with Dr. Meade, who would have slowly but relentlessly talked him into submission. "Now tell me, Mort," I could hear him saying in his deep voice, "correct me if I'm wrong, but isn't Leslie my patient?"

There were bound to be problems for me as a woman, but I thought the real trouble was that I hadn't developed the right style to deal with people like Morton. Robert Fletcher would never have let him operate in the first place. That had been my mistake.

Two days later, a nurse from Kruger Hospital called me: "Dr. Meade is on call, but he can't come and we can't find his partner. There's a guy here who went through a car windshield. Can you see him? His face is smashed."

I did see him of course. His name was Tom. The ER doctor had sewn up his face, but his right cheekbone was resting almost on top of his teeth. Tom had no medical insurance. Robert Fletcher had remarked bitterly that Wallace and Meade were happy to refer to him patients who couldn't pay. I wondered if I was getting the same treatment. It was an unworthy suspicion and I put it out of my mind.

Tom, a lean blond in his early twenties, was sitting in bed looking miserable as he held an ice pack to his swollen right cheek and black eye. Even with the swelling, his face looked pushed in and flat.

"Are you from around here?" I asked him.

"Nope. Kentucky. I'm a mountain boy." He tried to smile.

"Once the swelling is down, I have to wire your cheekbone back in place. That's a major operation."

"Do I have to have it?"

"No, you don't have to. Your face will be lopsided and your eye will sag down, which will look odd and may give you double vision. But it won't kill you not to have surgery."

"Yeah, doc, I get you. I won't die, but I'll look like a horror movie. I'll be honest with you. I don't know how I'm gonna pay you. I'm a housepainter. This is a slow time of year and I got three kids. I can't get no health insurance because the kind of work I do is risky, so the premiums are too high."

"I'll do the surgery and send you the bill. You pay me what you can."

"Okay, doc, it's a deal." He winked at me with his good eye. He could see out of his right eye but he needed to be checked by an eye specialist to make sure he didn't have a detached retina or other damage. Dr. O. was on emergency call in ophthalmology. I had not met or heard of him, but he turned out to be a lean, elderly surgeon who gestured with both hands while he talked.

"His vision fine," said Dr. O. "You operate him Saturday? Good. I be there too."

"There won't be much for you to do," I said. "I plan to check the bones under his eye and wire his cheekbone back in place."

"I help. You need help. I check his eye again."

"You know he has no insurance?"

"Ya, ya. I be there. A nice girl like you want someone with her." He gave me a knowing wink and went off, chuckling. I didn't need his help, but I didn't mind his coming to surgery as long as he knew Tom couldn't pay.

Saturday morning at ten I was in the operating room with Tom. The swelling had gone down, making him look like a Charles Addams character. His cheek sank in so far that there was only a hollow under his eye. I made my incision marks under his eye and in his eyebrow with a blue surgical marking pen. Tom was already asleep. Dr. O. looked over my shoulder.

"What that for?" asked Dr. O., moving to my right side. He tapped my hand and tried to push it away. "You don't need." I ignored him and finished my markings. The anesthesiologist, Dr. Price, carefully positioned Tom with his head turned to the left, the right cheek up. I stood on Tom's right side ready to operate. Dr. O. went to the opposite side of the table.

"Epinephrine," I said, and Laura, the scrub nurse, handed me a syringe.

"What you do that for?" demanded Dr. O.

"It cuts down the bleeding." I slid the needle into the tissue under my incision marks and started to inject.

"You don't need," Dr. O. said disapprovingly, with a shrug. In an unexpected, awkward effort to be helpful, he pulled the skin of the cheek taut near my needle. The needle slipped and I almost injected epinephrine into Tom's eye, which might have permanently damaged it. I pulled out the needle and looked at Dr. O., appalled.

"I don't need quite so much help," I said.

"Ha, ha," said Dr. O. "Young lady surgeon act like young men surgeons. Independent. Independent. Don't want help. What you say, Tom?" He took Tom's face between the palms of his two hands and shook it playfully to and fro.

"What the hell?" said Dr. Price, jumping up to look over the drapes at us. "You're shaking my oxygen tube. You want to kill him?"

"No, no. Anesthesiologist kill patient," laughed Dr. O. "Surgeons save lives. Don't bother me. We operate."

Now that his attention was diverted to Dr. Price, I finished the injections and started to operate, cutting through the thin skin of the lower eyelid and gently pushing the muscles away till my scissors touched down on the broken cheekbone. I held the skin up gently with a fine hook in my left hand, and with my right index finger felt the broken bone to decide how much further to dissect. Surgery around the eye is delicate, and I was concentrating on the operation when Dr. O. slapped my left hand, dislodging the hook and almost ripping apart the skin of the upper eyelid. Then he forced a three-inch-wide retractor into my two-inch incision.

"Now you can see better," he said proudly. "Let's go. Don't waste time. It's Saturday."

I removed his retractor and held a moist surgical sponge over my incision, which had started to bleed briskly after Dr. O. forced in the large retractor.

"Dr. O., what do you want to do in this operation?" I demanded angrily.

"I help. You young pretty surgeon. I old man. I like to help." He chuckled.

"Right now I don't need help. What do you specifically want to do in this operation?"

"I check eye to be sure muscles okay. Okay?"

"When I get to that stage, I'll let you take a look."

"Good, good. You in charge, but don't waste time. My family at home waiting. I talk to keep you operating. I lived in Geneva a long time. Long, long time. I was a student in Europe. You ever been to Geneva, Dr. Morgan? Yes? No?"

"No." I returned to dissecting the broken bone. Conversation when I operate is distracting.

"No? Well, beautiful country. I go back often. I speak many languages. Spanish, German, French, English. I speak them all. That's pretty good, eh, Dr. Morgan?"

I didn't answer.

"What you think of an old man who speak many languages — what you think of that, Dr. Morgan?" He tapped Tom vigorously on the chest with the retractor he still held in his hand, but he kept away from my surgery.

"I don't talk much when I'm operating."

Dr. O. lapsed into a few minutes of hurt silence. "I wonder why he drink beer, this Tom," he said speculatively after a while. "American beer no good. German beer excellent. You ever had German beer, Dr. Morgan?"

I ignored him and finished my dissection. The broken bones under and around the eye were free now of fat and muscle caught in the broken bones. The broken cheekbone was loosened and I was ready to lift it back into place. I had dissected the bones under the eye. They were not broken into little chips, but there was one big fragment that I had repositioned to support the eye.

"My turn," chirped Dr. O. happily, grabbing a pair of large rat-toothed forceps off Laura's instrument table. His hand had a slight tremor, and with the large forceps, he grabbed the muscle under the eye and pulled the eye around.

With Mayo scissors — which have six-inch, blunt, broad blades for belly surgery — he poked aimlessly under the eye. The optic nerve, the nerve of vision, was a few millimeters away from his clumsy probe.

"This is the way to operate," said Dr. O., nudging the eye carelessly with the heavy scissors. "It is the way I learned years ago. I study in Geneva. I live in Geneva. Very famous surgeons teach me." He yanked the eye around a bit more. "I'm satisfied. You finish. I don't need to see him again. He be fine." He dusted his hands off proudly, pulled off his gown and gloves, and patted his tummy. "Now I go to lunch. My daughter-in-law is excellent cook." He walked out of the room.

I wired the bones back in place and sewed the wounds closed in peaceful silence. I waited in the recovery room, drinking hot chocolate until Tom was fully awake. I had to know if he could see out of his right eye. It was remotely possible that Dr. O.'s sweep of the scissors around the optic nerve had blinded him.

"He's awake now, Dr. Morgan," the recovery-room nurse said at last, after I had read for the third time the jokes and notices on the bulletin board.

"Tom?"

"Huh?"

"It's Dr. Morgan. I'm going to open your right eye." It was swollen shut from the surgery.

"Huh."

I propped open his eye.

"Quit that!" shouted Tom. "That light is bright!"

"How many fingers am I holding up?"

"Three, damn it."

"What does the sign over there say?"

"I can't say it." His speech was slurred.

"Spell it."

"O-X-Y-G-E-N." I let the eye fall shut.

"Thank you. I'm sorry to bother you, but it was important." He had fallen fast asleep.

Tom was lucky. His vision was perfect, and he was painting houses three weeks later. I sent him my bill — $750 for the three hours of surgery, the daily hospital visits, and the office visits. I scribbled an untidy note at the bottom of the bill. "I known you can't pay me now. We'd be grateful if you pay what you can afford, when you can." Tom sent me a check for $100 within a week. Six weeks later he called me.

"Dr. Morgan, you remember that other doctor?"

"Dr. O."

"Yeah, that one, who talked funny."

"Yes, that's him."

"Did you operate on me, or did he?"

"I did. He was at the surgery and checked your eye. What's the problem?"

"I got a bill from him."

"He knows you have no insurance. I told him. He'll understand."

"Yeah, well he don't. He's already got the bill collectors on me. I don't have the money, but I don't mind paying an honest bill. What I want to know is why is his bill almost five hundred dollars more than yours? He's charging me twelve hundred and I thought you did the work."

"I'll call him and see if there's a mistake."

"No mistake. I talked to him myself, but maybe you can tell him to make it reasonable."

I called Dr. O.

"But Medicare pay me twelve hundred dollars for an operation like that," he protested.

"Dr. O., I did the surgery, and Tom doesn't have insurance. I told you that."

"They all lie. He has insurance. He have plenty money."

"He has no insurance, a low-paying job, and three children." I had met them — aged three, four, and six — when he came to have his stitches removed in my office.

"They all have money," persisted Dr. O. "Patients lie all the time. Don't believe him. How much you charge him?"

"Seven hundred and fifty dollars."

"That all? That not enough. I tell you, I wanted to send you patients, but now I can't. You make me lose money on this. But you a sweet girl. I do him a favor. I charge him what you charge him. That is fair. But he have money, you should believe me. You should make him pay you more. You a doctor. You charge anything you want. You should be rich, not Tom."

Tom faithfully paid me every month until my bill was paid in full. Yes, my long training had left me too innocent, and I was lucky that I had no family to support and that my office debt was only $38,000 — but surely the medical profession shouldn't tolerate Dr. O. Other doctors must have known what he was up to. He was not a great eye surgeon — in fact, he could be dangerous. His time wasn't worth $1,200 for fifteen minutes, and he wasn't really needed during the operation. No wonder people like Tom felt bitter about doctors and wanted socialized medicine.

6

From Horses to Hamburgers

My practice was now busy enough to keep me from thinking about the Board exam results. Even if I had passed Part One (which seemed unlikely), Part Two, the oral exam, wouldn't come for a year or more. I wanted a social life. I knew that if I let things take care of themselves, my practice would absorb all my time and I would wonder at fifty why life had passed me by.

I wanted to make my practice work but I also wanted to have a social life, build new friendships, and make up for all the fun I had missed during my long years of training.

"And exactly how do you plan to do this?" said Jim when I arrived home one evening at nine after sewing up a man at Glamorgan who had walked through a plate glass window. Jim was scowling at the racing sheets in concentration. In college he had followed horse racing and had made astute bets. "You have to study horses to win," he advised me. "It's more interesting than organic chemistry." Those days were over, but a college friend had invited him to the Laurel Race-track for the weekend and Jim was handicapping horses again as a change from Wiser Oil and the yen. "This looks like a good one," he mumbled. "A sleeper. Lost her last two races but in a better class." He put a red star next to Bwana Baby. "Northern Virginia is suburb city," he said to me with scorn. "Everyone has two kids and a colonial home. You'll never meet anyone. I can't stand it. What do you think of my transferring to the London Exchange? I'd like to live in London."

I left him weighing the merits of Rambling Rufus and King Kong and turned to assuring myself that the medical societies would be a way to meet people and make friends. My Elwin County Medical Society membership application was pending. I had joined the D.C. Medical Society when I was thinking of opening an office in the city, because Society membership was a malpractice-insurance requirement. D.C. membership had been simple. All I had to do was to send in my application, a letter of recommendation, and $100 as dues. In a month I was invited to a luncheon for new members, to meet the president and the president-elect — a distinguished black orthopedic surgeon and a woman psychiatrist.

The Elwin Society, by contrast, was solidly conservative. After sending in my application, I waited for weeks and waited some more until I was notified that the next Tuesday at 8:00 P.M. I would be interviewed in City Hall by the membership committee. I entered City Hall promptly at eight, followed the Society's directions, and found myself in a county supervisors' hearing on zoning regulations. Finally, with the help of a directory and a freight elevator with the hiccups, I was in the fluorescent-lit waiting room of the Elwin County Medical Society. The walls were gray, the rug a faded avocado green, and the chairs the inescapable black-and-orange plastic. Ten other young doctors were already there, sitting in grim silence. One was a woman. There were no free chairs, but a pale young man gave me a tentative smile and dragged out a folding chair from a stack behind him.

"Thank you," I said. He gave a brief, nervous smile, but

115

said nothing. In the glaring light we all looked pale green, like dead souls on the banks of the River Styx. A murmur of voices came from beyond a closed door marked PRIVATE CONFERENCE ROOM. A fat, rumpled man, slumped in his chair, looked up. He had a surprisingly deep voice.

"What do you think they're doing to him in there?" he growled.

"Torturing him," said the pale young man next to me with a cheerful smile. He turned to me. "I'm Murray Miller, a G.P. I may be joining a group practice over here. What about you?"

I gave him a rundown and asked about the others. The woman was a pediatrician. The rumpled man was a radiologist, as was a shy, polite Oriental doctor on his left. Suddenly the door to the conference room opened and a shell-shocked figure staggered out and bolted away. A fierce, tough type appeared in the doorway.

"Dr. Miller," he barked. My new acquaintance jumped to his feet and was ushered in. The door slammed shut behind him. Silence descended again on our group of nine. Five minutes later Murray Miller walked out, waved good night to us all, and the other woman went in. She, too, left in a few minutes. In half an hour it was my turn.

"Dr. Morgan," barked the tough. I followed him into the conference room, where five other fierce men, all in their forties, broad-shouldered, in rumpled gray suits, sat in a haze of smoke, studying copies of my application. They looked like the villains in a *film noir*.

"Have a seat," said the tough, surprising me with a jovial smile. "I'm the chairman. So you're Elizabeth Morgan, plastic surgeon?"

"Yes," I squeaked.

"We aren't going to eat you. Where'd you do your training? University teaching hospitals?"

"Yes."

"Good places." He looked down at my credentials. "Pretty impressive. Did you forge them?"

"No."

"Some do. That's why we go to all the trouble. We caught a man last year. So why did you choose Elwin County?"

"My family has lived here for thirty years."

"Oh. Anyone else lived in Elwin that long?" The chairman looked around the table. "Nope. Okay. That's a good reason. You plan to get rich off face-lifts?"

"No. I want to do general plastic surgery, reconstruction and cosmetic."

A skinny older man at the end of the table gave a cynical laugh. "That's what they all say. At first. Did you see Angleton on TV last night?"

"No."

"He's a fellow plastic surgeon of yours in this city. He was on TV for an hour last night, hustling face-lifts. Two thousand dollars a shot. I can't tell the difference before and after." He puffed on his cigar. "Do you do breast reconstruction after mastectomy?"

"Yes."

"Would you do an immediate reconstruct or let the gal wait?"

"Either way."

"Good. Meade did an immediate reconstruction on one of my ladies, and I'm very pleased with the results. Anyone else have questions?" Five heads shook in the negative. "Thank you for coming, Elizabeth. We discuss each applicant behind closed doors, but you'll get a notice in the mail." The six men stood up, smiled, shook my hand, and wished me good night. The initiation was over.

Two weeks later my notice came. I was now a member of the Elwin County Medical Society. I was invited to attend the next meeting. I was also invited to pay $75 in dues within a week. My D.C. Medical Society dues were $100, and my D.C. Plastic Surgery Society dues were another $100. The Virginia Medical Society and the AMA were $250 each. It is expensive to be a respectable member of organized medicine. I wondered what all this money was used for. The next week I got a letter inviting me to contribute another $250 to VAMPAC — the political arm of the Virginia Medical Society, which made contributions to political candidates. I threw away the letter.

"They think I'm made of money before I've earned any," I complained to Jim one evening while I was getting ready for my first dinner meeting of the Elwin County Medical Society. "VAMPAC wants two hundred and fifty dollars!"

"It may not be a bad idea. If medicine wants certain political concessions, it has to buy them. Listen, juice is getting very big."

I thought for a moment. "Maybe," I admitted, still thinking about organized medicine, "but according to the D.C. Medical Society, they contribute to all candidates, regardless of their platform, in the hopes that if they are elected they'll be kind to doctors."

Jim slowly lowered the *Wall Street Journal.* "The D.C. Medical Society contributes to political candidates regardless of whether they are for or against medicine?" he asked in shocked tones. I had his full attention.

"So they said at the meeting I attended. The president-elect was rather proud of it."

Jimmy raised the *Journal* again. "Only a doctor could be proud of doing something so incredibly stupid. If I had bought a thirty-thousand-dollar orange-juice contract yesterday, I could have doubled my money. The citrus groves are in trouble. I should have gone long on orange juice." He sighed. "Listen, if you meet any doctors interested in commodities, give them my name. I can't wait for the real estate crash to come. Then the market will get big."

No one at the Society meeting was interested in any commodity except a stiff drink. I arrived at the Mayfield Motel, signed my name in the logbook, and watched in astonishment as five hundred thirsty doctors tried to buy cocktails from two bars. The noise of five hundred people talking loudly in a small banquet room is overpowering. I stood on the edge of the crowd, feeling rather lost.

"Hi," said a friendly voice. "I'm Lucy Knight. I'm a pediatric urologist in Medfield. Now, are you a new doctor, or are you a doctor's nurse or a secretary?" She was a small, bright-eyed woman in her fifties, wearing a red suit. She had the friendly air of a robin.

"I'm a doctor." Lucy grabbed my arm enthusiastically. "Wonderful to have another woman doctor. Here's Odette de Blanchaud. Have you met her? Good. She's an internist. What we need is one of these men to come over and offer to buy us drinks. I will not fight my way to a bar. We have to set standards."

Odette de Blanchaud was looking dashing, as usual, in fur-trimmed boots and a matching hat. "I'm alone tonight," she told me. "My husband is working late. It is crazy to marry a doctor. Elizabeth, try not to fall in love with a doctor. Find a nice lawyer. We never have time to see each other. Right now I make more money on salary than he does in practice, and it kills him. He hates it. I tell him his practice will grow. It is only two months, but he doesn't want to wait. I need a drink, don't you?"

A balding elderly man with a handlebar mustache turned around. "Odette, hello! What can I get you?" he asked gallantly, removing a pipe from his mouth.

"Bourbon on the rocks for me and Lucy. A whiskey sour, Elizabeth?" I nodded. The mustachioed doctor replaced his pipe and shouldered his way through the crowd to the bar. "That is Dr. Duggins," explained Odette. "You know the type — divorced older man trying to act young, but he's harmless. He likes to flirt, but no action. You have to get to know all these men." She swept her hand around the room. "They will send you cases. It is better if they know who you are. You have to get known. They will refer you more patients if you are pretty."

Dr. Duggins reappeared beside us with three drinks in his hands, his pipe clenched between his teeth. "Odette, you must introduce me. This young lady is a secretary?" Odette made a face at him. "No, not a secretary, but your nurse? No, I'm wrong again. She's a medical student?" He studied me with mock seriousness.

"This is Dr. Elizabeth Morgan," said Odette severely. "A surgeon. A plastic surgeon. Women doctors are not all pediatricians and internists."

A handsome man in his forties walked over to join us. He looked healthy, happy, and confident, as though he had spent his life outdoors. "You can't have all the women to yourself, Duggins. I know Odette and Lucy. Now this young lady is the Society secretary, isn't she — or is she your office nurse? What happened to the pretty young thing with the blond hair you used to have?"

Odette winked at me as Dr. Duggins introduced me as "the new plastic surgeon, of course, Elliott. Where have you been that you haven't met Elizabeth before?" Elliott was Elliott Knowles, a cardiologist. "You're opening your own office?" he asked me.

"Yes. I'm in solo practice."

Elliott nodded energetically. "Good girl. That's the way to do it. I started out alone. Most of us did. You'll do fine."

Static and a humming sound suddenly filled the room, followed by loud raps on a microphone.

"Gentlemen, let's get seated. We're late. Let's have some consideration for our waiters and waitresses."

Dr. Duggins grabbed Odette and Lucy, steering them to a table with three seats left, and Elliott placed his hand firmly on my shoulder, pushed me past a dreamy little man with an unpronounceable foreign scrawl on his name tag, and guided me to another table.

"Tell me about yourself,' 'he said, pouring us some wine from a carafe.

"Butter," demanded a man on my left, pointing to the butter dish in front of me without bothering to identify himself. I handed it to him silently.

"Of course, you don't know anyone here!" said Elliott in surprise. "Let me introduce you to these doctors. Gentlemen, this is Elizabeth Morgan. A new plastic surgeon. On her own, come back to her hometown."

"You got a lot of competition," grunted the butter man on my left. "Hope you make it. I'm Doug Fanning. Radiologist."

"Dr. Ho," said the Oriental gentleman sitting next to him. "Family medicine." He smiled at me.

"Dr. Tang," said the third doctor, also Oriental. "Allergy." He smiled and nodded politely.

"I'm Cohen," boomed the next doctor. "My friends call me V.C. I do everything. What are you interested in? Making a billion bucks off boobs and faces?"

"No, I like general plastic surgery, Cosmetic and reconstruction."

"Ha. That's what they all say. Listen to her, Elliott. Set her straight. You gotta make money." He looked around the table and laughed.

"Al Farook," said a quiet, wary man on Elliott's right. The introductions had come full circle. "I am a cardiologist. I haven't got an announcement of your office opening."

"No, I'm still in a temporary office. My new office is being built."

"Building your own building already?" asked V.C. "That's a smart move. Where is it?"

"I'm renting," I explained. "It's a new office in Twickenham." He lost interest and turned away from me.

"So, Al," said V.C., "did you decide to buy that apartment building in Mattaponai?"

"No," said Dr. Farook, shaking pepper over the mixed salad a waiter had slid in front of him. "I don't think I want to buy another apartment building now. I am going to build my own office."

"No, don't do that." V.C. lit himself a cigarette. "I built a three-story medical building near Mattaponai. Buy your apartment and rent an office from me."

Al laughed. "Maybe I should buy the apartment building and rent an apartment to you, V.C."

Elliott Knowles turned to me. "Your big problem is going to be money. You don't believe it now, because you're starting, but you'll have many money problems. Your overhead will take a lot, but you've got to protect what's left. Otherwise, it all goes in taxes. Buy a house and deduct the interest. Buy a car. It is a business expense. Incorporate. Those are the usual things. V.C. and Al are into real estate. I'm not a businessman. I decided to enjoy myself. Virginia is hunt country, so I got interested in horses. I run a string of polo ponies."

I looked at him in astonishment. "Polo ponies?"

He buttered a slice of bread with pride. "I've got money set aside for my children's education and they're almost grown. Life is too short not to enjoy it. I'm a widower, so I have the time. As a doctor, you can meet people you never dreamed you could." His eyes lit up with enthusiasm. "I played polo at Palm Beach and met Prince Charles last year. Do you ride?"

I shook my head. "I used to, but it's expensive, and the last time I rode a horse it threw me off, tripped over me, and fell on top of me. After that, I was too scared."

"What are you doing tomorrow at four?"

"Nothing. Patients aren't beating down my doors to see me."

Elliott smiled. "They will be. Enjoy your free time while you can. Why don't I call you tomorrow when I leave my office. Meet me at my place and we'll go riding. My younger son is a great rider. We'll have you hunting and jumping in a few months."

I liked Elliott Knowles, and I accepted. I had gone riding in medical school and was given a horse that bolted. It all came back — my foot caught in the stirrup and the hooves barely missing my face as the horse reared, stumbled, and fell on top of me. It was time to get over my fear of horses.

During dessert, Elliott tapped my wrist with his teaspoon. "See that man?" He pointed the spoon at a strikingly thin, blond man with light green eyes and a peacock-blue jacket who was striding slowly across the banquet room. "That's Roger." A doctor from another table called to him and Roger turned to bestow a slight, unsmiling bow. Elliott Knowles called out, "Roger! I'd like you to meet Elizabeth Morgan, a new plastic surgeon."

The pale eyes inspected me as though I were a package of bacon. He decided I was inedible, nodded, and moved on to another table.

"Who's Roger?" I asked.

"Roger Bly — a rheumatologist, very powerful politically. He's on a lot of medical committees. Started his practice a few years ago, and now he's very rich. He's made millions in real estate already. He bought a house near mine. I can tell he likes you. Get to know him. He could be helpful in getting contacts for your practice."

"Is he American?" I didn't like the idea that my success might depend on a man's favor, and especially not a self-important foreigner.

"No, he's from somewhere in Europe. I think he went to medical school there, but that doesn't matter. Half the doctors in America are not American. We Americans are the real minority. There are so many Iranian doctors in Washington that there's an Iranian medical society. That's one reason you'll do well. People like a doctor who can speak English."

Elliott advised that I shouldn't let my practice interfere with my social life, but he was a poor example. He was called out during the after-dinner speech and had to leave for the hospital. A patient of his had had a heart attack.

"I'm the lucky one," he whispered on his way out. "I hate speeches. See you tomorrow."

He was right. The speaker was dull and talked for an hour about economic forecasting by computer. During the speech, the Society's secretary handed me a note from my brother Jim saying he was having a drink with a friend and would meet me in the hotel lounge at ten-thirty for a ride home. When the meeting broke up I sat in the lounge waiting for Jim and watching the hundreds of doctors laughing, grumbling, and commiserating about patients as they filed out through the lobby. Doctors are a sociable group. I was glad to be one of them. I noticed that Roger Bly was talking on the telephone. When he had finished, he walked over and sat down beside me.

"Elizabeth." It was a peremptory command, not a greeting. He gazed at me detachedly, as though sizing me up. "I understand you did some of your training where I did. We might have been out there at the same time. When were you there?"

I told him.

"We must have overlapped. We'll have to have lunch

sometime." Another command, not an invitation. I was annoyed but flattered.

Jim came in then and inspected the lounge warily before joining us. "Did you do your training in Chicago?" Jim asked Roger after I introduced him.

"No, but I was in the Midwest for a while. In medical training, as your sister knows, one travels around." Roger spoke slowly now, as though each word was important. He and Jim studied each other.

"What made you come to Washington?" Jim asked him, almost aggressively.

Roger shrugged. "It's a good place to practice medicine. I like New York, but I wouldn't want to live there." He smiled, and started to ask Jim a question, but Jim interrupted him.

"Where are you from? Did you go to medical school in this country?"

"No. No. In my home country. I am afraid I must say good night." Roger smiled at me, straightened his jacket, bowed slightly to Jim, and strode away. Rocking back and forth on his heels, Jim studied Roger's back carefully.

"Stay away from him," he said.

"Who? Roger?"

"Yes, Royal Roger. He's a crook."

"He is not a crook, Jim. He's well trained and he's a powerful physician in this area. You spoke to him for less than five minutes."

"How do you know he ever went to medical school? Listen, I've been around pool halls and racetracks, and if there's one thing I can spot" — Jim took one hand out of his pocket and snapped his fingers — "like that, it's a con artist and a crook. You can dress him up in a custom suit and put a diamond stud on his silk shirt and call him a doctor, but a con is a con. Do yourself a favor and stay away from Roger." Jim shrugged.

Solo Practice

"You shouldn't have trouble. He knows I spotted him as soon as I saw him. He may take you out to lunch to prove he's not afraid, but he'll leave you alone."

Roger took me to lunch a week later. I met him in his office, a downtown clinic decorated in salmon wallpaper with matching couches. His nurse had a crisp English accent, his car was a lemon-colored Rolls-Royce. I amused myself at lunch trying to find out more about him. Roger told me nothing. After a two-hour lunch I did not know his medical school, what country he was from, or where he had trained, except for a one-year fellowship. I heard a lot about how he had made his first million dollars by buying cheap apartment houses with borrowed money, renovating them, and raising the rents.

"America is the land where the grass is really greener," he told me over lunch. "I married a beautiful American girl, and that, plus 'M.D.' after my name, establishes my credentials. I can borrow money from any bank around here, and I've borrowed millions. I haven't risked a penny of my own money. I haven't paid a penny in income taxes. Your country is not for the poor. The laws are made for the rich businessman. America, the land of green," he repeated with relish.

Roger made the newspaper headlines a week later. One of his patients was a very old man living on his Social Security income of five hundred dollars a month. Roger's office had misled him about the cost of an evaluation and physical therapy. The charge was hundreds of dollars for work that cost Roger less than a hundred dollars to do. Roger was suing to collect what the man couldn't pay. The reporter had also uncovered some of Roger's medical training — one year of internship at a tiny private hospital; half a year's residency, which ended when he quit without notice; and a year of training in another hospital. Somehow he had convinced a university hospital to accept him for a rheumatology fellowship for which he was not eligible. His M.D. apparently was from a European university, but that could not be confirmed because the school was closed for holidays. All Roger would say was: "America is the land of opportunity. That man owes me money." The medical society convinced Roger to drop his suit. He's still successfully practicing, but he's not so powerful or so much admired by the other doctors. I had a European patient who knew Roger, it turned out. Roger's family was poor, and Roger had sent money to his mother through a friend of my patient's. "My friend gave Roger's mother the money. She was a poor old woman, but she wouldn't take it. She told him to tell Roger to send her a letter if he loved her, not money. It was very sad."

I showed the newspaper to Jim. "Elizabeth, of course I was right," he said, shrugging. "I told you I can spot a con artist a mile away."

Horseback riding with Elliott Knowles was fun. His polo ponies were so well trained that I gave them all sorts of instructions I didn't mean to. My pony backed up, turned to the left, took three steps forward, and stood still, waiting for further orders.

"You squeezed with your knees, shook the left rein, shook both, and pulled in," said Elliott. "These horses will listen, so tell them what you want them to do." All I wanted was not to fall off, and I squeezed my knees firmly to stay on. At once the pony broke into a fast trot, but two hours later, to my astonishment, I was cantering, breathless but still on, not under, the horse. Elliott was an excellent teacher.

I enjoyed this sociable life, but my parents had reservations. My mother was afraid of the horses. She herself had injured her hand riding as a teenager, and she knew that a college friend of mine had suffered a severe concussion when she was thrown by a horse.

"Elizabeth, be careful," she begged me.

"I will be careful."

"And wear a hard riding hat, in case you get thrown."

"I will wear the hat. Elliott won't let me ride without one."

"Don't let him put you on a horse you can't handle."

"These are polo ponies, mother. They're so well trained they almost speak English."

"I know I'm silly, but inexperienced riders do get hurt." She wasn't silly. A doctor in Elwin was permanently paralyzed from the waist down after a horse threw him.

"So who is Elliott Knowles?" my father wanted to know.

"He's a cardiologist, Daddy."

"How old is he?"

"In his mid-forties."

"That's too old."

"Daddy, I'm over thirty now."

"Date someone young."

"Elliott is young."

"He isn't younger than you."

"No, I wouldn't want to date a younger man."

"What about that nice boy you dated in medical school? Larry, the football player."

"He got married, divorced, and went crazy. The last I heard he thought he could fly and tried to jump out of an airplane."

"Oh. Well, I don't like you dating this Knowles man."

"Daddy, you haven't met him."

"I don't like your dating him."

"Of course not, Daddy. You're my father and you probably wouldn't think any man was quite right."

"No, I'm open-minded."

He loves to direct people's lives. It's his profession and he's a superb psychologist, but I was too old for him to be interfering with my life. I left to go riding again with Elliott.

I was having fun, and I loved being a woman as well as a

surgeon — not just a surgical resident who happened to wear a skirt. My family gave me lots of advice about the right kind of man for me. My father advised me to look for a younger man, "perhaps twenty-five or -six years old so you can direct him." Rob, my younger brother — now a lawyer in a Washington firm — said to find someone three to ten years older, preferably a lawyer. Most of his friends were either too young or married, but Rob promised he'd keep me in mind in case they got divorced. Jimmy asked me one Sunday at breakfast if I wanted to marry someone rich. He had won at Laurel Racetrack on a 7–1 long shot called Wabbit and was feeling expansive.

"Of course I'd like to marry someone rich. Who wouldn't?" I passed him the butter-pecan ice cream from the freezer. "I've been telling *you* to marry a nice rich girl for years. I'd love to have someone hand me fifty million dollars. Maybe I should put an ad in the *Washington Post* — 'Single woman surgeon seeks fabulously wealthy tycoon for a life of idle extravagance.' "

Jim shrugged. "If you're not going to be serious, I won't give you any advice." He turned to the sports pages.

"I'm sorry," I said penitently, putting back the ice cream after he was finished dishing out a bowlful. I hadn't meant to hurt his feelings. "I'm ready and listening."

"Horses!" said Jimmy, folding up the paper and leaning back in his chair. "I've given this a lot of thought, and I've got the field worked out for you. You're a woman surgeon. Socially, that's a disadvantage. A lot of men find the idea of a woman doctor intimidating. So you're starting with a big negative. On the plus side, it means you're self-supporting. I'm sure you could find a lot of men willing to live off you, but you wouldn't be interested." He ate some ice cream, deep in thought. "But, another plus is that women surgeons are a rare commodity, like oats in a hot year. There aren't many.

Result — you need to find a man who doesn't want to live off you but someone who won't find you intimidating. A good bet would be a self-made businessman, but they tend to work in their offices all day, so they marry their secretaries. That leaves the idle rich. Now, you can offer a rich man something his money can't buy — surprise value. An idle rich man doesn't do a thing to justify his existence, and he'd like a woman who looks like a normal woman, but bingo! There's a booby trap — she's also a woman surgeon. It's a showstopper at a cocktail party."

"So that's what eleven years of medical training gets me? A cocktail gambit?"

"Elizabeth, I'm being realistic. You want to meet a nice man and sooner or later get married. I'm telling you where you're a marketable commodity — at a racetrack."

"I'm not a horse."

"It doesn't matter. The idle rich spend their time hanging around horses — watching their horses race, or hunting, or playing polo. Now this man Knowles is a perfect example of the idle rich. He hunts and he's into polo."

"Jim, Elliott Knowles is a very nice man, but he is certainly not idle and he's also not independently wealthy."

"Are you kidding me?" Jim sat up with a jerk. "You told me he runs a string of polo ponies. Now, a string is nine horses. A polo pony is not just any pony — they're specially bred and trained to stop and change direction in a split second according to the feel of the reins. That kind of hourse isn't common. The only good polo-training ranch is in El Paso, Texas."

"You're right," I said. "Elliott said so."

"Of course I'm right. Now, ponies cost three thousand apiece and one polo string costs maybe ten to thirty thousand a year to keep up. The guy has a twenty-acre, million-dollar minifarm, three children, keeps a polo string in his backyard, takes a month off to play polo with Prince Charles at Palm

Beach — and you don't consider that rich? What more do you want?"

"Now that you put it that way, I suppose he must be. But he doesn't seem rich. He's nice and normal."

Elliott played polo every Saturday and invited me to come and watch him. I was one of the chic group of women, each belonging to a polo-playing man, who gathered on the "private" side for the afternoon. "A plastic surgeon?" asked a sapphire-ringed woman in yellow silk. "What do you think of my face? I might come to you. I don't like Taylor."

"Your face is beautiful," I said charitably. It was a social outing. I wasn't hunting for patients.

"Oh." She raised her eyebrows in disappointment and turned away. After the game Elliott sent his "boy" to take the horses home, and we climbed into the Mercedes of a friend, a Maryland millionaire, and drove off to his house to spend the evening with the rest of the polo team, their wives, girl-friends, and other horse-lovers. We sipped champagne and nibbled on caviar and I listened to talk about horses. Priceless blue-and-green Chinese rugs, Ming porcelain vases, and Post-impressionist paintings were strewn around the house. The piano was an antique Steinway concert grand. The still life on the wall was a van Gogh. The chair I sat on was real Chippen-dale. And the conversation was all about horses — riding, racing, jumping, breeding, and buying them. I was surprised. Lots of money to me meant glamour, and I had expected the rich to be exotic.

"The hunt these days doesn't kill the fox, does it?" I asked someone. He was horrified by my ignorance.

"Elizabeth, don't associate with him," interrupted Elliott. "He's a degenerate Englishman. We Virginians don't send those terriers down to drag the fox to his death."

"Old Francis won't be out at the hunt for a while, will he?"

said the Englishman. "Steeplechased his new filly and broke both his legs." He burst into loud laughter.

A white-haired man in riding boots joined us. "You can't keep Francis down. Last year he hunted with a cast on his leg."

"Of course, Francis is a great rider," said a hearty woman. "Swanson tried to follow Francis and came to grief in the mud."

"He joined the Quantock Hunt this year," said Elliott.

"The Quantock Hunt?" asked the hearty woman. "Why, they can't ride. We let them call themselves a hunt," she explained to me, "but the only rider they had was a Frenchman. I have to laugh. That man who calls himself 'a master huntsman'! No shame at all."

The white-haired man turned to me. "Will you hunt with us?"

There was no snobbery. I was welcomed and included. Even the disappointed face-lift lady patted me vigorously on the back and assured me I would be a marvelous huntswoman. I knew so little about horses that after a while my attention began to drift. The Steinway grand piano was beautiful. The carved leaf-green jade Buddhas in the wall niches were magnificent. The Regency drawing room continued out into a spectacular tropical conservatory. I had always found wealth fascinating, but I had never mingled with the rich. Everyone in the room except me was rich, at least by my standards, and I was startled to find myself bored. Elliott was not boring. I enjoyed his company, but after two hours everyone was still talking about horses. Perhaps I was being unfair. I sat down on a sofa and my host, a plump elderly man with a white mustache and carrying a glass of champagne, joined me.

"Are you interested in tropical plants?" I asked after he had leaned back on the sofa comfortably. He looked at me blankly.

"You have a lovely conservatory." I motioned to the adjoining room, which was bursting with tropical plants, in full bloom.

"Oh, that. No, no, my dear. Some sort of a garden service takes care of all that."

"I see." I was about to ask about the artwork, but he was one step ahead.

"The decorator does the room. My art curator looks after all that stuff on the walls. I just live here." It was a joke, and he laughed happily, slapping his riding britches. "That's a good one. Elliott Knowles! This young lady asked me about my plants and my artwork! I had to tell her I just live here!" It was a good joke the second time, and he and Elliott and I laughed. Everyone else in the room stopped talking and demanded to hear the joke. It was told a third time, and we all laughed again, and then someone asked Elliott how large a horse trailer a serious hunting man should buy. At this point my beeper went off, and the butler kindly directed me to a telephone on a carved mahagony desk in the conservatory. I couldn't imagine who was calling me. I wasn't on emergency call at Metropolitan yet, but I yearned to be able to say honestly that I had to leave for the hospital. I had overdosed on horses. The call was from Jim.

"Not bad, Elizabeth! I'm testing your beeper for you. How does it feel to have your own beeper, kid? Make you feel like a real doctor? I was sitting here in the office and I figured I'd take a break and see if it works. I thought you might want to go and catch an ice-cream cone or dinner with me. Sandy" — Jim's current girlfriend — "had to go home because her mother's sick, but I guess you're too busy living it up with the VR's."

"Who?"

"VR's — the very rich. Having a good time?"

A lively discussion drifted in from the living room — on

the relative merits of the hunt masters of the Mendip, Teesdale, and Quantock hunts. The butler came into the conservatory and offered me more champagne, but I waved it away.

"Yes," I said, "I'm having a good time."

"What's wrong? You sound like a stuffed frog."

"Nothing. I'm having a lovely time."

"Oh," said Jim, "I know the trouble. You're out with the horsey set. Great people. Give you the shirt off their back, but get two of them together and all they can talk about is horses. Well, I warned you."

"You did not!" I hissed indignantly (if you can hiss without *s*'s).

"Didn't I? Hell, Elizabeth, I shouldn't have to. The horse is just a dumb animal, but it's time-consuming. Anyone who chooses to spend all his time around a horse isn't likely to have conversation that is interesting to people who don't, but if you want to mingle with the rich, you can't have everything. I'll see you later."

I joined the party again.

"Now Francis was in the Quantock Hunt," the Englishman was saying, "but that was years ago. I think all the good people are now in the Mendip Hunt, if they aren't in Teesdale."

"Sure," said Elliott giving me a friendly smile as I joined the group. "Quantock Hunt people don't have good terrain. Just a couple of coops."

"Now foxes in the Teesdale Hunt," said my host, "they're quite —"

My beeper went off again. Glamorgan Hospital had a child with a tiny cut, but the mother insisted on a plastic surgeon. Would I be obliging enough to come?

"Yes, I'd be happy to come."

"Sorry to call you on a Saturday night."

"I don't mind at all."

Elliott was excellent company — intelligent and witty — and I liked being with him. He was devoted to his patients, despite his advice to me to protect my free time. One evening he took me to meet the invalid Francis, who lived on his own horse farm. We commiserated with Francis about his two broken legs, and Elliott and Francis discussed the various bones Francis had broken through the years jumping horses over fences. They then analyzed the relative merits of the bone doctors serving the Teesdale, Quantock, and Mendip hunts. I gazed with interest at the family oil portraits that hung on the walls of the oak-paneled library. The armchairs were green leather, the tables mahogany; the maid had lit a fire. It was a comfortable room.

"That's nothing," said Francis, noticing me studying the portraits. "If you want real art, take a look in the bar next door." He turned back to Elliott to describe in detail how a spirited three-year-old gelding had thrown him off thirteen years before. "Landed on my back," he said proudly. "Broke one arm, four ribs, the collarbone, and a vertebra."

"Similar thing almost happened to me in the Teesdale Hunt in 'seventy," said Elliott. Francis was over sixty. He was brave to jump horses over fences that no professional jockey would go near, but wasn't it silly? I thought. I wandered into the bar. It was the size of a cocktail lounge, with a white leather counter, black stools, and half a dozen round glass tables lit by antique Tiffany lamps hanging from the ceiling. The artwork was floor-to-ceiling photographs of Francis and horses: Francis sitting on a horse, Francis standing by a horse, Francis patting a horse, Francis jumping over a fence on a horse — and sometimes just the horse going over the fence without Francis.

My days of mingling with the horsey set were soon over, because my practice didn't leave me time to learn to hunt. A hunt takes all day. If you don't ride and hunt, you can't travel with the horsey set, because you can't talk about horses. My practice was taking more and more time, but I was still looking for some way to have fun — and someone to have fun with — that would fit in with my career.

Two weeks later, Rob, Jim, and I went to Rob's college alumni party. The announced intention of the party was to hear arms-control expert Paul Warnke speak on SALT II at the Newport Club. Two hundred alumni and guests politely listened, questioned, and discreetly applauded Mr. Warnke. There was a two-second pause and everyone stampeded for the buffet table. These meetings always have good food. A serious young man looked around in annoyance when a matron jostled his arm as he reached for the vol-au-vent. Turning back to the food, he caught sight of us.

"Rob!" he exclaimed, and slapped Rob on the shoulder.

"Lester!" said Rob.

"What are you doing here?" demanded Lester.

"I live in Washington. What are *you* doing here?"

"*I* live in Washington."

The crowd made movement as well as conversation difficult, but after collecting a roll with roast beef, a pickle wrapped in ham, and some lemonade, I emerged from the fray and joined the others.

Lester Duckworth had been a classmate of Rob's. He had the hungry eyes of the man who lives alone and can't cook. He soon ducked back to the buffet table and returned with a tray piled high with shrimp, cheese rolls, turkey, roast beef, strawberries, apple tarts, and ham.

"I'll help you eat those," said Jim. "Nice of you to go back for all of us." He handed me a shrimp and selected an apple pastry. "Not bad," said Jim, and he distributed the rest of the food among the four of us.

"I was going to eat all of that," said Lester.

"And events turned out so you didn't have a chance. What are you up to, Lester?"

"I'm a senior executive assistant to the first under secretary. It's not important. Just government."

"What exactly do you do?" inquired Rob, with a lawyer's interest in facts.

"Push papers," said Lester, finishing off the last shrimp.

"What sort of papers?" asked Rob. "Do you set policy? Work with Senate committees?"

"Beats me," said Lester. "I collect a paycheck and do what the big boys say. I've been in Washington six years and it's my sixth change. I hate government work. I'm getting out."

"What field are you getting into when you leave the government?" asked Rob.

"I've got applications in at the Department of the Interior, for a Treasury post, and at the FCC."

"I see," said Rob. "You aren't getting out of government work. You're leaving one department but staying in the government."

"No, I intend to leave the government. I hate the work, but you can't leave all at once. I'm waiting for the perfect job offer, something with some excitement."

"Try commodities," said Jim with a straight face. "It's a great field. Man I know pulled in six million dollars last month going short on soybeans. It's exciting." He had Lester's undivided attention. "And lost seven million this month trading corn," he added.

"Yeah," said Lester, losing interest. "I want a job that's exciting, but it's got to pay well and have security, too." He turned to me. "What do you do?"

"Elizabeth is a plastic surgeon," said Rob. "Reconstructive, not just cosmetic surgery."

Two days later Lester called me.

"Lester here," he began. "Would you be interested in catching a movie with me tonight? It's a 1941 Bogart showing at the Circle."

"Certainly." I liked movies but had seen almost none since medical school.

"I can't pick you up. Meet me there. We'll get a bite afterwards."

The movie was good. Dinner was a McDonald's hamburger and a Coke.

"You sure are a sport not to mind McDonald's," said Lester. "I haven't found a single decent restaurant in this city yet. Have you?"

"A few."

"I had a rotten day. Government corruption is incredible. My boss is a woman, the worst kind of prune. A mindless stickler for the rules. I was a Modern Thought major in college and it's wasted." He banged the table softly with his fist. "One day I'll expose the entire department," he warned me.

"What did you do today?" I asked. "Anything special?"

"I was so sickened that I had lunch with some friends doing top-secret work in electronics to compare notes. We talked till four. We're all going to quit. I'm collecting information on corruption, and once I do, I'll blow Washington sky-high."

It was, for me, a relaxing and passive evening. All I did was watch the movie and listen to Lester. It was a pleasant change from the way I had spent the day. I had operated in the morning and made visits to local doctors all afternoon, introducing myself so I would get known. "It's awful," said Odette, "but how else do they know who you are? Everyone goes through the same thing."

Lester drove me home, parked in front of the house, and

pulled out a copy of the newspaper movie guide from under the front seat.

"Let's catch *Advise and Consent* this Friday at the Kennedy. Starts at six. If you come in and pick me up at the office, we can catch it on time. I may have to work late. How often have you seen it?"

"How often? Never. I don't see many movies."

"You will with me. I think I've taken in this one only four times." He drove off.

Jim was on the phone trying to persuade a client to buy an option on General Motors. The problem seemed to be that the client didn't know what an option was. After fifteen minutes of overhearing Jim's explanation I was still confused, but the client wasn't, and he agreed to buy a GM option.

"It's a good hedge for your position," said Jim. "I think it's a wise move." He hung up the phone. "See a movie?" he asked me.

"Yes, *The Maltese Falcon*."

"Give you dinner?"

"We ate at McDonald's."

"Seeing him again?"

"We're going out to a movie this Friday."

"Going to give you dinner?"

"I imagine so."

"Picking you up?"

"No, I'm picking him up at the office."

There was a short and intensely disapproving silence before Jim spoke again. "That figures," he said. "Gas is expensive."

"And exactly what is that supposed to mean?"

"A movie is a cheap date," said Jim, and went to bed. I was insulted. Older brothers have no business interfering in their sisters' social lives.

I saw a lot of movies after that. At four o'clock one Friday,

Lester called me at the office. "Say, when you come in, why don't you bring a couple of burgers from McDonald's. It's a double feature, so we better eat before we start."

"Fine."

"Big Mac, fries, and a Coke for me, okay? See you at six." It was routine by now.

I picked him up at five-thirty, and we ate our McDonald's dinner parked outside the theater while we waited for the movie to start.

"Big problems in the office today," said Lester after finishing the last of his french fries. "I complained to the under secretary today. I had to take most of the day off to calm down. I had lunch with my top-secret buddies and didn't get back till four-thirty, but it's all paper-pushing, so who cares?"

The movie finished at ten. He bought popcorn and we ate it on the way home. It was my car, and I dropped him off at his apartment.

"Tuesday is one you have to catch," said Lester, producing the movie guide from his coat pocket. "A double feature. Two Fellinis. It starts at six-thirty. I'd appreciate it if you'd pick me up at work. I'd take you out this weekend, except I have to go to a sort of training course for work. It's the worst. The inefficiency and waste you wouldn't believe."

On Saturday morning Clare and I worked in the office. She had insurance forms to fill out and I had an emergency patient from Friendship Affiliated Hospital whose stitches had to come out. At one o'clock we stopped and joined my mother for lunch at a coffee shop. Clare had become a good friend. She could not be ruffled. We could have an office full of patients, children screaming, all the phones ringing, the emergency room demanding my help, and she took care of everything. All I had to do was see my patients.

"How is your boyfriend?" she asked as we sat down to lunch.

"Fine. He was a good friend of Rob's, you know."

My mother toyed with her fork. "Rob knew him," she said, turning to Clare. "But they weren't exactly friends. He sounds like a pleasant young man."

"A nice speaking voice on the telephone," said Clare. She and my mother exchanged looks. Neither of them would say so, but I knew they both thought it was time Lester took me out to a proper dinner. In fact, I did too.

"I thought Rob and Lester were friends in college," I said.

"Rob made a point of telling me last night that they were not exactly friends."

"What?" said Clare and I together. Rob is friends with everybody. The only people Rob has ever spoken against are Adolf Hitler and a judge who was rude to Rob's fiancée, Janice.

"Your life is your own," my mother said to me later, "but it is perhaps foolish to become entangled with someone simply because you are over thirty and feel it is time to get married."

"Marriage! Mother, we go out to the movies. This is strictly teenage."

"When a man of his age," my mother said delicately, "is interested in a woman of your age and his behavior is decorous, it suggests he is thinking of marriage."

A week later, Lester and I stopped off at McDonald's before going to the movie. I had a cheeseburger for a change. "Lester," I said suddenly. "Look at that van on the other side of the parking lot. Is that smoke coming out of it?" Three agitated men were inspecting the van's engine.

"Oh, my God!" Lester hurriedly started up the car. "Those vans can explode! Jesus! I've got to get out of here fast!" He handed me the trash from his Big Mac and Coke. Leaning across me, he opened the door and pushed me out of the car. "Dump it in the trash. Then run and meet me."

He backed up and screeched off, stopping a quarter of a mile down the street. The van didn't explode. I walked slowly to the car.

"Sorry about that," said Lester, "but you have to react fast to danger and get the hell away. I could have been killed."

"Really?" I said coldly. I was the excess baggage that had been jettisoned.

"Absolutely. Army training."

The movie was another Fellini double feature. Afterwards, I explained to Lester that my schedule was so unpredictable, I couldn't make a definite date to see him again.

"I'll call to check," he said. "There are a lot of movies I have to take you to see."

"Like hell you will," I said to myself as I stalked in the front door, slamming it behind me. Jim was on the phone with a friend of his, a New York lawyer, trying to convince him not to buy Kodak or Chrysler. "Guy, I tell you. Buy them, but it's against my advice. They're duds. I know you think they're honest, but their balance sheets aren't strong." He covered the phone with his hand and grinned at me. "You look like Lulu Liz, the local tornado. Did he make you pay for the movie this time? Yes, Guy, I'm listening. Yes, I think you're smart. You're brilliant. You know that. If I wanted to float a billion-dollar loan, I'd call you, but you don't know a damned thing about stocks. You buy Chrysler, and I'll bet you four to one it's down fifty percent by Easter. It's a deal." He hung up.

"I did not pay for the movie," I announced from the kitchen. I was mixing myself a strong rum and Coke. "But I'm not seeing him again."

"If Lester were sixteen, he'd be a real Romeo," laughed

Jim. "So, he doesn't get to marry the doctor. Rob and I have already discussed your situation. If you'd gotten serious, we had planned to have you committed to a mental hospital. He's not your type."

"He won't call again," I snapped.

I was wrong. Lester called five times over the next few days. I said I was busy, and each time he said he'd call again. After that I had Jim answer the phone and say I was out. Lester kept calling.

"I'm not answering it either," Jim finally said. "He wasn't dating me, Elizabeth. You pick it up or we let it ring." The calls continued, four times that evening, and each time we let the phone ring and ring and ring. Finally Jim picked it up.

"Yes, I know it's you, Lester. You've been calling all night. . . . Why should I answer it? . . . My sister is a surgeon and she works hard. She isn't always in to answer the phone. . . . Good-bye."

Jim turned to me. "From now on, you answer the phone."

"No."

"Yes."

"No."

"I'll strangle you."

"Okay, I'll answer it."

The phone rang the next night. Jim waved a dictionary threateningly at me and I answered it.

"Elizabeth, it's Lester."

"Yes."

"I've been trying to get you."

"Yes."

"Did Jim give you my messages?"

"Yes."

"Last time I took you out, you didn't want to go out with me again."

"Yes."

"I'm getting annoyed. I call four times a night. I even called you at two A.M. last night, but you must have had the phone off the hook."

"Yes."

"Are you playing hard to get, or what?"

"I'm busy with my practice."

"I hope you're making a lot of money, but you can't be too busy to see a movie with me."

"Yes, I am."

"Well, what about me? I got used to taking you out. What am I going to do with my time, huh? I think you're pretty selfish. I don't think it's fair. Golly."

"I'm sorry, Lester."

"Ha. I'm sorry for myself. College stinks, the government stinks, and now you." He hung up.

"Don't let it bother you," said Jim.

"I feel awful," I said, "but most men wouldn't have kept calling."

"He's like a kid. He wanted to annoy you. He wasn't calling to be nice. Listen, would you be interested in a pilot? This guy I know flies his own plane. On second thought, he's probably making his cash in cocaine. It's not good for your image to date a drug dealer." He pondered my plight for a moment. "I know — I've got it psyched out. Random chance. If your practice gets busy, sooner or later the right guy is going to klutz up at home and chop his toes off with a lawn mower. You'll be called to see him in the emergency room, and it's love at first sight! Perfect. Now we don't have to worry about it. By the way, if you ever make any money, give it to me to put in a company called AAR. It's a sleeper."

7

New Year's Celebration

A weekend later I decided to read the entire *Sunday News* over breakfast. During my seven years' training I never read a newspaper, because I started work long before the papers were delivered. I had been so out of touch that I did not know we had landed a man on the moon until a nurse mentioned it during an open-heart operation. Now that I was a normal person once more, I felt I had to read the paper. I was unhappy to find a front-page feature on cosmetic plastic surgeons. "It costs a hundred thousand dollars a year to run my operating room," said one, "but in a million-dollar practice like mine, it's a welcome tax deduction." Another coyly remarked that his practice earned "well into seven figures." He seemed to be prouder of his income than of his patients. I sighed. Jim, huddled in a blue bathrobe, winced at the sound and covered his ears. He had been out late the night before. He was managing to read the business news by propping his head up with one hand and running a finger under each word. The phone rang and Jim clapped both hands over his ears, groaning. I picked up the receiver.

"Hey, kiddo, it's Sven Ohlsen here. Listen, I'm going to

do you a favor. The holidays are coming up and I'm going to give you my emergency call on New Year's Eve. You can make a mint." He paused. "Actually, I'm pulling a dirty trick. I've had to take New Year's Eve call for the past hundred years. I bitch and groan and tell Ronald Meade I won't do it, but he always gives me New Year's. This year I want to celebrate. You won't get any sleep for a week, but you can hack that. You're used to it from residency. I'm too old for night work." I laughed; Sven was a mountain climber and in great shape. "Elizabeth, can I tell the emergency room to put your name down starting December twenty-sixth?"

"Certainly, but I thought it was New Year's."

"That's when the call starts, but you won't be busy till New Year's Eve. You'll love it. Just ride with the punches, kid."

He hung up and Jimmy slowly removed his hands from his ears.

"Jim, are you hung over?" I asked in astonishment. Jim never drinks more than two glasses of wine.

"No. I saw an opera and it gave me a headache." He groaned again. "What about this?" He handed me the business section, which claimed that surgeons' earnings averaged a hundred thousand dollars after taxes.

After working with Morton Jones and Dr. O., I wondered if the money a surgeon makes is inversely proportional to how much he cares about his profession and his patients.

In private practice it can be hard to tell who is a first-rate doctor, who is a good doctor but preoccupied with money, and who is one of the few who are, regrettably, either greedy and deceptive or ignorant and incompetent or both. It is easy for a resident to tell which is which. Within a few days of working with a doctor full time, you can tell whether he cares about his patients or if he's sloppy. Now, out on my own, when I met a friendly colleague with a thriving practice, I tended to assume that he was a good doctor. I might be wrong, but I had no way to tell unless I worked with him closely. I looked forward to my New Year's emergency call. It was a chance to work with some more doctors. The emergency room, like the OR, is stressful and brings out doctors' bad traits as well as their good ones.

My first call came at eleven in the morning, the day before New Year's Eve.

"Dr. Morgan? This is Dr. Jim McPherson, the Metropolitan emergency-room doctor. Sharpen your scalpel. A lady was hit by a drunk driver head-on in her car this morning. She went into the windshield and she's a mess. Can you come in?"

"Yes. It will take me about fifteen minutes. I live close to the hospital."

"Are you kidding?" he yelped.

"Is that all right? She's not dying is she?"

"I'm not complaining. It's next to impossible getting a plastic surgeon to come in. I'd settle for fifteen hours!"

"Family are not allowed in without a doctor's permission," said a pink-uniformed volunteer at the front desk when I arrived in the ER.

"I am a doctor."

"You're a doctor? I'm sorry. You look like family. Go through those doors, and one of the nurses will help you." I went through the doors and was taken aback. I had not yet been in the Metropolitan emergency room. It was clean, organized, well lit and freshly painted, and the equipment was new — a startling change from the only ER's I knew firsthand, those in the old inner-city hospitals where I had trained. The ER's in those hospitals were staffed by residents in rumpled scrub suits, frazzled types working frantically or waiting, exhausted, for more action, incessantly smoking and complaining. The medical staff here included experienced doctors in private practice, relaxed professionals smartly dressed in suits and white coats. There was an air of well-heeled efficiency about them.

On one side of the main ER were monitors, built into the wall, that recorded by remote control the heart waves of patients in the cubicles. Two secretaries manned the telephones.

"Dr. McPherson, pick up on line six, please. Hello, Metropolitan Emergency Room, can I help you," said the secretary all in one breath.

There were sixteen cubicles, each with two or three patients. There was no screaming, no shouting, and there were no derelict drunks sleeping on stretchers in the hallway. The suburbs were a different world.

"Can I help you?" a nurse asked me.

"Yes, I'm Dr. Morgan, the new plastic surgeon. Dr. McPherson called me to see a patient."

She looked at me blankly for a moment, and then: "That must be the lady with the face. She's in room —" An alarm in the bank of heart monitors began to shriek and she jumped to a red intercom built into the wall. "Metropolitan!" she snapped.

"We've got an MI coming in," buzzed a voice with much static. "Can you read us?"

I was fascinated. The faulty heart wave on the monitor was that of a woman in an ambulance four miles away, beamed by radio to the ER so the doctors and nurses could direct her treatment. Inner-city teaching hospitals don't have the funds to buy such elaborate equipment. I had seen such devices only on TV medical soap operas.

"Got you," replied the nurse, turning the knobs on the monitor. The flickering outline of the abnormal heart came into sharp focus.

"We're giving her lidocaine," crackled the intercom, "but she's still got the PVC's."

A doctor swiveled around in his chair to look at the monitor. "She has less than ten a minute," said the nurse to the intercom. "She should be stable now." The doctor nodded and turned back to his desk. The heart waves suddenly became wildly irregular and then stopped.

"Straight line," screamed the voice from the ambulance. "She's arrested!"

"Shock her!" commanded the nurse. The doctor, swiveling back again to look, nodded approval. Almost immediately the wail of the siren became audible through the door to the ER, grew louder, and then stopped as the ambulance approached the hospital. The nurse ran out to the ambulance at the emergency ramp. Reluctantly I tore myself away. Had I made the right choice by becoming a plastic surgeon? Internal medicine and general surgery had the real drama. How exciting were a few cuts on the face?

"Can I help you?" another nurse asked me.

"Yes, I'm Dr. Morgan, the new plastic surgeon."

"Room fourteen has your patient, doctor. It's nice to meet you. Dr. Meade told us all about you." She opened the door for me. "This is Mrs. Archer, and I'm Audrey, your nurse. If you need anything, I'll get it."

Mrs. Archer was a limp form covered with a white sheet, with a blood-soaked bandage wrapped around most of her face. Her jaw and upper neck were swollen into a great mound.

"Has she been seen by anyone else?" I asked.

"No, Dr. McPherson took a look at her face and called you immediately. We are very busy today."

Besides her face injury, Mrs. Archer could have had a punctured lung or a ruptured spleen — but no one would have known it. A smashed face looks so awful, disfigured and dripping with blood, that even some doctors recoil. Mrs. Archer's untreated bleeding face wouldn't have killed her, but an undiagnosed injury in her chest or abdomen might have.

"Don't trust anyone," Robert Fletcher had warned me. "The ER doctors are better at Metropolitan than anywhere else, but they aren't surgeons and they don't understand chest and belly trauma. My first night there I was sewing up a kid's face when he went blue and started to wheeze. I hadn't listened to his chest and when I did, there was no sound. He had ruptured both lungs and I saved his life sticking the needle of my novocaine syringe into his chest. Don't let it happen to you."

I opened my purse to get out my stethoscope.

"Can I get something for you?" asked Audrey.

"I'm looking for my stethoscope," I explained. She whipped one out of her uniform pocket and put it in my hand. "Tell me what you need. I'm here to help you."

Nurses may like, hate, bully, or help residents, but they don't wait on them. Nurses treat private doctors with great respect. I wondered if it contributed to — or was the result of — the arrogance some doctors showed toward nurses.

"Mrs. Archer," I said leaning over the stretcher, "I'm Dr. Morgan." She couldn't see because of the bandage wrapped over her eyes, and her mouth was too swollen for her to speak, but one hand loosened its grip on the side of the stretcher and waved. "I'm going to examine you and then take off your bandage to have a look at your face."

She had no other injuries that I could find. Audrey handed me gloves and whisked away the bloody bandage as I cut it off. The right side of Mrs. Archer's face and neck was thickly studded with jagged fragments of windshield glass.

"Are my eyes all right?"

"Your eyes?"

"My eyes."

I reexamined her eyes. Her vision was fine. Her eyelids were not injured. "Do they hurt?"

"No, but I had an eye operation two years ago. If they're all messed up, I don't know what I'll do. That operation was painful."

"No, your eyes are fine. I'm going to ask you some silly questions to be sure you haven't had a concussion. Can you tell me your name?"

"Yes, I know that one. My last name is Archer."

"And where are you?"

"Where am I?"

"Yes, where are you?"

"I don't know."

"Are you at home? At work? At a hospital?"

"Hospital. Metropolitan, isn't it?"

"Yes. What day of the year it is?"

"I don't remember, but tomorrow is New Year's Eve."

Her answers were sensible, her voice was confident, and a concussion seemed unlikely.

"Good. I'm going to sew up your face today, but your jaw is broken. You'll need an operation after the swelling goes down."

I went out to talk to her husband, who was pacing in the hall.

"How did the accident happen?"

"I wasn't with her, but she was driving to work. The police told me another driver, dead drunk, going the wrong way down a four-lane highway, hit her at sixty miles an hour. Will she be all right?"

She was lucky to be alive. I explained about her broken jaw and the lacerations on her face.

"What about her mind?" Mr. Archer bit a fingernail. "I'm anxious. She seemed to come and go when I was talking to her. I guess after an accident, that's natural?"

"When I was speaking to her she was quite coherent," I assured him, and I returned to her cubicle.

I found Audrey, another nurse, a doctor, and an orderly struggling to hold Mrs. Archer on the stretcher.

"I have to get to my office," she explained, clutching my arm.

"Mrs. Archer, you've been in an accident. Your office knows you're not coming in."

"I'm sorry," she said, suddenly lucid. "I'll be good."

The other doctor and the orderly left, and I turned to the small operating stand that Audrey had prepared.

"She needs to be restrained, doctor," said Audrey quietly. I turned to find Mrs. Archer sitting up with her legs dangling over the edge of the stretcher, undoing the snaps on her hospital shift.

"My husband is expecting me at home," she said. "I want to give him a call."

"No, he's here now — out in the hallway." I had been taught in medical school that asking the "concussion questions" as I had would give a diagnosis that was "virtually one hundred percent" accurate. I now wondered how I could have believed that. In medicine, nothing is one hundred percent certain. The professor who taught me was a specialist in the spinal cord of a cat; he never saw human patients if he could avoid doing so.

Mrs. Archer took my hand. "Please. I don't know what I'm doing here. Don't make me stay. I don't like hospitals."

"A little strap around your ankles," said Audrey kindly, wrapping a felt band around each ankle and tying them down to the stretcher.

"And your arms," said another nurse who had come to help. Gently but firmly she tied Mrs. Archer's hands to the side of the stretcher. "We can't let you fall off a stretcher. You have enough problems for one day."

"You're right," said Mrs. Archer, lying back, breathing slowly. "Doctor," said Mrs. Archer in a sudden panic, "I haven't done my grocery shopping!" She tried to sit up and struggled to free her hands and feet, which were entangled in the white sheet. Audrey straightened the sheet and tucked it back in place. "I can't keep my appointment with you," said Mrs. Archer, raising her head to inspect an imaginary watch on her left wrist. "I know you had to keep me waiting, but I'm much better, and I have to do the groceries. I'm giving a party." She obviously had a severe concussion in addition to her extensive facial injuries, and yet, as is the way with patients who suffer a concussion, her personality was still apparent. She thanked me profusely for helping her and was most anxious to be sure that her husband was all right and that her children were safe at home.

An orderly gently held Mrs. Archer's head still while I injected the novocaine so I could dig the glass out of her face.

"My jaw feels swollen," she said suddenly. "Did I fall down?"

"You were in a car accident."

"Oh. I have to go to a party tonight."

"You told me you were giving one." From the swollen, bleeding mass of tissue that was her face and neck I extracted the slivers of glass, dropping the pieces with a clink into a stainless-steel basin. There were bits of steering-wheel plastic under her chin, and gravel was studded everywhere.

"No," Mrs. Archer laughed. "I don't have time this month to give a party. I like to go to parties."

"You'll miss your party tonight," said the orderly, a blond

teenage boy whose emergency-room work was part of a college course.

"Why?" Mrs. Archer gazed up at him. I pulled glass fragments out of her ear.

"You were in an accident," he explained.

"Accident? I thought I fell."

"No, a car accident."

"It wasn't my fault, was it?"

"No." I extracted four jagged glass splinters from the side of her mouth. Each time I pulled out a piece of glass, the cut bled anew. Mrs. Archer's face was a patchwork of small gauze pads soaking up blood from innumerable cuts. It took two hours to remove all the glass and sew up her face, and every fifteen minutes or so, after engaging in normal conversation, Mrs. Archer asked to leave for her office. She became more and more confused and agitated, folding her legs in a sort of yoga position at the foot of the stretcher in an attempt to cast off her restraints and go home. I wondered if she had a brain injury more serious than a concussion and decided to consult the neurosurgeon on call. I got his answering service.

"Dr. Hoff is not on call," they told me.

"Yes, he is. I'm in the emergency room, and his name is posted."

"I'll call him," said the answering service wearily. "He won't be pleased."

I shrugged, waited, and in ten minutes he called me back.

"Hello, Dr. Hoff? I'm Elizabeth Morgan, a plastic surgeon."

"So?" said a peeved, disagreeable voice.

"I have a patient in the emergency room who was in a car accident. She is very confused and I'm worried that she has a brain injury that I've overlooked."

"So?"

"Would you be kind enough to see her?"

"No! You don't need neurosurgeon. When she have seizure or something like, you call me." He hung up. I stared at the telephone.

"Something wrong?" asked **Dr. McPherson**, who was sitting next to me, writing a prescription.

"I need a neurosurgeon, and the one on call isn't interested."

"Who was it?"

"Hoff."

"Oh, he hates Metropolitan. He won't see a patient until they're on the operating table after paying him cash in advance. Try Andy Rothman. He's not on call, but he's good. He may come in."

"Sure," said Andy Rothman when I called him. "I'll check on her till she's back to normal."

After I hung up, Dr. McPherson grabbed my arm. "Don't escape," he said. "There's a hand waiting for you in room four."

Audrey arranged for Mrs. Archer's admission. I talked to her husband, wrote orders, and went to see "the hand."

It belonged to a restaurant owner who had cut a tendon to his long finger while opening a cracked five-gallon glass jar of mayonnaise.

"You will be in a cast for three or four weeks while the tendon heals," I told him.

He winced. "I wish you could make it shorter, doc. Can I watch you operate?"

"As long as you keep still. Have you had lunch?"

"Why?"

"I'd prefer that you didn't have food in your stomach. Watching makes some people feel sick."

He lay back, looking pale. "I'm one of them. Go ahead and get it over."

"Got another hand for you, Liz." Dr. McPherson looked

into the cubicle. "He's in the room next door. You're lucky," he said to the restaurant owner. "You've got our only woman plastic surgeon working on you."

He walked out laughing.

Emergency work always takes longer than I expect. It was five o'clock by the time I had repaired the tendon, put on a cast, written instructions for the patient, dictated the surgeon's note, and spoken to his wife in the waiting room. She naturally wanted everything explained to her, and I obliged. I hadn't had lunch, though, and I was famished. I decided that the next patient could wait till I made a short trip to the vending machines around the corner.

"Hey, plastic surgeon, don't forget me!" shouted someone from the room next door. It was the second "hand," a long-haired, disheveled teenager. "Don't go home. I've been waiting for you," he pleaded.

"I'm going to get coffee and a candy bar and I'll be right back. Are you having pain?"

"No. It's not bad. I only need you to put on a cast. I've done this before."

"What happened?" I picked up the X rays by his bed. He had broken a bone in his hand, but it was not out of place.

"I got mad and smashed my hand into a brick wall. I do that when I'm mad."

"I hope you're not a concert pianist."

"No, are you kidding? I'm in the CIA. Spies and all. Top secret. I file memos. You know the kind of thing — Stansfield Turner ate a hot dog with mustard. Top-secret baloney."

"Let me see your hand." He held it out. "Make a fist."

"I know that routine. The position is good. See?" He opened and closed his fist, and he was right. The fingers were in good alignment.

"I'll forget the coffee and put the cast on now, on one condition."

"Don't worry. I have good insurance."

"It's not that. Don't hit any more brick walls this weekend."

"Okay." He lay back, holding his hand over the edge of the stretcher so I could put on the cast. He yawned and asked, "Can I smoke in here?"

"No. We'd blow up. There's oxygen in the wall."

"Okay." I put on the cast and let it dry while I wrote out instructions for him.

"I'll see you in my office next Tuesday. The cast comes off in three weeks."

"Right." He took the instructions and stood up. "Thanks a lot, doc. Last one I had for this gave me a big speech on emotion control. A real bastard. See ya."

"Listen, Liz," said Dr. McPherson as soon as I was done. "There's a cute little blond girl here with her lip cut up. I'd hate a pretty girl to have her lip scarred. Can you see her? You'll find fresh coffee in the back room."

While I was repairing the girl's lip, Dr. McPherson found himself faced with yet another "hand." Since I was too busy to handle this latest emergency, he asked another surgeon, Dr. Aylor, who was waiting for his own patient to be X-rayed. I finished the lip and was washing my hands when Dr. Aylor came into the cubicle to talk to me. He was a cocky man in his late thirties. To him, every patient was a snap. He had a relaxed confidence that I envied.

"Hello, hello, Elizabeth. How are you today? I'm taking care of a finger for you. Vanessa. She's Haitian, but they have insurance." I listened carefully, because he spoke so fast that he was sometimes hard to understand. He rustled the emergency-room check-in sheet. "A good insurance policy. Listen, in any of these amputations I always ask someone to make a note on the chart to protect me in case there is a malpractice suit — just to say I do the right thing. Of course, we all do the same thing, but it's good for protection, you know. You have to think protection. So, when our hands are dry, write down you agree with what I do, okay?"

"I'd be happy to. What will you do?"

"Oh" — he raised his hands to indicate that the problem was too simple to bother with details and said quickly, "the fingertip is cut off very sharp with a knife. It's hanging by a piece of skin. I'll put it back and fix it up."

At least, that was what I thought he said.

"You're going to put the tip back?" I asked to be sure, but he was already out the door. When I was free, I went into the next cubicle to see Vanessa.

"I can't understand what that doctor says," complained the child's mother. "I wish he'd talk slower. Vanessa, honey, show the lady doctor your finger."

Shyly, but with the air of someone performing a dangerous mission, Vanessa pulled her left ring finger out from the moist cotton gauze wrapped around it and, with a smile, held it up for me to inspect. Her mother hid her face in her hands while Vanessa and I solemnly inspected the injured fingertip.

"Does it hurt?"

Vanessa shook her head.

"Would you like to put it back in the gauze pad?" She nodded her head. "Then, you can do that."

"Thank you." Vanessa carefully wrapped her finger in the gauze again. I turned to her mother.

"Dr. Aylor will explain to you what he's going to do, but he's already told me and I agree with his plan." I could have said more, but it's best not to. The same thing said by two doctors in different words can cause confusion. All that Vanessa's finger needed was for Dr. Aylor to fold the tip back in place over the bone, put in one stitch, and put on a dressing to protect the finger till it healed. Her finger would have a scar but would look more or less normal. I wrote on

Vanessa's chart: "I agree with your plan to replace the finger-tip. Completing amputation is not indicated."

Twenty minutes later I was up to my arms in plaster with a boy who had fractured his hand. I like the mud-pie feel of wet plaster, and I don't mind the mess since it washes off with water. Dr. Aylor poked his head into the cubicle.

"Here you are, here you are. I've been looking for you. Where have you been? You seem to be busy. That's good for your practice. I took care of that little girl. She's fine. I sent her home."

"Good." I dipped a plaster roll into the water bucket.

"Listen, I changed your note. I explained to you what I wanted to do, but you did not listen. I didn't want to put that tip back on. Too much trouble. It wouldn't live anyhow." I straightened up and looked at him in surprise while the plaster roll hardened in my hand. "I cut off that useless piece of finger and cut the bone back to shorten the finger. It'll heal underneath fine. You listen to me. I do that all the time. Insurance pays much, much more if you shorten the bone and make it a complete amputation. You get nothing for putting the tip back. I changed your note to 'Amputation *is* indicated.' It's all over anyhow. Water under the bridge. Listen" — he smiled from the doorway — "you do nice work, but you have to remember how much you'll be paid. I'll keep you in mind and send you patients, but now I have to go to the operating room. Bye-bye." He ambled away.

"What was that all about?" asked my patient.

"Nothing." I threw out the hardened plaster and dipped a new roll in the water.

Dr. Aylor was not a stupid man. He was a specialist. If I hadn't done hand surgery myself as a resident, I would not have known that Vanessa's fingertip could have been saved, for a few hundred dollars less. Her life would not be ruined because her ring finger was short and stubby, but she needn't have had an ugly finger. There was nothing I could do.

Dr. Aylor's secretary called me the next morning. "Dr. Aylor was wondering if you would see a patient of his at Kruger. He's a forty-year-old who injured his arm in a car accident. He's in room six-eleven. Dr. Aylor wants you to do a skin graft on his arm."

The man's arm wound was healing well. It did not need a skin graft. I saw Dr. Aylor at the doctors' lounge later. "Your patient's arm is healing beautifully. He doesn't need a thing."

"It heals better with a little graft," said Dr. Aylor, smiling.

"It will heal faster without," I said firmly. "A skin graft takes two weeks to heal. He'll be healed without it in less than a week."

"He has good insurance," Dr. Aylor said, quietly touching my arm.

"He doesn't need a skin graft."

Dr. Aylor shook his head in disapproval. "You lose four, maybe five hundred dollars. It's a safe operation. It wouldn't hurt him."

"He doesn't need it."

"Okay, okay. I tried to do you a favor." He turned away, hurt and offended.

That was Sunday, New Year's Eve. I had worked in the ER all the night before, slept a few hours in the morning, and got called back in the afternoon. I was still at work in the ER Monday morning, New Year's Day — my eyes gritty and my dress rumpled. I had had four hours sleep in forty-eight hours, and I felt as though my residency had never ended. My last patient was a middle-aged man called Roy. He had come in at three A.M., but he was too drunk to cooperate until six, and anyhow I was too busy to see him earlier. New Year's Eve is a constant stream of car accidents, family fights, and barroom brawls. Roy was one of the hordes of celebrants with facial cuts and injuries in the aftermath. I was examining him when I heard Odette's voice in the corridor complaining to Dr. McPherson: "Every year we need extra help on New Year's Eve. Every year, the same charade. We need more doctors for a night like this, because all hell is breaking loose. Next year, I do not come in!"

Odette came into my cubicle calm and smiling, despite her impassioned proclamation. "You look tired. You must have been up all night." She looked at Roy and whispered to me, "He didn't cut himself shaving, did he? I'll see you later."

If I looked tired, I felt worse. At eight o'clock my New Year's call would be over. The room reeked of liquor from Roy's clothes and breath. He was in a deep sleep, snoring, and the stale stench of exhaled alcohol drifted into the hallway. His clothes were torn and bloody. He had no insurance. Tonight, for the first time, I found myself resenting that I wouldn't be paid. I wanted to go home. I wanted to sleep. I wanted to sew up Roy's face quickly. Any ER doctor could easily have done it. He had a long, straight cut on his forehead that would be simple to sew closed. If I had not already been in the emergency room, I would not have been asked to do it. I was sewing up Roy only because I happened to be free and the ER doctors were busy. My skill as a plastic surgeon was irrelevant.

"Roy, I'm Dr. Morgan."

He snored peacefully

"I'm going to numb your face and sew up your cut."

Snore.

I put on gloves, drew up the anesthetic, and gently inserted the needle. Thin, sharp needles cause almost no pain. Pain comes from a large needle, or too quick an injection. I was impatient, and injected quickly, anxious to get this over.

"Holy Christ," shouted Roy. "What the hell are you doing to me?"

His alcoholic breath engulfed me and I felt sick. He waved his arms angrily. "Leave me alone, you bastards."

"Right here, doc," said a large orderly, coming in from the hall. "Let me hold his head. I won't let him hurt you."

The orderly held his head but Roy was agitated and shook his head to and fro relentlessly. Injecting the novocaine became almost impossible. I ground my teeth and cursed Roy under my breath as I struggled to hold on to the syringe, but I knew it was partly my fault. If I had been gentle, he might have stayed asleep.

"Dr. Morgan, can you come to the phone?" asked Audrey, who had come to work on the morning shift. "It's about Mrs. Archer. I'll put the phone to your ear so you don't have to change gloves."

"Hello, Dr. Morgan? This is Mrs. Sloane, the night nurse on Eight-W. Mrs. Archer slept well."

I made a face in irritation. Surely she wasn't calling to tell me this.

"Ten minutes ago," continued the nurse, "she woke up and said she had to go to work. I thought I'd better check with you. She wants to sign out against advice and seems reasonable and persuasive, but if this is from her concussion, you wouldn't want her to go."

"Absolutely not." I felt ashamed of my irritation. "She's confused and she may hurt herself. You may have to restrain her again."

By the time we finished talking, Roy had fallen asleep once more. Gently, I injected his cut and started to sew up his laceration. All at once the sedative effect of his alcohol wore off and he woke up, irritable and disoriented.

"I've got a good hold on his head," said the orderly.

"Lemme go," said Roy, shaking his head vigorously.

"Hold still." I tried to tie a stitch.

"I've got him, doc," said the orderly grimly.

"Lemme go, you bastards," shouted Roy.

I focused on part of the laceration and flicked in a stitch quickly, coordinating my sewing with the rhythm of his shaking head.

"Hold still!" I commanded.

The orderly wrapped his arms around Roy's head and upper chest.

"I took wrestling in high school," he explained.

"Bastards!" barked Roy. He couldn't move his head, so he puffed his cheeks in and out. I knew I wasn't hurting him, because he didn't shout when the needle went through his skin.

"Please hold still. I'm trying to sew you up."

"I don't want to be sewn up. Lemme go!" This was absurd. I decided to try reason.

"Roy, look at me. I'm a doctor, a plastic surgeon. I'm trying to help you by sewing up your face. Your forehead is slashed open. If you want to go home right now, all you have to do is keep moving. You move one more time and I'm going home," I threatened. Almost everyone, no matter how confused, has moments of lucidity, and talking harshly to him brought him to reality for a moment.

"Okay, I'll be still."

"Got a good hold on him, doc," the orderly whispered.

I put in three stitches, and Roy started to puff his cheeks and curse again. My threats had been silly. I knew he couldn't help his behavior, and I wasn't going home until his last stitch was in. At nine o'clock I was finished and his wife came in. I gave her my card, a pain prescription, and written instructions.

"That's one you won't get paid for," said Audrey. State and county aid pays a hospital for taking care of indigent patients, but it doesn't pay the doctors, which is why many doctors, including surgeons, won't take emergency calls. If the case is complicated, a surgeon may have an emergency patient in hospital for months, needing several operations. The surgeon loses time, sleep, and fees, and often gets little thanks in return. I was beginning to understand how private doctors so easily can become obsessed with money.

Audrey handed me a bottle of hydrogen peroxide. "You have blood on your dress and your shoes. You'll want to take it off before you walk out."

I scrubbed the blood off in the hall, sitting at the doctors desk.

"Elizabeth!" said Odette, joining me. "Do you want a broken nose?"

"Yes. If you give him a pain prescription and tell him to keep ice on it, I'll see him on Thursday. I can't set a nose until the swelling is down."

"Good. Isn't it fun being a plastic surgeon in private practice? Nothing to do. No night call," she teased me. "After a few more nights like this, you may change your mind about cosmetic surgery and money. You look beat."

Another doctor looked over at us. "What's wrong with money?"

I returned his stare. "I don't think a doctor should get rich off his patients. To live well is one thing, but getting rich is another."

His brows flew up in amazement. "Honey, medicine is business. If you don't make the money, someone else will." He scowled and turned away. I said good-bye to Odette and left at last. I had been working nonstop for thirty-six hours.

Two weeks later the formerly drunken, shabby Roy came to my office to have his stitches removed. He was now well dressed and clean-shaven.

"Your scar will be red for several months then start to

fade," I explained to him. "I'd like to see you in six months, because if it doesn't look good, I might be able to improve it."

He nodded. "My wife says I was a pain in the neck when you sewed me up."

"That doesn't matter. Everyone's drunk on New Year's Eve."

"Thanks, but I'd like to apologize. I left an insurance form with your secretary."

After he left, Clare handed me $250 in cash. "Roy gave it to me. We haven't even billed him yet."

I sat down to think. I gave Roy excellent care, but I had resented him because I thought he couldn't pay. Now I felt guilty. I knew I had to make my practice profitable, but I must not let money become priority number one. I made a New Year's resolution. Regardless of loans and debts, my patients had to come first.

8
Nothing Is Safe

RICK HAZELTON, my real estate agent, was right. My new Twickenham office was completed by New Year's and Clare and I moved in that week. I was proud of my office. I had designed the layout and chosen the furniture myself, with my mother's advice and Clare's. They both have a better eye for color than I do. We had all agreed there would be no black-and-orange plastic chairs. The office was on the first floor, with its own entrance. The curtains were a blue Williamsburg print. The waiting room had blue velvet chairs and love seats in rust-colored velvet, and the walls were decorated with Audubon prints of birds. One wall displayed all my professional certificates and diplomas. I now had almost thirty — from college, medical school, the teaching hospital, certification boards, licensing bodies, and medical societies. Clare's office opened on to the waiting room. Down a short corridor were a bathroom, two examining rooms (one set up for minor surgery), and my office, which had bookshelves, my desk, and comfortable upholstered armchairs. Clare did most of the packing and my father directed the movers. I did very little to help because I was busy with my four patients from New Year's Eve in Metropolitan Hospital.

Mrs. Archer had recovered abruptly and completely from her concussion, to my relief as well as that of her family, and I had wired her broken jaw back together. She would stay wired for three weeks.

She ran a flourishing interior-design business in Washington and had a wide circle of devoted friends. "I'm successful because I take time," she said slowly through her teeth (they were wired together too, to let her broken jaw rest). "Women buy houses and don't understand how to decorate them. I help my clients do their decorating before they buy the house. I've gone all over Washington to help a woman find a pattern to match the drapes in a house she wanted to buy. I love it."

The wires in her mouth were uncomfortable and sometimes hurt her, but she never complained. She was a brave woman, and once the grotesque swelling in her face and neck subsided, she proved to be beautiful as well, despite the scars on her face.

"I am a mess!" she said, laughing at her reflection in the hospital mirror. "The worst is I don't remember anything for the five days after the accident. I don't like losing five days of my life. It's eerie. Will these scars go away?"

I explained they would improve but never vanish. "They may become invisible, but I can't promise. It depends on how your body heals." My beeper went off twice while I arranged for her hospital discharge.

I hated that beeper. I wished I'd never rented one. It never gave me a moment's peace. I was called out of a grocery store one evening by a patient who wanted to change his appointment. Another time I was called out of a movie by a woman who found my name in the Yellow Pages and wanted to know all about face-lifts.

"Tell me about the scars and the complications and how much younger I'll look," she had demanded.

"I would have to see you in my office to explain all these things. I can't tell before I see your face."

"Yes, but you'd charge me. Your secretary said there was a consultation fee."

"Certainly, because it would take about an hour of my time to discuss a face-lift."

"I don't want to pay for that. Don't you answer questions for free? Carpenters and everyone else do that — it's the same thing."

"Perhaps you can find a plastic surgeon who will give you a free consultation."

"Yes, but I want a woman doctor."

"There are two other women plastic surgeons in Washington. You might call them."

"I have. They charge, too. I need a lot of questions answered. What you read in the magazines is confusing."

"If you can't afford a consultation, you can't afford a face-lift."

"But I really need one. Don't you do surgery for free?"

I disengaged myself at last, but the beeper continued to haunt my life. It went off again while I was checking on my other patients at Metropolitan. This time it was Jim, a pleasant surprise.

"Do you have any Brascan?" he demanded tensely.

"We have Brasso, in the cupboard under the sink."

"Brascan. Daddy says he gave you a hundred shares when you were in college."

"Then I must have them still." I thought for a moment. "Yes. I know I do."

"Okay. Get them now. I'm going to sell you out. It's urgent."

"Why?"

"Daddy bought them at a dollar a share. They've been at thirty."

"How can a stock be an emergency?"

"Dad called five minutes ago and said he'd been reading the *Journal* and you had to sell. I know he's excitable, but he has amazing intuition and insists Brascan is going to tumble, soon. If he's right, you could lose two thousand dollars. Are you sure you have a hundred shares?"

"Yes."

"Listen, Elizabeth. The tape shows they're already down to twenty-five. I'll sell them now. Good-bye."

He called me at the office at four. "Did you get your Brascan?"

"Yes," I said irritably. I had been late to the office because of stopping at the bank to get the Brascan stock out of the safe deposit box. There were people waiting to see me.

"Good. I sold you out at twenty-three. They fell to fourteen just fifteen minutes later and the Board suspended trading."

"Heavens. Daddy was right, wasn't he? How did he know? He's a genius."

"I wish I had his intuition," said Jim. "He makes the market analysts look like kids. Did you know Mrs. Spencer-Neville is in Highcliff Hospital? Rupert called me this morning. It may be her heart."

Rupert's mother was an older Englishwoman, classically beautiful, self-possessed and extremely kind, the granddaughter of an earl. I drove to the hospital to see her after I finished with my last patient at the office, a carpenter with a broken finger who came late because he stopped for dinner. Mrs. Spencer-Neville had been admitted to the cardiac intensive-care unit, but it turned out that her heart was fine. Her problem was stomach pain.

"Dr. Pusey, the specialist assigned to me, says I will need to see a surgeon next week," she told me.

"Next week? Why not now?"

"I don't know. I really didn't think much of him. A third-rate young man. Not like a doctor at all." She was ill but her spirit remained. "No surgeon he recommends is operating on me. I'd prefer my local butcher."

"I'll find you a good surgeon," I promised.

I like general surgeons and general surgery. After all, that was my field for five years and I am a Board-certified general surgeon. It is my general-surgery training that enables me to do good reconstruction and care for severely injured patients.

I wasn't very familiar with the local general surgeons, but I knew what to do. The chief resident in surgery was on the phone at the nurses' desk when I found him. After he hung up, I introduced myself and asked who the best general surgeons were. I knew that only the residents would know and feel free to say.

"There are quite a few. Dr. Lippman, Dr. Alexis, Dr. Eastman, Dr. Mukerji. I'd let any one of them operate on me."

I knew them all by sight. "What about Parnell?"

"Never. He doesn't give a damn."

Mrs. Spencer-Neville decided on Eastman because she had heard of him. In any case, Dr. Mukerji was on vacation and Dr. Alexis had the flu. Dr. Pusey finally agreed to call Dr. Eastman for a consultation.

"Is there a medical reason why I should be kept under Dr. Pusey's care for a week first?" Mrs. Spencer-Neville inquired. "Wouldn't it make more sense for me to at least see a surgeon in case I need surgery right away?"

"Much more sense," I replied. "I'm not sure why he didn't ask Dr. Eastman in earlier."

"Well, I'm sure," said Mrs. Spencer-Neville with cold disapproval. "It's his fee, obviously. He can't charge me once I'm no longer his patient."

Dr. Eastman was from London and he and Mrs. Spencer-

Neville got along very well. He was energetic and loved to operate, but his great concern was that his patients get good care. He had a reputation for displaying a fiery temper if even a small detail was overlooked.

"You didn't refer her to Pusey, did you?" Dr. Eastman asked me one afternoon. "No? That's good. If I'd seen her immediately I could have removed her gallbladder then, but now it's too inflamed. She has to wait six weeks, but she'll be home in the meantime. She's a charming woman. It's a shame we have to have men like Pusey on our staff. They should be out where any doctor is better than none."

Dr. Eastman operated on Mrs. Spencer-Neville six weeks later. She had no complications, and Dr. Eastman had her home in five days. She was fully recovered in a month — a tribute to her constitution and his skill. I became friends with Dr. Eastman, and later with Dr. Alexis.

Dr. Alexis and his wife were from Belgium. They had survived the Nazi invasion, and after the war they came to the United States. Dr. Alexis was intense but handsome. His serious, almost solemn, expression softened when he smiled. One day, after I finished a five-hour reconstruction of a plumber's injured hand at Metropolitan, I stopped in the doctors' lounge as usual for coffee. Dr. Alexis was sitting by himself and asked me to join him. "I'd like you to see a patient for me, Elizabeth. She's a welfare case, and you know how much they'll pay you."

"Yes, they paid me thirty-five dollars for a four-hour operation to repair a cleft lip." Clare had indignantly shown me the check just the day before. It had taken six forms, three long-distance phone calls, and four hours of work for her before we got paid even that. Most doctors, like me, lose money trying to collect from welfare.

He nodded sympathetically. "We all face the same problem.

It won't pay your gas to the hospital for postoperative visits."
He shrugged. "But this lady is a sweet patient with a delightful
family. They'll be forever grateful, which sometimes is more
satisfying than money. She's an unfortunate victim of our
country's involvement in the Vietnam War. Years ago, long
before the government started using napalm, American
troops burned her village. Vietnamese women wear pants,
and hers caught fire, burning both legs. She was not poor, but
they lived in a small village with no doctors. She was in her
sixties and it took two years for the burns to heal. Later, her
family moved to Saigon, and her granddaughter-in-law got a
government job. When the Viet Cong were about to invade
Saigon, she was told, 'If you want to go to America, you and
your family should report to the airstrip in two hours.' "

"They all got out?"

"On the last plane before the Communists drove into the
city. Oriental families are very close. No one would leave
unless they could all go together. Five generations of the Gaus
came. My patient, her husband, her children, her grandchildren, and their children and grandchildren. They live together, and those of them who can work, do. They're on
welfare now, but they won't be for long." He sat silent for a
moment. Perhaps he was thinking of his own escape. Most of
his family had died in World War II.

"Oh yes, about her legs," he went on. "The burn scars on
her legs keep breaking down into ulcers. At this point, she
has an enormous ulcer on her right leg. She has constant pain
and she can't walk. Mrs. Gau is almost eighty, and she doesn't
work, but she has done all the cooking for the family. Now
that she can't walk or cook, she has agreed to come to the
hospital. The Vietnamese never go to a hospital except to die,
so you can imagine how she feels. See if you can get her healed.
She and I would be grateful for anything you can do. The

Vietnamese are wary, and she may not let you operate without my approval."

I agreed to see her, of course. It was a compliment to be
asked. I came back to the hospital that night at eight, after
office hours. I had never treated such a burn, and I felt it
was but a small thing I could do measured against the horror
and injustice of the war.

Mrs. Gau was in room 802, a frail lady with such smooth,
unwrinkled skin that it was hard to believe she was nearly
eighty. She was sitting up in bed. In a chair by her bedside was
a beautiful Vietnamese woman in her thirties.

"How do you do, Mrs. Gau. I'm Dr. Morgan. Dr. Alexis
asked me to come."

Mrs. Gau smiled graciously from the bed and bowed to
me, while the younger woman translated. Mrs. Gau listened
attentively, smiled, and bowed again. I bowed back, clutching
my medical bag in front of me.

"My grandmother was expecting you, doctor."

They had a discussion in Vietnamese and then the younger
woman turned to me. "Dr. Alexis said you would come to see
her. I am her granddaughter-in-law."

"You must be the one who helped your family come here?"

"No. That is another granddaughter-in-law, Dr. Morgan."
She laughed shyly. "We are a big family."

I put my bag down on a chair and turned the sheet back to
inspect Mrs. Gau's legs, which were wrapped from toe to
knee in gauze bandages. The bandage on the right leg was
stained with dirty yellow-green drainage from the ulcer
beneath.

"I think I'll ask a nurse to help me." I rang the bedside bell
and sat down on the bed to unwrap Mrs. Gau's bandage.
"Does changing the bandage hurt her?"

The granddaughter-in-law asked Mrs. Gau in Vietnamese,

then said, "No, doctor, it does not hurt now. Would you like her to tell you if it does hurt?"

"Yes indeed." Mrs. Gau smiled encouragingly and pointed a finger to her bandaged leg to indicate that I could begin. I bowed again and unwrapped the dressing.

When I removed the bandage, I let out an involuntary gasp. The right leg from knee to toe had no normal skin, merely a shiny, tight, thick scar covered with a fragile skin that could almost be wiped away with a sponge. An open ulcer covered half the leg. The tissues were green with infection and gave off a semisweet smell of decay. When I pulled off the last of the gauze, Mrs. Gau spoke.

"She says it hurts, but not too much. She wants you to go ahead."

I looked at Mrs. Gau, who smiled but averted her gaze from the ulcerated leg. I studied her leg with care. It was soft with infection and there were areas of gangrenous skin. At the bottom of the ulcer was bone — not normal bone, but a heavy sheet of bone made by the body in a bizarre attempt to heal the neglected burn. American doctors do not often see such "ectopic" bone in burns, because such badly neglected wounds are uncommon here.

"Very bad, isn't it, doctor?" said the granddaughter-in-law.

"Had she had any treatment in Vietnam?"

"Only Communist doctors, and they are not good like American."

Long-neglected burns can develop a rapidly fatal cancer, and I was afraid the burn ulcer was cancerous. Dr. Alexis doubted it, I learned when I called him later to discuss Mrs. Gau's condition.

"It doesn't look like cancer, Elizabeth, and it hasn't behaved like it over the months I've seen Mrs. Gau, but I agree a biopsy is a good idea."

Her left leg also had thickened scar, thin skin, and ectopic bone, but only a few tiny ulcers. It too needed the painful scar removed and skin grafts, but it didn't look cancerous.

Mrs. Gau and her family agreed to the biopsy and to removal of the gangrenous skin and ectopic bone on both legs, but only after Dr. Alexis gave his formal approval the following day. I took her to the operating room that same evening, because I had other surgery booked for the next two days and I didn't want her to wait longer. The beauty of operating at Metropolitan, which was the best-run hospital I had ever seen, was the attitude. I didn't have to cajole or argue in order to operate on Mrs. Gau. The operating room was well staffed, and if I, the surgeon, wanted to operate, there was no argument. Emergency cases had first priority and I might have to wait sometimes, but I didn't have to fight with a hostile bureaucracy in order to give good care. First-rate hospitals are rare, and I was fortunate to be able to work at one.

I had worked at hospitals where there were no evening- or night-shift operating nurses — where emergency surgery meant dragging in an "on-call" team over the protests of the nursing supervisor, who saw her job as keeping overtime pay to a minimum. Sometimes a hospital had the OR nurses available, but the anesthesiologist did not want to come in at night; to do evening surgery meant tedious, time-consuming arguments with the anesthesiologist about whether the operation really had to be done. Operating rooms reflect the attitude of the hospital administrator, and unless the administrator is anxious to provide good care, it can be an uphill battle for a surgeon to get time to operate and to have trained assistants to help. Fortunately, Metropolitan was so well run and the nurses were so good that I became accustomed to a level of help and cooperation that would have been miraculous almost anywhere else.

Once Mrs. Gau was asleep in the operating room, I cut away the diseased skin and scar and sent it to the lab for a frozen section — a quick microscopic exam for cancer. While we waited for the report from the pathologist, I fidgeted, rapping the tips of the Metzenbaum scissors on the ectopic bone.

"It sounds solid," said Stella, the scrub nurse. "That's not bone, is it?"

"Yes, ectopic bone."

"Hi there, Dr. Morgan." A pathologist whose beard and mustache were sticking out on all sides of his mask poked his head into the operating room. "I see scar, infection, and dead skin. No cancer." He withdrew. Dr. Alexis was right, and I now had a chance to reconstruct Mrs. Gau's legs. If the biopsy had indicated burn-scar cancer, even amputation would have been futile. She would have died within months.

"Now what?" asked Stella.

"We take out the bone, clean up the infection with dressing changes for a week, and when the wound is clean, put on skin grafts."

"She's almost eighty! Will she survive?"

"I hope. She can't live the way she is now."

The ectopic bone had grown in the leg for some fifteen years and was enmeshed by scar. For ten minutes I struggled with heavy rat-toothed forceps and with progressively larger clamps, trying to work the sheet of bone out from the scar. I made no progress. The bone was stuck.

"Scalpel, please." I took a number 10 knife — a big, wide blade — and tried to cut through and pry up the bone. I made a little progress. The inch-thick bone loosened in the scar, but it was still trapped. I couldn't get through it or under it or around it.

"I need some heavy bone-cutting instruments," I told Stella.

"I think you'll need a chain saw. Want us to steal one of the open-heart kits so you can use the chest splitter? Dr. Cushoff would die if we used his heart kit, but he'll never know."

It was a good idea, but the vibrating chest saw would be too big to insert under this ectopic bone.

Alice, the circulator nurse who handed us supplies as needed, staggered in with an enormous metal basin wrapped in sterile green towels. It held the heavy bone cutter. The bone cutter took two hands to use, and I still got nowhere. It wouldn't cut through this bone.

"A mallet and a chisel."

"All right, Michelangelo." Stella handed them to me. "I hope you don't take her leg off by mistake."

No one spoke as I pounded the chisel into the bone. The ringing sound of steel on the ectopic bone was unnerving. Normal bone has a hollow marrow cavity that dulls the noise. The ectopic bone was solid, and the operating room echoed with the sound. I chiseled the bone into pieces and pried the fragments out. To my surprise, the tissue beneath the bone was pink and healthy, despite the pus around it.

Two hours after surgery, I visited Mrs. Gau in her room and found her awake, sipping a cup of hospital tea cradled in both hands. Her eight-year-old great-great-grandson now sat at her bedside. During her four weeks in hospital she was never once alone. Several times I stopped to see her at two or three in the morning after I had been working in the ER. A relative was always curled up asleep in the chair by her bed. No one is sure why, but patients with loving friends and family heal faster.

Mrs. Gau put the tea down. "Herro, dachta."

"My great-great-grandmother is learning English," said the boy proudly.

Mrs. Gau bowed energetically.

"Would you tell her the surgery went well? She will need another operation in a week to put skin grafts on the open wounds on her legs. She will be in bed for two weeks after that." It sounded easy, but the surgery would take hours.

Mrs. Gau's great-great-grandson translated my message into Vietnamese. "She says that is fine," he told me. She no longer needed Dr. Alexis's approval.

"Good. What is 'thank you' in Vietnamese?" I asked him. If Mrs. Gau tried to speak English to me, I should try to speak Vietnamese to her.

"*Dau*," said her great-great-grandson.

I turned back to Mrs. Gau. "*Dau*."

Mrs. Gau looked bewildered. Her great-great-grandson explained in Vietnamese that I was speaking Vietnamese. She raised her eyebrows. "*Dau*, dachta," she said politely.

A week later Mrs. Gau was on the operating table again, for her skin grafts. She looked up at the operating room light, an enormous steel circle suspended directly over her head, and put her left arm up as though to protect herself.

I patted her hand. She said, "*Dau*, dachta," and fell asleep, as the anesthetist injected Pentothal.

A long operation is stressful, especially for an elderly lady. Any mistake or delay could be disastrous.

"She is nearly eighty," I told the circulator nurse. "I want this to go fast. Spray her legs with the iodine. I'll take the grafts first." When I was gowned, Stella handed me the dermatome, a giant automatic straight razor. I shaved skin strips off Mrs. Gau's thighs to use as skin grafts on her lower legs.

I gave each strip to Stella. "Don't throw it away by mistake." The removed skin is wrapped in a wet sponge and can easily be tossed into the trash bucket by mistake. Stella set the skin aside in a sterile bowl.

"Knife." I cut off the scarred, burned skin on Mrs. Gau's right leg. "Specimen." I handed the skin to Stella. "Dry lap pads." I put them on the raw tissue to soak up the blood.

"Knife." I started on the left leg. Stella put the scalpel in my right hand and a wet sponge in my left.

"Stella! This has skin! Where are the rest of the grafts?"

"Oh, my God." She sorted frantically through the sponges on the instrument table. The eight grafts were mixed up with used sponges, ready to discard, but we found them all. We looked at each other and sighed with relief. Accidents happen. Losing skin grafts in the trash bucket is the plastic surgeon's nightmare.

The surgery took three hours. Finally the grafts were in place over the raw wound where they would grow, like grass, to the tissue beneath.

"Can I wake her up?" asked the anesthetist. The operation had gone smoothly and he was bored.

"Not yet. I have to put plaster on each leg."

"Hurry. She'll be awake in about two minutes."

Mrs. Gau woke up, calm and dignified. She coughed, and tried to move her hands, but they were bound to the operating table. She relaxed and closed her eyes.

When a patient of almost eighty has two major operations in a week and spends weeks in bed, you expect some complication. Mrs. Gau had none. Once she could walk, she visited all the wards, leaning on her granddaughter's arm.

A week later she was ready to go home, and once she got home, she did all the cooking.

Medicaid paid me $75 for the two operations, twenty-one visits to the hospital, and many office visits afterwards, but I didn't mind. Mrs. Gau shyly kissed me when she came to my office the first time.

"We are very happy with you, doctor," said her granddaughter. "She can walk without pain for the first time in twenty years. We would like you to have this." She handed me a box that held two beautiful black China vases.

"We don't have money," she said, apologetically, "and these don't cost much money, but you can't get them in this country."

The vases have been on display in my office ever since. I love to look at them.

Mrs. Gau's gift was a touching end to a busy and anxious day. After office hours ended at six and Clare left, I sat down with the office books while the cleaning men vacuumed around me. What remained of the original loan money was dwindling rapidly as a result of my rent payments (close to $1,000 a month), Clare's salary, the phone bills, electricity costs, and office-supply expenses. Everywhere I turned I needed more money.

I was sitting at home that evening, eating hominy grits because I was feeling poor, when I noticed a dull ache in my side. I decided that my ulcerative colitis, a legacy from the Tewkesbury days, was coming back because I was worrying so desperately. The body is influenced by the mind. Too much stress, emotional as well as physical, makes it sick. I had to control my anxiety about money or I would get sick; that meant I had to turn a profit in my practice to pay off my debt. Jim walked in, burdened down with a weeks' supply of the *Wall Street Journal*, a computer printout, two investment books, and a briefcase. "The crash is coming," he announced happily. "The bottom will fall out of the real estate market. You've got to go to gold. Gold, silver, tangibles. That's why I like commodities." He tossed the newspapers on the top of the refrigerator. "What's the matter with you?"

"Money and my colitis." I was feeling sorry for myself. I saw myself in the hospital, dying after surgery.

"What are you eating?"

"Hominy grits."

"Not the ones in the cupboard?"

"Why not?"

"They probably caused the colitis. They're eight years old, the roaches have been in them, and a mouse or two."

A short gray mouse hair floated to the top of the cereal bowl.

The grits went down the sink, and my stomachache subsided. "Don't worry about being in debt," Jim continued, unfolding his computer printout. "A New York commodities broker lost six million today on a wheat contract. If he can lose that in a day, you ought to be able to make forty thousand. Rustle up a few face-lifts."

"Not for the money, Jim. A lot of women don't understand the complications, and once they do they may not want a face-lift. I'm a doctor, not a face-lift salesgirl."

"Why are you so concerned about complications?" Jim leaned back in his chair. "You're a surgeon. You should operate."

"Ten percent of face-lift patients have a complication."

"They don't die."

"No, but they may not be happy with the result, especially if they think it's like a haircut with guaranteed results. That's why I have to be honest about what a face-lift will do."

"If you talk people out of surgery, you can't pay your bills." Jim's chair fell backwards and he scrambled to his feet. "You have to be practical. You pay malpractice insurance. If something goes wrong, you're covered."

"Would you push a junk stock just for commission?" I demanded. He was shocked by the very suggestion.

"Do you have your appointment book?" Jim asked later. "My real estate friend Eddy has a friend who wants to meet you. I've researched him. He's from Baltimore, worth a couple of million, a widower, no children, fiftyish." He ticked the items off like pork-belly prices. "Eddy wants to arrange a lunch for the four of us. I said I'd sound you out."

"It sounds lovely."

"I'll tell Eddy to set it up if you give me a day you're free. It sounds reasonable except for his age. He may be too old for you."

"We could still join them for lunch."

"True. Also, I want to move into the city. If I can arrange a three-bedroom apartment on Connecticut Avenue, would you want to share?"

"I can't afford it, Jim."

"The rent is two hundred each. It's a good deal. It's a late-nineteenth-century building, like a New York East Side special. It's rent controlled and the owner runs it for something to do. He's seventy and he doesn't need money. Our apartment also has eight walk-in closets, two bathrooms, a separate dining room and a butler's pantry. Not bad."

It sounded too good to be true, but it was perfect. We moved in two weeks later. Actually, Jim, Rob, and Dad insisted on moving my things. I was doing a nerve graft most of moving day.

"I like feeling helpful," said my father, carrying out my sofa. At sixty-nine he was still as strong as either of his sons, and liked to prove it.

The next afternoon Odette called me from the Metropolitan ER. "Elizabeth, I can't find Sven Ohlsen, who's on call, and I have a fireman who had a fuse box explode in his face and set him on fire. His face, hands, and chest are burned. Not that badly, but *assez*. It's Workman's Compensation, dear, so it's not for free. Can I admit him to you?"

"Of course, Odette. Can you see that he has a chest X ray, pain medicine —"

"It's all done, the bandages, the IV. I take care of everything before I call. All I need is to know when you will see him. His wife is anxious."

"Six-thirty."

"She's worried, so she won't be happy, but he can wait. I'll tell them. This place is a zoo today. Take care!" She hung up.

At five o'clock Clare stopped me between patients with a call from Metropolitan.

"Dr. Morgan, I'm calling about Mr. Brandon, the fireman with the burns? He's having pain."

"Didn't Dr. de Blanchaud order Demerol?"

"Yes, but he won't take it till he sees you. He's afraid of addiction."

"He won't get addicted if it's for pain."

"I told him that, but he wants to see you first."

"I can't come in before six-thirty."

"Oh dear. Mrs. Brandon is very angry because she thinks you ought to have been in to see her husband sooner."

I knew what Mrs. Brandon didn't know. The burn had done its damage. Her husband had had emergency care. I would examine the burns and then we would have to wait to see if the burns would heal on their own or if they needed skin grafts. I could do nothing useful by rushing to hospital.

At five-thirty Clare said, "Metropolitan called again about Mr. Brandon. I told them you would come at six-thirty." Half an hour later, as I said good night to my last patient, Clare was saying politely, "No, Mrs. Brandon, Dr. Morgan is not free now to come to the phone. She will come as soon as she is finished here." I gritted my teeth as I listened. I try my best, and it upsets me to be harassed. I couldn't be in two places at once.

At six-fifteen I walked into Mr. Brandon's room. His wife was a young, attractive blond in a green suit. She stood in front of the window, her arms folded, tapping her foot impatiently and biting her fingernails. I could see why she was upset. Somewhere under a thick coat of white antibiotic cream was her husband's face. Only a thin layer is needed, but the ER nurses had been too thorough and put on enough cream to turn his face into a frightening white mask. No wonder she was in a panic. His eyelashes and forehead hair were burned away. His arms and hands were wrapped to the shoulders in bulky dressings.

"It's about time you got here," said Mrs. Brandon sharply, looking me over.

"I'm sorry."

"So what do you think?" she demanded in a tight voice. Mr. Brandon stared at me through the white mask.

"I can't see anything yet."

It took me an hour to scrape and wash off the cream from his hands and face. His face was slightly blistered, but needed no treatment and would heal without scars. His hands were badly burned. He had used them to slap out the flames on his burning shirt. They would need dressings, lots of physical therapy, and maybe surgery.

"I feel so much better now that I can see your face!" Mrs. Brandon exclaimed, forgiving me and hugging her husband. "I've been in a state of panic all day." They were extremely nice people, and Mrs. Brandon was embarrassed to have been so impatient. Her husband's chief concern was to get back to work. "Don't let him go home too soon," she pleaded with me. "He'll be at work the next day." I didn't let Mr. Brandon go anywhere. Without physical therapy, a burned hand can rapidly stiffen so that the joints are locked and the hands permanently crippled even when the burn is healed.

I ordered that Mr. Brandon be given penicillin for two days to prevent strep infection. He also got lots of physical therapy, and I changed his bandages daily. That was all he needed. The boredom of the hospital irked him, but he adapted by getting to know the other patients and he turned the ward into a social club. His hands healed rapidly. He ingeniously invented a contraption to fit a spoon onto his bandaged hand so he could eat without help. He was almost healed when he suddenly developed a fever of 100. There was pus in a blister on the back of his right hand, and the laboratory reported that it was a staphylococcus infection. An infection now could destroy the healed skin, so I prescribed oxacillin, a staph-killing antibiotic, and went home to dinner, confident that I had done the right thing.

At four in the morning a nurse called me. "Dr. Morgan, Mr. Brandon has a fever of a hundred and three."

"When did that start?"

"An hour ago."

I sat up, shivering. It was snowing and I had left the window open. "Give him ten grains of aspirin for the fever. Also, increase the oxacillin to a gram every six hours." She hung up and I stared out at the falling snow, thinking it strange that Mr. Brandon should have a fever now. His hands were not that badly infected. In the morning his hands looked even better than the day before and he had no fever, but at four in the afternoon it was 103 again. By the time I came to the hospital to see him after office hours, his temperature was back to normal and he was watching "General Hospital," sipping apple juice and feeling fine. I examined him meticulously and began to worry that the staph had settled on a heart valve or in the kidneys, starting a dangerous hidden infection.

I increased the oxacillin to the maximum safe dose and decided to ask an infectious-disease specialist to see him the next day. I knew from my textbooks that Mr. Brandon couldn't be allergic to the oxacillin. Such a reaction could cause the high fever, but he had had penicillin the week before without trouble and the two drugs are chemically similar.

At one A.M. his nurse called again. "Dr. Morgan, are you awake? Mr. Brandon just spiked to a hundred and six."

"A hundred point six, you mean."

"A hundred *and* six."

"He can't."

"He has."

"A fever of a hundred and six will cook his brain and kill him."

"I know. That's why I called you."

"Do everything — put him on an ice blanket, put a fan on him, rub him down with alcohol. I'll be in."

My new apartment was downtown, ten miles from Metropolitan, but I arrived in the hospital ten minutes later.

Mr. Brandon laughed when I walked in. "I'm kind of glad to see you doc. What's causing this?"

"I was going to ask you. You don't look sick enough to have a fever of a hundred and six."

"What if it won't go away?" He didn't sound worried but I knew he had to be.

"It will." I spoke with the empty confidence doctors assume when they are baffled.

I examined Mr. Brandon for the third time that day. His burned hands looked superb. They had healed completely. I ordered an emergency chest X ray. It was normal. His throat, his eardrums, his blood oxygen were fine. Everything was normal except that he had a fever of 106, and even if it didn't kill him, it might damage his brain.

I left his room and sat in the nurses' lounge studying every page of his chart, my notes, the nurses' notes, his laboratory tests. His fever chart looked like the Himalayas. I stared at the ups and downs. Since the oxacillin, the fever had become much worse. What if the textbooks were wrong ? What if you could be allergic to oxacillin but not to penicillin?

I remembered a medical professor who taught me that

smoking cigarettes doesn't cause lung cancer. All the textbook chapters he had written were wrong, but it took me several years before I realized that cigarettes did lead to lung cancer and many other diseases, such as emphysema and atherosclerosis, despite the professor's claims. He was learned and wrote his opinions in textbooks, but he was still completely wrong.

Mr. Brandon's nurse rushed by, clutching an IV bottle. "I've mixed up the oxacillin. I'm going to start it now."

"No!" I shouted. "Don't do that."

"Dr. Morgan, you wrote it in your orders," she said quietly.

"Cancel the order. No more oxacillin." I had made up my mind. Regardless of textbooks, Mr. Brandon didn't look sick enough to have an overwhelming infection. He had to be allergic to oxacillin. Eight hours after his last oxacillin dose, his temperature came down to normal and stayed there.

"What caused the fever?" his wife asked me the day he went home.

"He had a severe allergy from the oxacillin. He should never take it again. I don't know why it happened — medicines are unpredictable."

The Brandons were grateful for all my help but I didn't feel I had done much. He didn't need surgery. The physical therapist kept his joints loose, and I had nearly killed him. It was sobering. I met Odette in the doctors' parking lot on my way home.

"Elizabeth, it was a terrible day," she lamented, propping herself against her car. "I gave a teenage boy three cc's of novocaine to sew up a cut and he almost died from a heart arrhythmia. It's frightening. People don't understand. Nothing is safe in medicine. Nothing."

She was right. The best doctors are the least confident, because they know that things can unexpectedly go wrong. Medicine isn't a line of products and services supplied with a warranty, but a mélange of science, skill, intuition, and experience. I realized with pride that I was a better doctor in private practice than I had been as a resident a few months before. My solo practice had forced me to think independently, even if it meant discarding "facts" I had believed for years.

9

Like a
Ton of Bricks

LATER that evening I visited my parents to see how my mother
was. The week before she had come down with the flu, but
had kept working all week. She looked terrible. My father
was out in the country. With the bossiness of a doctor-
daughter, I put her to bed and told her to stay there.

"What about my patients?" she asked anxiously as I helped
her upstairs, but she didn't object to getting in bed. Her face
was pinched and had gone dead white, and she was so tired
she lay flat in bed. Sitting up was too tiring.

"You can't see your patients, Mother. You are sick. S-i-c-k."
She smiled. "If you bring me the appointment book, I'll call
them and explain."

"No, I'll call them and explain."

"Your father will be terribly upset. I've never been sick
before except when I had pleurisy, and that was almost thirty
years ago." She started to shiver and pulled the blanket up to
her neck. "At least I'm sixty-five now, so I have Medicare.
Elizabeth, I feel very sick. Do you think I could have leukemia? Do you think I'll get better?"

"Good heavens, Mother. You'll be up in a week." But I
knew it wasn't true.

"I've wanted to retire," she said. "I know now I won't work again. I won't be able to. I've overdone it once too often."

She had the drained look people get when they are going to die — not soon, but in a month or two. I made an appointment to take her in to Dr. Hamilton, our internist, and to have the lab next to my office do blood tests. Leukemia had occurred to me, too, but I refused to admit it.

"Sick?" my father said when he came in from the country. "Sick? In bed? Toni's never been sick."

"She is now, Daddy. I've put her to bed."

"What about her patients? What will they do? I can't cancel them." He couldn't take it in.

"I've done it, Daddy. It's all arranged."

When I left he was upstairs sitting on her bed, still in his frayed blue jeans, holding her hand, staring at her anxiously.

"Daddy, I got dinner ready. It's downstairs. All you have to do is make the coffee." He nodded, on the verge of tears, unable to speak. After that I stopped by every day after my office hours, always trying to get there in time to make dinner. My father turned the heat up to 80 to be sure my mother stayed warm, and he rushed out to buy a huge supply of steak, ice cream, strawberries, and champagne "to keep up her strength."

"Don't forget our lunch today with Eddy," Jim warned me sternly a few days later as I was dashing out of the apartment on my way to the operating room. It seems I have never arrived anywhere on time. I'm always exactly ten minutes late, yet it never fails to surprise me.

"Yes, yes," I called to him. "Where did I put my camera? I need to photograph my surgery today. I need photographs for the Board exam." I ran back into my room.

"Don't be late for the lunch, too, Elizabeth. These are big-time real estate men and their time is just as important as yours."

"I can't find my keys!"

"You left them in the door."

"Oh — thank you." I ran across the living room. The apartment was vast and I couldn't see the keys from the far end of the room.

"And don't rush or you'll have an accident and miss the lunch."

"I'm late!"

"Other doctors have been late. The nurses won't give you demerits," he said, turning back to his desk-top computer. "The franc, off at twenty-three and an eighth. The pound up to two dollars and a quarter," he murmured blissfully.

I was not late to the hospital as it turned out. I had forgotten it was Monday. Surgery at Metropolitan on Monday starts half-an-hour later than usual, after the nurses have finished a teaching conference. I had time to see and reassure the parents of my patient, a beautiful seven-year-old Hawaiian girl with an unsightly birthmark on her leg. I then calmed down, had another cup of coffee, and relaxed.

"Anything special on this case?" Stella asked, coming in to the nurses' lounge.

"No. I'm removing a giant hairy nevus and doing a skin graft on a little girl. I will need the baby Padgett dermatome, but otherwise just give me a regular plastic kit."

"How old is she?"

"Seven, but she is absolutely tiny. You'll love her. She's quite grown-up and completely unperturbed about having an operation." I paused and Stella looked at me sympathetically.

"You look tired. You should take a vacation." She went

off to get the operating room ready and to set up her instruments.

I was indeed tired, but at last my practice had passed the break-even point and I was beginning to pay off my debt. The turning point had been a reconstruction I did on a man visiting from Tennessee whose wife had tried to kill him by driving a pickup truck over his head. He survived, miraculously, but his face needed a lot of surgery. I didn't think he had insurance, and neither did he, but a social worker found out that he had excellent coverage through his employer. His insurance company paid me three thousand dollars at the same time as other insurance checks started to come in, even some late ones from my New Year's emergencies. The money came just in time. I had used up all but five hundred dollars of my loan and had already arranged an appointment with a banker for a second loan when the mail arrived with the checks. Clare stacked them on my desk with a triumphant smile, and we canceled the bankers' appointment. John Napier, my former plastic-surgery professor, was wrong; I was making it on my own without hustling face-lifts. I was paying a price, though. I had my emergency call at Metropolitan, and often Ronald Meade and Sven Ohlsen asked me to take part of theirs as well. I covered St. Barnabas's emergency room for a week each month, Mattaponai for two weeks a month, Radnor for another week, and Highcliff all the time. When one emergency room was quiet, another would usually have a patient for me. If they all happened to be quiet, I was kept busy operating on my regular patients; and if all the emergency rooms were busy, Clare would have to make frantic calls to postpone my surgery and rearrange all the office appointments. I was not exhausted, but I knew I couldn't go on at this pace, and I dreaded what would happen to me as my practice grew. My time was overbooked already and I was almost as busy and harassed as when I was a resident — only now I had the responsibility of being the surgeon in charge as well. I desperately wanted the normal social life that was eluding me.

"We're ready in five," crackled Stella's voice over the intercom, and I got up, ready to work. I caught a glimpse of myself in the mirror as I left the lounge. My face was pale and my eyes looked unnaturally large. My hair was drawn back, ready for the surgical cap, and I was wearing an extra-large rumpled cotton scrub top and pants — the only size on the laundry cart that morning, cut to fit a fat surgeon of six foot four. I looked like a coolie heading for the rice paddies. No wonder my patients looked shocked when I greeted them before surgery. I found myself a most depressing sight and resolved to buy some scrub dresses, as the nurses did, rather than wear the hospital-issue scrub suits.

At 11:30 I was finished with the skin graft on my little Hawaiian girl and I was looking forward to my lunch. It would be fun, an escape from the world of surgery. It was a comfort that Eddy and his friend would never know how dreadful I looked in a scrub suit. As usual, I was not going to be on time. I called Jim.

"I'm going to be fifteen minutes late."

"No problem. I'll call Eddy."

"Where are we going?"

"Meet us there."

"Where?"

"Chez Rostang."

"Where's that?"

"Elizabeth, where have you been all these years?" he asked incredulously. "You were the one who was telling me it would be easy to combine a surgical practice and a social life, and you don't know where Chez Rostang is?"

"Jimmy, don't give me a hard time. Just tell me how to get there."

"Relax, kid. Unwind. The lunch will be a ball. Ritzy French

food for free. You can't beat it. It's the restaurant near the Metro on K Street."

"I know how to get there," I said with relief. "See you soon."

Washington streets are a maze of one-ways and no-left-turns. Lunches run predictably late, and I called Clare to be sure she had not scheduled any patients for me until four. Of course she hadn't. Without Clare, my life would be chaos. I made the thirty-minute drive into D.C. and found Eddy and Jim already seated at a table with a waiter hovering around them.

"Jeff Clark's on his way," said Eddy cheerfully, "so he shouldn't be more than an hour late." Eddy was a friendly, good-looking man in his late thirties with the expansive manner that accompanies successful speculation in high-rise office and apartment ventures. Big-time real estate men must take lots of risks; outwardly, at least, they don't worry.

"Jeff and I have been buddies for almost twenty years, but I've never known him to be less than an hour late. He's a busy man. Too many people need his okay. He's big in his field. What are you drinking, folks?"

Jim had iced tea. Eddy had a Bloody Mary and I had a whiskey sour. I don't drink at lunch, and the whiskey sour is a happy solution. Since it is a sweet drink, you can't taste the alcohol, so most restaurants don't put any alcohol in. Eddy talked to me in a confidential manner.

"Listen, Liz. I hope you like Jeff. I met him before either of us had a dime. He's a great friend of mine but I'll be honest with you. Since his wife died, years ago, he hasn't dated much and, as far as I know, only for sex. He's almost fifty and you're both adults. You're on your own with him." Jim grinned at me over his iced tea. He had warned me that Eddy was a character.

194

"Jim tells me you like china," said Eddy.

"I do," I replied enthusiastically. I can browse happily for hours around the china department in stores and if I had money I'd buy more patterns than I could use.

"What period? Ming? Ch'ing? My wife collects *famille verte.*"

I hadn't realized he meant "china" as Chinese antiques at twenty thousand dollars a piece. I had once visited the Altman Collection in the New York Metropolitan Museum, and remembered the beautiful rose-colored vases that are the pride of the collection. I tried to take Eddy's wife's china collection in stride. "*Famille verte*'s beautiful but I prefer *famille rose.*"

"We can't afford *famille rose,*" said Eddy, impressed. "One small vase sells for a quarter of a million now, if you can find any. Where do you get yours?"

"Me?" I laughed. I was on the verge of explaining when Jeff arrived. He was tallish, fit, tanned, and exuded self-assurance. He apologized for his lateness with a charming smile. His eyes were friendly, and when he turned to look at me I fell in love like a ton of bricks. I was so dazed I ordered soft-shell crabs, which I detest.

"What did you think of him?" Jim asked later as he walked me back to my car.

"He's very nice." Jim gave me a funny look and rubbed his left ear. "Yes. He's a smart guy."

Back in the office Clare handed me an envelope with my mother's test reports from the laboratory. I looked at it, prepared for the worst. "Oh. Thank God. At least Mother doesn't have leukemia. Her blood count is normal."

"I'm so relieved," said Clare. "I knew you've been worried. But what is making her so sick?"

"I don't know. It may be the flu, or it may be something

strange, like histoplasmosis. There have been thousands of starlings around the bird feeders my father keeps in the back-yard and they can carry histo. I'll ask Dr. Hamilton."

Office hours ran late as usual, and we didn't finish until seven-thirty. The last patient was a young man who had been crushed by a truck that was backing up. He had spent a month in the hospital and had returned home to find that his wife had eloped with another man after sending their two children to her parents in New Jersey.

"Doc, I've gotta get my kids. I have to have them. I don't understand this woman I married. Can I go on a plane with my leg in this cast?"

Clare helped him make the plane reservations and I talked with airline officials to make sure he would be attended to on the plane. At last the day was over. I drove over to make my "house call" on my mother and to get dinner ready. Cooking is a mystery to my father. All he knows is that if you put it in a pot and boil it all day, it won't be raw, whatever it is.

"I'm feeling much better," my mother said emphatically. "Much better." But her eyes were sunk back into her head with dark circles around them and she had started to have drenching sweats at night.

"I'm so glad I don't have leukemia. How was the lunch with Eddy?"

"Lovely," I said with a dreamy smile, thinking of Jeff. My beeper went off. "Damn it." I struggled with a desire to throw it onto the floor and jump on it, but instead I called the answering service.

"A Mr. Jeff Clark called, but he's not a patient of yours. Do you want his number?"

"Yes. Please."

He was calling to invite me to dinner the next day, and I accepted with delight, bouncing happily on my mother's bed. My beeper went off again. This time it was Mattaponai calling about a garage mechanic with a broken finger, and I was happy to be called. I would have been happy whatever happened. The most wonderful man in the world had appeared in my life and I didn't have a care in the world; debts, my burgeoning practice, my mother's illness — all seemed to recede in the distance. Somehow he would make everything turn out right.

"You have love the way some people have measles," said my mother laughing at me when I said good night. I walked to the front door but my father stopped me.

"How is she?" he asked in a whisper in the living room, pointing up to the bedroom.

"I think it's a terrible case of the flu, Daddy. At least it's not leukemia."

"Not leukemia? What is it then? I want a diagnosis."

"Daddy, the serious and fatal diseases are often easy to diagnose. As long as she gets better, I don't care about a diagnosis. It's not surprising she's caught something. She has worked too hard for ages."

"I want a diagnosis. I want her better now." His voice began to rise, urgent and agitated. "And who is this man you had lunch with?" he demanded.

"Jeff Clark. He's in real estate in Baltimore."

"Is he black? Did Jim introduce you to a black?" His eyes flashed.

"Daddy, no, he's not black, but what difference would it make?"

"How old is he?"

"About fifty."

"Fifty!" My father was shocked. "Fifty!" he repeated. "He's old enough to be your father." He walked away into the kitchen, muttering angrily. I heard him pull dinner out of the oven and onto a tray with a slam and utter an oath as I left for Mattaponai. He had always been moody, but never like this. My mother's illness was almost too much for him to bear.

Mine is a temperamental family and one reason Jeff appealed to me was his complete calm. He took me to dinner the next night at La Gioconda, and to The Golden Pheasant two nights later. On Friday — I had been operating all day and all the night before and was exhausted — he drove out to Virginia at ten at night, picked me up at my parents' and whisked me off for *faisan à l'orange*. We were both in love. We even agreed we didn't like Chinese food or soft-shelled crabs. I had never met such a perfect man. The night he picked me up at my parents,' my father glowered at him from the front door.

"You mustn't mind Daddy," I told Jeff. "He's worried about my mother." Dr. Hamilton had called to tell Daddy he found nothing seriously wrong with her except fatigue and the flu and some scars on her X ray that two lung specialists agreed were the harmless result of her pleurisy years ago. My father was dissatisfied and again had been demanding a "diagnosis" from me when Jeff arrived.

Jeff and I were inseparable (whenever I wasn't operating or seeing patients or visiting my mother or going to meetings, or he wasn't out of town on business). We faithfully called each other on the days we couldn't meet. One night I called him at two A.M., after I had finished sewing up a boy with a lacerated face from a car accident.

"I don't mind," said Jeff, very composed, when I apologized the next night over dinner. "All the years my wife was ill, I would come home for an hour to join her for dinner and then go back to the office. I can work all night. Working late is a habit now. I'm always awake when you call."

"You didn't see much of your wife."

"No. I gave her money, bought her everything she wanted, but I led my own life. I decided that I was entitled to my own life when she got diabetes a few years after we were married.

I could have divorced her or put her away in a home. Many men would."

He spoke without feeling and it struck a discordant note. I was in love with this man and I didn't want him to say things like that. It sounded so callous. Diabetics don't get "put away" in nursing homes. Many lead perfectly normal lives.

"How sick was she, Jeff?" I wanted her to have been a terrible invalid with brain damage or something incapacitating to justify his coldness. He shrugged, detached.

"Oh, she was in and out of the hospital a couple of times a year when she misjudged the insulin dose. Her circulation was poor and she tired quickly. She had diabetes," he added again, as though it explained everything. His attitude jolted me. I was forced to admit to myself that he had not once spoken to me about his family or any friends with real interest or compassion, and he had had plenty of opportunity. Most of the time we were together I listened to him talk about himself. He told me stories about his clever business negotiations — how he bought up land shortly before the urban revival made the value rise steeply — and about the clubs he belonged to and how well he skied. I liked listening to him. He was witty and amusing, but he listened with perfunctory politeness when I talked about my practice or my patients. It flattered him to be listened to and I enjoyed flattering him. Sometimes I was simply too tired to talk. My practice was running my life. I had no time or energy to sort out my feelings. Sometimes I had misgivings that Jeff might not be the perfect man; at other times I knew he was. Between fatigue, the demands of my practice, my mother's illness, my father's depression over her condition and his antipathy toward Jeff, I never had time to think clearly.

My father simply couldn't look after my mother calmly. "Eat more. Eat, Toni," I found him urging her one night, holding a huge plate of cookies and an enormous dish of ice cream. "You have to eat to get better. Don't you want to get better? Please, eat some more."

"Bill, I can't eat more," she protested feebly. She needed a nurse or a companion to shake out her pillows, change her sheets, keep her company, and let her rest. My father could do everything but let her rest. He behaved as though he could forcefully drag her away from the virus and back into health with his own energy.

"Do you want me to get a nurse to come in, Mother? Would that help?" I asked after my father left the room.

"No! No!" she raised herself on one elbow in alarm. "It would only upset him more. Please, don't. He'd hate it. I don't want a nurse hovering over me." She lay back. "What is that funny feeling in my chest?"

It turned out to be premature ventricular contractions, the abnormal heartbeats that everyone has occasionally — but a cardiogram the next day showed that she was having five or six a minute when she felt her worst. Though Dr. Hamilton and a cardiologist agreed the arrhythmia didn't need treatment till there were ten or twelve irregular contractions per minute, I was frightened. I had treated patients for PVC's — and I had seen a few of those patients become worse abruptly and die. Just then I hated being a doctor and knowing all the nightmares that could happen to my mother. I also knew that Jim was going to have to share our glorious city apartment with someone else. My mother would only get well if I looked after her. As women have known through the ages, the best person to nurse a mother back to health is her daughter; and I was my mother's only one. She had stood by me for years. Now it was my turn. I was glad I had come home after residency. There was only one trouble: although being a plastic surgeon was all very fine, I wished I'd also been trained as a nurse.

Before I could move home, I had to spend a week out of town in CME — continuing medical education. CME started in the mid-seventies with a well-intentioned government commission that reported that doctors in practice should periodically update their education to keep up with medical advances. The American Medical Association decided to accredit certain conferences as part of CME, and many state medical societies now recommend or require that doctors have fifty hours of CME credits each year. This has spawned a large group of educational entrepreneurs who set up CME symposia. The approach is self-defeating. The doctors who don't want to bother to attend a conference choose one in a pleasant resort, sleep through the morning lectures, and spend the afternoon on the beach or on the ski slopes.

A letter from the state medical society informed me that continued membership required fifty credit hours of CME a year. The letter was followed by a brochure advertising "The Mid-Atlantic Plastic Surgery Hand Course." It was a one-week workshop, with two days of cadaver dissection, and was accredited for thirty CME hours. That plus miscellaneous conferences and other meetings would meet my yearly requirement. The small print at the bottom of the brochure mentioned a fee of $500. It was expensive, but Janice, my brother Rob's fiancée, would let me stay in her apartment. Jeff was away on business, so I decided to go to the hand course.

The first day of the course I walked into a dimly lit foyer furnished with three long tables, each supervised by a secretary. The first secretary directed me through the milling registrants to the third secretary. The third secretary had glasses, gray hair, and looked efficient. She had me sign three cards and then said. "You're late. Lectures begin at nine-fifteen *sharp*, doctor." She studied my signature with suspicion, as though she suspected me of check forgery, and handed me a plastic black bag containing preprinted lecture notes and a white coat for the cadaver dissection. I was the only woman and saw no one I knew, not surprising in a plastic-surgery course restricted to two hundred people. At 9:15 *sharp*, the lecture hall doors opened with a flourish and we shuffled in.

"Hey, Liz. I thought you knew all this stuff." It was Percy Peregrine. We had been together at medical school. I went over and joined him. He was a whiz kid who had wanted to be a plastic surgeon since he was ten. By the time he graduated from medical school he knew more about plastic surgery than anyone except the professors, and before his surgical training was over, he knew more than the professors, which made him generally unpopular with all but the best of them. He was thin, and dark-looking like a Spanish grandee.

"Hey, Dave, over here," shouted Percy jumping up and waving his black plastic briefcase. Dave Herzog, a stocky, blond plastic-surgery professor we had known in Illinois, vaulted across knees, feet, and empty seats and slid into the seat next to mine.

"Hey, you kids. You must know all this stuff. What are you here for?"

"The cadaver dissection appealed to me," I said. "I haven't had a chance to dissect a hand since medical school."

Dave shook his head sadly. "Poor girl. Look what medical training does for a woman. Sick, very sick." We waited for half an hour,

At 9:45 an elderly white-haired man climbed onto the auditorium stage. "Good morning. Good morning. This is the fourth year we've given this wonderful course, and it gets better every year."

"Does he realize we've paid already?" whispered Percy.

"If you'll look down the list with me," droned the elderly doctor, "you'll see that we have forty lecturers to teach you. I've followed Walter Zuckerman's career with interest for many, many years. We're lucky to have Walt with us. Olaf Haas is next. He's an old, old friend. Unfortunately, Olaf can't come, so we'll miss having Olaf with us."

"Don't tell me they charge five hundred dollars for this," said Dave.

"CME is a money-maker," said Percy. "Two hundred in the course is a hundred thousand dollars. Subtract thirty thousand for guest-lecturer expenses, and it's seventy thousand profit in five days. You can't beat it."

After thirty minutes of introduction, the podium was turned over to Dr. Scott Sylvester. His hair was wavy, his skin was tanned, he wore a nautical blazer. He directed us to the dissection laboratory where coffee, doughnuts, and cadavers awaited us.

Soon Dave, Percy, and I were standing around a gray, pickled human arm, severed at the shoulder, lying on a stainless-steel table. None of us were interested in the coffee and doughnuts.

"I'm joining you," said a voice firmly. "I'm Mel Johnson, an orthopedic surgeon. There's one cadaver arm for every four of us, and I'm your fourth."

Four people grouped around one arm are a lot of hands for a small area. The pickled arm was dry. The fingers had curled almost closed. Dave tried to straighten them, but the joints were stiff, and he would have had to break the fingers to make them straight.

"Why am I here?" Dave asked gloomily. "I hate cadaver dissection."

Mel and I started to dissect the upper arm, Dave and Percy worked on the hand. The instruments provided were dull and rusty.

"This is awful," muttered Percy in frustration while he tried to cut off the skin. "Can I use my teeth?"

"Sick," muttered Dave unhappily. "Very sick."

Mel and I dissected the median nerve, had trouble finding one of its muscle branches, and asked an anatomy instructor to help. The instructor shook his head with a smile. "They asked me to teach, but I never operate in the arm. I'm a finger-replant man."

"We're working on an arm, not a finger," said Mel rudely.

The instructor shrugged, uninterested. Three hours later, Mel straightened up and looked around the room. All the "instructors" had left. "I'm disgusted. This is a waste of time." He stomped off.

After lunch, Dave disappeared for good. The afternoon started with a lecture by Dr. Black, a microsurgeon. "This afternoon," Dr. Black barked, "I'm going to show you what microsurgery can do." In a blur of slides he showed us pictures of his hospital, his laboratory, his operating room, and the emergency room he covered. There followed countless pictures of amputated fingers and toes, and then arms and legs. He was teaching us nothing.

"Canned lecture," said Percy. "I heard this one three years ago. The next slide is a mouse, and then a rat."

The next slide was a mouse, and then a rat. Then Dr. Black showed us pictures of experimental dogs, cats, and pigs. Percy fell asleep. I doodled.

The next lecture was by Dr. Basel, a microsurgeon from Canada. Incredulous, Percy and I watched as he showed us slides of his hospital, his laboratory . . . I fell asleep. Percy doodled.

Percy woke me for the anatomy lecture by an Australian professor, Dr. Widemere. "I have two hours to cover hand anatomy," he announced crisply. "I will not use slides. In the hand, the brachial plexus from the upper arm. In three cords. Remember three. At the elbow, the ulnar wraps around the humeral epicondyle. In the finger, the extensor indicis proprius is the ulnar-most extensor . . ."

Percy and I looked at one another in confusion. Dr. Widemere had traveled from the armpit to the little finger and back to the wrist in sixty seconds; he mentioned the brain, the arm, the monkey's leg, and got back to the hand. I had no idea what he was talking about and neither did he himself. At four o'clock he began his second lecture, on pain.

"Pain," said Dr. Widemere, "I want the audience to consider pain. Pain," he repeated, "follows injury." A man on the aisle got up quietly and left the lecture hall. "Nerves feel pain." Dr. Widemere pulled a pin from his lapel. "If I prick my finger with a pin, I feel pain!" He sniggered. "Of course, in the United States the verb 'to prick,' has several — ah — meanings."

Percy nudged me. "Let's go." The back half of the auditorium had already emptied.

The next four days were as bad as the first. "Well, at least you got your credits," laughed Robert Fletcher when I returned. "You didn't expect to learn as well, did you? CME is big business."

CME also allows you credits for publishing medical papers. I had begun one back when I was a resident in general surgery. It started as a short report on a patient we operated on for a rare stomach tumor called carcinoid. Dr. Brody, my surgery professor, was my coauthor. In doing the research, I paid thirty dollars for a computer search that gave me eight pages on Japanese throat cancer and nothing on carcinoid, but I finally tracked down the 132 known cases of stomach carcinoid. I wrote a draft and sent it to Dr. Brody.

He wrote back that Dr. Hwang, a pathologist, should do the part on the microscopic findings and be a coauthor, too. Then Dr. Brody wrote again, reminding me that Dr. Ferguson, the chief of surgery where the operation was done should be a coauthor. It's a surgical tradition.

Dr. Ferguson was pleased to be invited to join us. He worked on the paper with me and suggested that his colleague, Dr. Grant, be a coauthor too, because he reoperated on the original patient. It was a surgical tradition. He liked to help his junior colleagues.

Dr. Hwang called me to say that he liked the paper and that we needed more slides. He didn't have time to do them, but his associate Dr. Kelly would do the slides if he were listed as a coauthor.

"We already have five authors," I told him.

"Another won't hurt," said Dr. Hwang.

My next project was to review the X rays of the patient. Dr. Schwann, the chief of radiology, was helpful. He sent me the X ray photos with a note saying he was delighted to be a coauthor (I hadn't invited him) but Dr. Pope had to be a coauthor because he did the original X rays.

The little paper now had as its authors three department chairmen, their three colleagues, my professor, and me: Morgan, Brody, Hwang, Pope, Grant, Schwann, Kelly, and Ferguson. Before I left the Midwest for private practice, Dr. Hwang called to say his other colleague, Dr. Wilson, had done some special stains and was another coauthor to be added.

I protested. "I have been working on this paper for three years. We have eight authors on a three-page case report."

"Another won't hurt."

I mailed the finished paper, complete except for Dr. Hwang's associate's slides, to Dr. Brody the day before I left my residency. That was the last I heard. I wrote once but he didn't reply.

When I returned, disgruntled, from the CME hand course, I remembered carcinoid and wrote to Dr. Brody again. Ten days later, he called. "Elizabeth," his deep, cheerful voice crackled slightly over the wires. "Are you sitting down?"

"No."

"Sit down. I have the finished paper in my hands. I finally got the slides from Dr. Hwang."

"I don't believe it."

"Fact. Absolute fact."

"How many authors are there now?"

"I have the paper in front of me: Morgan, Brody, Hwang, that's us; Grant and Ferguson, two more surgeons; Kelly, a pathologist; Schwann and Pope, the X ray men; then Alini and Wilson. That's ten."

"Who is Wilson?"

"Hwang's second associate."

"Then who is Alini?"

"Oh." He paused. "Hell, Elizabeth, I don't know. I'm going to send it to *Gastroenterology* for publication." A short time later he wrote to say the report had been rejected. They said it was too insignificant a paper for so many authors.

10

Goats Were
the Last Straw

My mother was looking slightly better these days. I visited her one day and found her guarding at her bedside a letter to me from the American Board of Plastic Surgery.

"Clare brought this," she said, holding it out. "She thought you might not want to open it in the office."

"In case it's bad news," I said despondently, taking the envelope from her reluctantly, as though a tarantula — the nonhuman kind — might crawl out of it.

The form letter told me that I had passed Part One of the Plastic Surgery Board Exam and was now eligible for Part Two, which would next be given in May. I had to let them know within two weeks if I intended to take the oral exam then. My examination number was 1001.

"I passed!"

"You passed?"

"I passed Boards!" I shouted, jumping up and down. My father burst into the room.

"What's wrong?" he demanded in agitation.

"Daddy, I passed Boards!"

I called everyone — Clare, Jim, the recently married Rob and Janice, and Jeff, of course — while my father hurried downstairs intent on finding a bottle of champagne so we could celebrate.

"Now tell me, what is Boards?" asked Jeff when I called him. I had told him before but impatiently I explained again.

"Well, that's very nice, dear," he said absently, as though I were a tiresome child. "I'm pretty tied up with meetings the next few days, but I'll take you to dinner Friday. I have to leave for that Australian business trip on Tuesday." His tone was patronizing and I wanted to vent my anger and hang up with a slam.

"I'll see you again over the weekend before you leave, won't I?" I asked instead, anxiously. There was a pause and then he laughed quietly.

"No, my dear," he said and hung up. I felt humiliated. He was taunting me deliberately. I was baffled, until I remembered his saying once, "I dated a lot of women while I was married. I had a right to do that because my wife was an invalid."

"Did she know about your affairs?" I had asked, feeling sorry for that sickly diabetic woman. It seemed I had a bond with her, loving the strange, elusive man she had been married to for years.

"She knew but she never dared to ask me about them," he replied.

Sometimes I wondered whether I could really be happy with him. I wanted him to be the most wonderful man in the world. This time, suddenly, for a brief moment of insight, I realized that he wanted me to think he was dating someone else, that he wanted me to be jealous and uncertain of his affection. I knew that his pastime was cheating, teasing, and lying to women.

"He's upset you again," said my mother sharply. "I don't like this man, Elizabeth."

"You do sometimes, Mother." I was indignant.

"Less and less. It's not his age. After all, Clare has been

married for many years to a much older man and so has Sophia Loren. It's not his age and it's not his style. He has a polished, courtly manner, but I have yet to see any sign that he cares for anyone but himself."

"Mother!" I was outraged.

She lay back, prepared for an outburst.

"You don't understand him. He's a very unusual man," I protested. I remembered the time he told me he had reached the semifinals in his bridge club tournament and my surprise, upon glancing at the actual standings, to see that he had really been beaten in the second round. I remembered also the charity on which he was bestowing his stock profits. By the way he talked he led me to believe he was giving at least a half a million dollars. One night I asked him more about it and I soon realized he was giving much less. It was still a fortune to me, but I wondered why he pretended to be richer and more generous than he was. Now, for a moment, I also realized that Jeff must be stringing me along, as part of a game. But my flash of common sense faded. Emotions prevailed and I assured myself there was nothing he could do wrong. He was just tired, and I was reading much too much into the way he had laughed. Everything would be all right. Jeff would look after me.

My father bustled in, beaming, with champagne and glasses, and mother and I stopped talking. Jeff was a forbidden subject with him.

During Jeff's long business trip to Australia I had little time to think about him. My father helped me move back home but I could not give my mother enough time. My practice was frantically busy and I had to prepare for the oral board exam. I wrote to Jeff often, got an occasional postcard in reply, and missed him all the time.

"You have thirty patients this afternoon," Clare said one

Wednesday. "Elizabeth, you can't keep this up. And you have an Elwin Medical Society meeting tonight."

"Fine." I put on my white coat and got to work. I had dictation to do and letters to answer, as well as patients to see, stitches to remove, tumors to evaluate, reconstruction to explain. I also had to talk with men and women interested in cosmetic surgery. One was Mrs. Dawes, a woman of seventy who wanted a second face-lift. Her first had been in the 1930's. "I know I was foolish to have it," she confessed to me. "Plastic surgery wasn't respectable then, but I thought I looked old. I saw an ad in the paper, and went in. I don't think the man was a doctor at all. He told me that if I had the cash — two hundred and fifty dollars, a lot of money in the 1930's — he could do it right away." She showed me the ugly scars in front of her ear. "He did the surgery in a hotel room, and left town that week. I never saw him again."

Quacks calling themselves "plastic surgeons" still travel from city to city. These days they illegally inject liquid silicone into the breasts of women who "can't afford" a reputable plastic surgeon. The liquid eventually inflames the breast, which may become painful, or even gangrenous, and have to be amputated.

I took care to explain in detail the risks and the probable result of a second face-lift for Mrs. Dawes. I knew that the waiting room was filling up and that I was running late, but I had to be honest with her. "Mrs. Dawes, let me be sure you understand," I said after I examined her. "First of all, the face-lift will improve mainly the jawline and upper neck. The eyes are a different operation, but they can be done with the face-lift. The face-lift leaves a scar all along here." I ran my finger from behind the hairline on the temple, in front of the ear, behind the ear and back into the hair above the neck. "The surgery can lead to thinning of the hair in these areas."

"I don't want that," she said. "My hair is thin already."

"I don't want that either," I replied, "but it can still occasionally happen. The scars are permanent. They usually don't show but sometimes they get short and thick and may be rather ugly, especially behind the ear. This can usually be avoided, but it can happen, even in the best hands. Very rarely, you can get gangrene — death of an area of skin, either from infection or because it is pulled too tight. It usually heals, but the scars are noticeable and ugly for months. They improve with time. What the operation does is to lift all the skin off the side of the face and upper neck and pull it up and back to tighten the face. Not much skin, less than a inch, is actually removed. It's changing the direction of the pull that makes the main difference.

"The complications include bleeding. This can be a tiny blood collection that needs no treatment but leaves a hard nodule for a few months; or it can be massive bleeding under the skin, which requires emergency reoperation within a few days after surgery. Such severe bleeding is very rare but it can happen. If it happens to someone else, it doesn't sound so bad, but if it happens to you, it's a catastrophe." Mrs. Dawes nodded, listening carefully, and I continued. "Infection is another possible complication. The face has an excellent blood supply and infection is rare, but it can happen. I saw one patient who, for no apparent reason, developed a massive infection on one side of the face less than a day after surgery. She was very sick, had a fever of a hundred and four, and had fluid and pus drain out of her face for a week. She healed quite well, eventually, but was first miserable for several months. So, infection and bleeding are risks.

"Another is facial paralysis. When I was training I saw one patient, a man, whose surgery had been done by a well-qualified plastic surgeon, but the main facial nerve, which runs close to the ear, had been cut in half. I saw this patient two years after the face-lift. He was permanently paralyzed on one side of his face. I don't know why it happened. Maybe the nerve came abnormally close to the skin. Such a complication is very, very rare. The man had several operations to improve his face, but he will never look normal. Minor nerve injuries are not uncommon. A branch of a nerve to the forehead or the lip may malfunction for a few weeks or months, but the feeling usually returns in time."

"It sounds disgusting. Why does anyone have it done?"

"Most people don't have complications. Most of the complications are minor. They are upsetting but don't affect the final result."

She looked down at a list of questions scribbled on the back of an envelope. "How long does it last?"

"I can't tell you. The average time we say is five years, because naturally you're still growing older. A face-lift doesn't stop or reverse aging. It only tightens the face. In some patients, especially ones with full faces, the effect may be gone after six months to a year, because in them it's harder to get the proper lift. I know of one surgeon who tells many of his patients to plan on a second face-lift within a year. You have a thin face. I don't think this applies to you, but I can't promise. It depends to a large extent on how you heal."

"It all sounds too horrible," she said, "but I've made up my mind to have it done. I'll hope I'm lucky and it all goes well." She asked that I have the surgery booked for her as soon as possible.

Clare appeared as soon as Mrs. Dawes left. "Your next is Navy Commander Rowe. He wants a nose operation."

"Another?" He was the fourth man within a few weeks who had asked me for a nose operation. Divorced, in his forties, with crew-cut red hair, blue eyes, and a boyish smile, he was in uniform and his manner was poised and confident.

"I want you to fix my nose," he announced cheerfully as I examined him. He had a broad, square face and a well-proportioned nose.

"Why don't you like your nose?"

"Come on," he said laughing. "It's a big ugly nose." He ran his finger over the tip of it. "I don't like the bump here. I hate feeling this bump. And my nose is too big."

I talked to him about nose surgery, the most delicate of plastic-surgery operations. The nose is complicated, made of interlocking cartilage and bone. To "fix" a nose is not like carving wood. A nose operation that takes a fraction too much or too little can make the nose uglier than before. Commander Rowe studied my diplomas and the two large Audubon prints on the wall.

"Wait a minute, doctor." He jumped up and walked to the other end of the room and squinted at the framed prints from a new angle. They were huge — about three by five feet and in heavy frames. "They're off center, you know."

"They're a bit off center, but that's the way they were hung," I said. "It's not perfectly symmetrical."

He frowned. "I can see where the two frames are off balance, but the whole display should be moved over three inches." He snapped his fingers in frustration. "I wish I had my ruler." He stepped back, and then moved up to the frames to try taking them down. They were heavy. They didn't move. He dusted off his uniform jacket as though he were on parade and sat down again on the examining table.

"A nose operation," I began, "is —"

"No, it has to be done now!" He sprang up, climbed onto a chair to reach the prints, and dragged one of them down. "You don't mind, do you?" he asked with a disarming smile. "This way you won't have to worry about it anymore." He waved me into a corner and lifted the second frame off the wall, staggering under the weight. "I think we're ready." He rubbed his hands together eagerly. "I lift a lot of weights. This won't take a moment. Do you have a hammer?"

"Commander Rowe —"

"No, don't worry," he said chivalrously, "I can do it." He climbed back onto the chair, took out a pocket knife, and took off a shoe. With the knife he dislodged the frame hooks and repositioned them, hammering them in a more symmetrical position, so they hung exactly in between the diplomas on either side. Finally, red with exertion, he picked up the framed prints and hung them on the repositioned hooks. "If you were stronger, we could have made it perfect by hanging them higher. You would have to hold them up. I don't suppose your secretary . . ."

"No," I said firmly, "Mrs. Ring is too busy to help me hold up pictures." As I spoke he was busy polishing the frames with his clean handkerchief. He straightened them one last time, brushed the wrinkles out of his trousers, and turned to me.

"Okay, when can you operate?" he demanded. "The money doesn't matter. I'm rich. I have plenty of money."

"It's not the money. It's what surgery can do, and the risks. It's not a simple operation, and there can be complications."

"I'll take the risks. I'm a Navy man. I can't stand this bump."

"Let me explain," I persisted. "Your nose is a good nose."

"I can't stand that bump."

"If I operate, I would not radically change your nose. A small nose would ruin your face."

"It's an awfully big nose."

"Not that big. You don't want a tiny nose."

"Look, doctor." He leaned forward to me. "It is too big,

too long, and the bump drives me crazy. I don't care exactly how it looks." We talked some more, but I didn't have time to ask him much about his home life and his family.

When I took photographs his face fell. "I'm an impatient man. I want to get this done right away. When will the photos be ready?"

"Monday."

"I'll see you Monday. You operate Tuesday."

Was I being unreasonable? He was eccentric, demanding, obviously used to giving orders, but his medical condition was not abnormal and his nose, though not as terrible as he insisted, could be improved by surgery. We scheduled the operation for two weeks later. Office hours ended at eight, three hours late.

Commander Rowe's surgery went smoothly. He was sedated and he snored peacefully until I had to break the nose bones so I could realign them. I positioned the chisel in the nose at the base of the bone.

"Tap, tap," I instructed Stella, the nurse assisting me. She obediently tapped my chisel lightly with a mallet.

"Holy Jesus!" shouted Commander Rowe, waking up. "What the hell is that?"

"Does it hurt?" I asked anxiously. The anesthetist dived under the drapes to inject some more sedative through the intravenous line.

"No, it doesn't hurt," said Commander Rowe, "but strange, very strange. What a sound inside my head. A bomb or an explosion. Christ! It's like war." He tried to sit up. The anesthetist slowly injected the Valium. Commander Rowe sighed and fell asleep again.

"Tap, tap," I said. Stella hesitated, tapped, but Commander Rowe only sighed. In a few minutes the bones were repositioned and I had put the dressing on his nose. He went home the same day, puffy-eyed from the surgery, still groggy, but happy. I gave him strict written instructions to stay in bed till he saw me in the office the next day.

When he came, I didn't recognize him. His eyes were swollen almost shut, black and blue.

"What happened?" I asked in alarm.

"I felt stiff so I worked with my weights and jogged. Then I got swollen." He laughed. "It won't do much harm. It makes me feel patriotic. I look like a flag — red, white, and blue."

"How did you get here?"

"I drove."

"You shouldn't drive. You almost can't see."

He laughed as though it were a compliment.

In a week the swelling was better, and I took the dressing off Commander Rowe's nose. He ran his fingers down his nose slowly and carefully.

"Hmmm." For ten quiet minutes he felt his nose and inspected his face in the mirror — left and right profiles, oblique and full-face views.

"It's a pretty ugly nose when you get right down to it, isn't it? I guess there's not much more you could do to it." He studied his face. "You've seen General MacArthur's nose?"

"Yes."

"You couldn't have made it like his, could you?"

"Impossible. I explained that before I operated."

"Yes. I remember." He looked at his left profile. "Okay, it'll do."

He left, grumbling and dissatisfied. A week later he marched in an hour late for his appointment but much happier.

"I have to tell you — my family is mad."

"About your nose?"

"Hopping mad." Commander Rowe smiled. "We have this family nose, you know, and did my parents hit the roof when

I saw them last night! I don't look like a Rowe anymore."
He stood up to leave. "The bad part is that they won't lend
me their jet to fly to Morocco for the weekend. I've got a
friend stationed on a ship in the Mediterranean."

He kicked the examining table in exasperation.

I felt equally put out, not with him but with myself. He
reminded me of Mrs. Schmidt, Dr. Villiers's patient who had
had a face-lift to keep money from her son. Cosmetic surgery
is to help people, not to be used as a weapon in a family feud.
I was making the same mistake as Dr. Villiers. I had too much
to do and too little time. Money was no longer my first
anxiety. I had paid off my last debt, a year and a half after I
opened my office. A quarter of my patients never paid me,
but I was working so hard I didn't care about bills. I had been
working twelve to eighteen hours a day almost every day,
including Saturday and Sunday, and I was getting busier —
too busy to give all my patients first-rate care. In the case of
Commander Rowe, I had cut back on the time spent explaining surgery beforehand — a mistake so many surgeons make.
Skimping is no way to be a doctor. I felt angry with myself
and with private practice in general.

My mood did not improve when I arrived late for a medical-
society dinner meeting and met Max, another plastic surgeon.
He was smooth and handsome, with a broad, empty smile. He
shook my hand firmly. "Glad to meet you, Liz. Let me get it
out in the open," he announced. "I'm interested in cosmetic
surgery. Faces and boobs — money. Sit at my table." He
pulled out a chair for me. "My wife and I called it quits after
fifteen years. She got the kids, I got the office. I couldn't
run my office without my girl."

"Your girl?" Did he mean his daughter or his secretary?

"My girl."

"I don't understand."

"My live-in lady. My girlfriend." He waved a buttered saltine in circles to express his emotion. "She is a beautiful person. A beautiful body. A beautiful relationship. You should meet her."

The six other surgeons at the table stopped talking and looked at Max oddly.

"Excuse me," said Max brightly, waving his saltine to encompass the group. "Who would you guys say is the best plastic surgeon in town? If I want to learn a new technique, which of you would I want to watch?"

There was an embarrassed silence. Every surgeon likes to think he or she is the best. "We're all the best," said one man diplomatically.

"I guess I won't get an answer from these guys," muttered Max to himself. "Do any of you guys do fanny-lifts? I've done them for years, but I'm still not sure how to do them." He turned to me and grabbed my elbow. "Come over tomorrow for drinks with me and my live-in. Make it this Wednesday. See you at eight."

The Mattaponai ER kept me busy and I couldn't make it to Max's on Wednesday. I wasn't anxious to go. He wasn't my type of plastic surgeon.

"Gee, Elizabeth, I'm sorry," said Max when I called to cancel. "I never do ER work. I like to make money. What with my new house and my round-the-world trip last year, there isn't much for the kids. I've done a lot of soul-searching lately, working on love and hate." He paused for breath. "I make a lot of money. I did two noses and a boob yesterday morning. Listen, am I keeping you? Come over Friday at nine."

This time I made it. When I arrived, Max introduced me to his "girl." Oddly at variance with her crisp, efficient manner, masses of tawny hair cascaded down her back in disarray. She and Max showed me around the townhouse and his adjoining office. The books on his office shelves were murder mysteries and collections of astrological advice.

After the tour, Max's girlfriend headed for the kitchen and he led me to the living room. He offered me a seat, sat down himself, propped his feet on a coffee table, and gave me his for-the-camera smile.

"So, are you going to make it, Elizabeth?"

"Make what?"

"Are you going to make it in practice?"

"I'm pretty busy."

"Answer my question. Are you going to make it? Or are you going to starve?"

"I'm not starving."

"Come on. How much?"

"Listen, Max, I pay my bills and I've paid my debt. I'm happy."

"Yeah," said Max, "I can understand." He leaned earnestly across the coffee table. "My girl is thirty but she has the body of an eighteen-year-old. It all depends on her state of mind."

I stared at him.

"Last year I tried transactionalism."

"Is that like meditation?" I asked.

Max frowned. "No. I used a therapist to reshape my body." He scowled. "We worked on pressure points. My therapist worked on my leg and brought out the universal pain, like a house. People are like their houses. My mind gets bigger and bigger, with this house. It's an active agency."

Max's girlfriend came in with drinks. She offered me an olive and sat on the floor. "My therapist kneaded my left armpit for an hour, until I developed a basic inner pain," she explained. "It's also basic nudity. A complicated idea. My therapist insisted I have my therapy in the nude."

"Is your therapist in the nude too?" I asked.

"No, he wears his undershorts. Max, does he take off his undershorts during *your* therapy?"

"No," said Max.

I looked at my watch and decided I could decently leave. "I'm afraid I have two patients to see tonight."

Max snorted in disgust. "You don't have to impress us, Elizabeth. That's an old trick."

"Max, I do have two patients to see and it's ten-thirty."

"Gee, that's too bad," said Max. "I wanted to get into your mind tonight. Listen." He looked at me wistfully. "Send me your cosmetic patients. I'd be happy to do all your boobs and face-lifts. It's easy money."

"Robert, he's out of his mind!" I exploded on the telephone the next day. I had called Robert Fletcher to see whether he was recovering from a painful hand infection he had developed.

"Don't let Max fool you," said Robert. "I know the guy, and he's a smart businessman. He may be odd but he's not dumb."

"He's lazy" was Jim's diagnosis. "He's going to try to take advantage of you. You have to beat on these turkeys to keep them in line, so watch out."

Two weeks later, on a Saturday at Radnor, a head nurse stopped me.

"Are you sending Mrs. Angelo home?"

"Who?"

She explained that Max had gone out of town without discharging one of his patients from the hospital. He had left a note asking that I write the order to send her home.

I went to see Mrs. Angelo. Her face was swollen, wrapped with gauze, and she was crying.

"Where's my doctor? I want to go home."

"He's out of town. I'm Dr. Morgan, but he asked me to send you home."

"I won't stay here another second," she sobbed. "I never wanted to come here. He was doing my face-lift in his office, and halfway through I started to scream, so he had to bring me here and put me to sleep to finish the surgery."

"That's unfortunate but it can happen."

She sniffed. "Did everything go all right?"

"I wasn't there. What did he tell you?"

"He said you would take care of me. When is my appointment?"

"I don't know. You'll have to call his office on Monday."

"If I have a problem this weekend who do I call?"

"I don't know who's covering for him. His answering service will know."

"I've tried to reach him before at night or on a weekend, and they can never find him."

"If you can't find him, call me." I gave her my card.

"Will the surgery help my depression?"

I stared at her.

"I got a divorce, and the doctor said a face-lift would help my depression. He said you'd give me a big prescription for Valium."

"If you're depressed, you shouldn't take Valium. Are you seeing a psychiatrist?"

"Yes, but he won't give me any Valium. Can't you?"

"Absolutely not, especially if your psychiatrist doesn't want you to have it. You might get depressed and take an overdose."

"Yes. I've tried to kill myself before."

Max called me on Monday. "Thanks for covering for me, Liz. I have to leave town often, but I figure my patients can call you anytime."

"No, Max. I'm not your partner."

"Oh."

"Your patient seemed very disturbed."

"Crazy. That's why I gave her Valium. It shuts her up. You can't talk to these patients. That's why I tell my answering service to say I'm out of town. Patients bug me at home all the time. I can't live like that. If they have an emergency, there are plenty of emergency rooms around. Listen, will you cover for me next weekend?"

"No."

"Hey, have I annoyed you?"

"I look after patients in a different way."

"Yeah. A matter of philosophy. See ya." He hung up.

At midnight a week later, I climbed into bed after operating all day. I was booked for surgery in the morning and would have to be out of bed at six.

My telephone rang. "It's your answering service, dear," said the midnight telephone operator. "Your patient Miss Holland wants you to call."

"I don't have a patient named Holland."

"She insisted she was your patient and said the call was important."

I dialed the number. "Hello," whispered a faint, sweet feminine voice.

"Is Miss Holland there? I am returning her call."

The voice sighed sweetly. "You don't know me, but I wanted to talk to a woman plastic surgeon. If I called a man he might get mad at me."

"You're not one of my patients."

"No. Another plastic surgeon operated on me to make my breasts bigger."

"Yes."

"I can't find him tonight, and I want some questions answered." Sure enough, when I asked, it turned out to be Max. "Yes. He operated two weeks ago," said Miss Holland.

"I can't help you. You're his patient. If it is an emergency, you should go to the nearest emergency room."

"That's what he told me, but it's not an emergency. I want some questions answered."

"I can't advise you. Your own doctor has to answer your questions."

"His secretary doesn't want to bother him, and she said for me to call you because you would be sympathetic."

"I'm not angry, but I'm not your doctor. I can't advise you about what he did in surgery."

"I only have a few questions," persisted Miss Holland.

"I'm sorry, but I can't advise you. It would be unethical." I hung up, fuming.

So this was private practice. There was nothing I or any other doctor could do. Max was a good surgeon, but there was more to being a good M.D. than that. I felt caught in a trap. There had to be some way I could practice plastic surgery and be happy. I was overworked, with too little time for my patients and none for myself. The alternative was to become a Max, a Morton Jones, or a Dr. O. I fell asleep trying to think of a solution and worrying about when I would find time to study for Part Two of the Board exam.

"You'd better be ready," Grant had warned me. "Tewkesbury will get you failed if there's any doubt at all. You'd better be hot stuff for that exam."

I had a confused dream about tarantulas, cosmetic patients, and Jeff, and I woke up thinking that my ulcerated colitis had returned. On top of everything else, I was now a hypochondriac. This was no way to live.

The goats were the last straw.

That Sunday I left my mother in order to make rounds checking on my patients at Metropolitan — a woman whose lip and jaw I had reconstructed and a child whose burned leg I had skin-grafted. My father was in the country on "the farm," a large tract of mountain land he bought twenty years ago. Rocks stick up from the soil, nothing has been harvested in years, but my father loves it. When grapes refuse to grow, he shrugs and cuts timber for his wood stove. He had lately added a herd of goats. "Meat prices are too high," he announced, "and I know the answer. We'll live on goat meat. Drink goat milk. You can learn how to make goat cheese, Elizabeth." He had five pregnant goats and expected them to deliver in a month.

When I got back from the hospital, I heard a sound like the squawk of a saxophone. A few moments later, I heard another squawk, like a car in the driveway honking. After the third squawk I ran upstairs to be sure my mother was all right. "Did you hear the noise?" she asked, lying comfortably in bed. "Have you seen them?"

"Seen what?"

"Go downstairs and look."

I went down to the basement.

"Daddy?"

"Squawk."

"Daddy!" I called out louder.

"Squawk, squawk, squawk."

I looked in the storage room and saw a fat brown-and-white goat with floppy ears, a swollen udder, and four baby goats trying to feed.

"They were born this morning," said my father proudly, dragging in another big goat that was bleating unhappily. She sniffed the kids suspiciously, then decided two were hers and let them feed.

"I hope you don't mind my bringing them home," said my father. "It's very cold in the mountains, and I thought they would be better here."

He hurried out to bring in hay and feed. One of the

mothers perched on top of an empty barrel and the babies crawled happily into a cardboard box and fell asleep.

The next morning there was a distinct smell of goat throughout the house. The babies chased each other around the basement. One mother stood on top of a file cabinet and refused to come down. My father boiled gallons of milk in case they didn't have enough to eat.

When I came home that night the goat scent was mingled with the smell of hay, molasses, corn syrup, spilt milk. The air was uncomfortably humid because my father had hosed down the basement.

The next day I came home to find my father walking the two mother goats on a leash in the front yard while the babies trotted behind, the two males bounding in the air and butting their sisters.

Jim came by that evening with a quart of almond fudge ice cream and a Trendline stock report.

"Read this, Mother," he said, handing her the stock quotations. "It's so dull it could kill those germs that are making you sick."

He sat down on the edge of the bed to talk with her and I went into my bedroom to try to study the synthesis of collagen for the Board examination. I was scribbling on a note pad when Jim opened the door.

"Can I come in?" He shut the door quietly. "How is she?"

"A lot better."

"What's wrong with her? She's so pale."

"Jim, I don't know. I've taken her to five doctors and none of them have any answers. It seems to be a terrible influenza infection that is taking her a long time to get over."

"She looks better than last time. Anything I can do? How's Dad?"

"You know how he is. He's terrified that she'll die. He'd do anything to help her, but he won't leave me alone. He can't stand Jeff. He's always telling me how to build up my practice. Build it up! The work is killing me. He tells me I ought to make a million dollars, how I should answer the phone, how I should study for Boards, and I'm going crazy. I'm working eighteen hours a day, looking after Mother, cooking the meals, and now these damn goats. I'm losing my mind. I'm going to fail Boards."

"No you won't. No you won't. It's difficult, I know. Can you cut back on your practice? No emergencies, no new patients for a while?"

"I don't think so."

"Maybe you'll have to."

"Ronald Meade would die. 'Another crazy woman doctor' — but I have to pass Boards and I have to look after Mother. I don't want to cut back after getting started so well, but I'll think about it."

Jim opened the door to leave and stopped. We could both hear my father's voice, bitter with anxiety, saying to my mother, "I don't want you sick. I don't like it, do you hear me?"

"Poor Dad," said Jim, and he went in to calm him down.

I thought about Jim's advice. Almost daily for the past eight weeks I had gotten up at six, operated, seen patients, worked on emergencies till midnight. I was exhausted. At this rate I would need a second full-time secretary, a nurse, a bookkeeper, an accountant, and a partner. Gone were my dreams of a small practice where I could look after my patients and still have time to think — to lead a life of my own.

"How are you, dear?" my mother asked the next day. "You don't look very happy."

"How am I?" I exploded. "I have no idea how I am. I've been operating like a maniac. I saw fifty patients in the office. Monday is going to be worse. I don't have time to return calls to my patients. I don't have time to talk to my patients. If I take time to talk, the day's schedule goes haywire." I sat down on a chair. "Now I need a bigger office. I walk into the waiting room — people are standing, babies are screaming, and people are upset because they have to get back to work and I'm running late. I don't have time anymore to be a doctor. I'm just a goddamned machine. Run here, run there, operate here, operate there. I hate it."

My father walked into the room with two boiled eggs, a large danish pastry, a bowl of ice cream, half a grapefruit, two oranges, and some jam for my mother.

"How are you, Elizabeth?" he said.

"I'm awful," I almost shouted.

He looked at me in alarm. "You ought to get more sleep. Don't stay up so late."

"Daddy, I've been operating."

"Eat all the food," he said to my mother severely. "I'm going to sit here and watch you."

"Bill, I'm not hungry. I can't."

"Eat it to get well."

"Please, Bill."

"Don't you want to get better, Toni?"

"Daddy, leave her alone," I snapped.

He walked out, slamming the door furiously. I tried to calm down and get a grip on myself. I knew there was no way out. I had to cut down my practice.

"Mother, I want to talk with you. I am going to cut back on my office — take no new patients and no emergencies for a while. I'll still see my old patients and operate on them. I'm booked for six weeks."

"Not for my sake, I hope," she said weakly. "I'd hate to ruin your career."

"You won't ruin it. I'll take a leave of absence, study for Boards, and look after you. It's for my own sake. I insist."

"Whatever you say, dear." She was too tired to protest.

It was an abrupt decision, one that could jeopardize my career, but not a bad one. I *had* to pass Boards, or eleven years of training would be wasted. I *had* to look after my mother. I *had* to find a way to practice plastic surgery without ruining my life or neglecting my patients. There must be a way.

11

Is My
Mother Dying?

I decided that I would have to take an indefinite leave of
absence from my practice. I would keep the office open, keep
Clare, and continue to see my present patients and do the
surgery already booked for weeks ahead, but I would take
no new cases. I also had to look after my mother and prepare
for the Board exam, as well as straighten out my feelings
about Jeff, who would soon be back from Australia.

My mother was the overwhelming concern. After weeks
in bed she looked no better, and spent hours every morning
lying flat, without a pillow, because even propping her head
up would make her feel dizzy. Wave after wave of "grisliness"
swept over her during the day. She felt better in the evenings,
but had drenching sweats all night that soaked through the
sheets. All of the laboratory tests were normal. Dr. Hamilton
found nothing wrong with her, and one specialist suggested
politely that she was having a depressive reaction to Rob and
Janice's marriage.

"Losing a son can be traumatic," he gravely explained to
me, his hands folded across his chest.

"My mother's not that type," I protested. "I know she's

sick. She adores Janice. She's happy they're married, and depression doesn't give you night sweats."

"Oh, she tells me those are better," he said lightly. "Don't worry, Elizabeth. It's not histo, it's not TB — probably a touch of the flu. She'll be fine."

He had written her off as a neurotic mother and I ground my teeth in exasperation. Of course she told him the night sweats were better. She wanted to be better. My mother would rather die than complain, and dying was exactly what I was afraid she would do. Important as my career might be, my mother was more important. What a horrible thing if I were too busy a doctor to look after my own mother — or too fatheaded to admit that all her normal lab tests meant nothing. I had seen many patients die with normal electrolytes and normal CBC's. The body gets sick in a thousand different ways. Lab tests measure only a few of them.

"Mother," I said one Saturday evening while sitting on the edge of her bed. "You know I'm taking a leave of absence from my practice. I'll tell Ronald Meade tonight."

"You can't worry about me. I'm much better. As I told you before, I'd hate to think I had interfered in your life."

"No, it's not for you," I prevaricated. "It's so I can study for Boards. I'll do all my studying here in your room and that way I can look after you at the same time."

"That's a good idea. You don't want to fail Boards, and I can help you study."

She knew as well as I did that Boards were not the real reason. I called Ronald at home.

"Hello, Elizabeth. What can I do for you?" He had helped me in the operating room the week before — an emergency repair on a stripteaser with abnormal hand tendons. I knew he was afraid my call was to ask him to help me in the OR again. I had been exhausted the previous week, having been up all night, and I had called when I couldn't find the injured tendon. It was the first time I had needed another surgeon's assistance in the operating room, but all surgeons sooner or later have to call for a helping hand.

"Don't be afraid to drag someone in if you get stuck," Dr. Villiers had warned me, his eyes flashing. "It's only the idiots who think they never need help." Ronald had been happy to help but he wouldn't be happy the second time.

"I'm not calling to ask you to come on to the OR."

"I wouldn't mind if you did," he replied gallantly, but there was relief in his calm voice.

"I'm calling about a fairly big decision I've had to make, Dr. Meade." I felt extremely guilty leaving my practice and I was nervously addressing him as Dr. Meade, as though he were my professor. I knew I was right to take a leave of absence, but I knew also that few people would understand. I was not abandoning my patients, but I was abandoning my colleagues and my career, even if briefly. It was an extraordinary thing to do, and my seven years of puritanical surgical training made me feel that no one had ever committed such a crime.

"Yes?" said Ronald slowly, as though it were a word of two syllables.

"I'm going to take a leave of absence from my practice. I'm not going to take emergency call. I'm not going to take new patients."

Nothing happened for a full minute.

"That's a big decision," said Ronald in a shaken voice. "You've thought this over, Elizabeth?"

"Yes," and I tried to explain my mother's illness, studying for Boards, the fact that my practice had gotten out of hand and that I needed to change the way I practiced medicine. He was too polite to say it, but he obviously thought me deranged. A perfectly good plastic surgeon, but quite mad.

"That is a big decision," Ronald repeated. "Well, well."

"I'm sorry, but right now I have to do it."

"It's happened before," said Ronald, wearily. "You help someone get started and as soon as they're settled in, they leave. Stuart Yancey wasn't here two years before he left for Oregon. Ford went to El Salvador and look what happened there. A revolution a month after he arrived. I hope you're going to be happy with your decision, Elizabeth," he finished gloomily.

"I'm not happy but I have to do it," I said firmly, feeling more guilty than ever.

There was a long pause. "Don't worry about emergency call," said Ronald at last. "Norman is back. He left and came back within a year. Maybe you'll do the same." Ronald's voice brightened. "He'll be happy to take your calls. My girl will call him in the morning." He lapsed into silence once again. "Well, it's a big decision," he sighed. "Let me know if I can help." He sighed again. "Hope you come back into practice. We'll be glad to have you back as one of us again." He said good-bye, a saddened man who had seen a stream of younger plastic surgeons pop in and out of his hospital, and I felt I had let him down. I hung up, relieved that it was over, but feeling as though I was betraying my profession. I went back to my mother's bedroom.

"Closing her office!" My father was saying in an intense whisper standing by her bed. "Closing her office? All that work of mine gone to waste. All that money wasted on her. She never wanted to be a doctor. She never wanted to be a surgeon. I should never have sent her to medical school. I've wasted my money on her."

I pushed open the door in a fury. "Daddy, if you want to say things like that, you say them to me, not to Mother. I'm not closing my office, and I'm still doing the surgery I have booked. I'm just not taking new patients or emergency call

so I can look after Mother and study for Boards. All right?"
I had never been so angry. I wanted him to leave me alone
and not complain about me, criticize, or interfere. My father
turned away.

"I wish he wouldn't get angry so easily," said my mother.
"He's so exhausting, Elizabeth!" She sat up in a sudden agita-
tion. "I have to get better. Soon. He can't take my being ill.
It's too much for him."

I was afraid she was right. My father, whom we all love
greatly, is eccentric and irascible at times, but he's also a
cheerful, gregarious, generous man. My mother had looked
after him and shared the running of their practice for years.
Without her, he was increasingly lost and increasingly angry.

The following weekend, while my father was in the
country, my mother got abruptly worse. She suddenly sat up
in bed and her eyes widened. "I feel as though I don't have
enough air," she said, and sank back flat, her skin white,
tinged with blue. I felt her pulse, which was weak, then rushed
out of the house to my car, dragged out my emergency
resuscitation kit, and rushed back inside. I had a horrible fear
that I would forget how to assemble the emergency oxygen
tank, but fortunately I remembered. The oxygen made her
feel well enough to let me help her into the car. I sped over
to Highcliff Hospital, the nearest one. "I feel fine now," she
said on the way, "but I still can't breathe." She insisted on
walking into the emergency room, and sat down while I
impatiently tried to get the attention of the volunteer behind
the desk.

"Yes, Susan, it's nice hearing from you," she was saying
chattily. "Well, I have to go now." She hung up, but the
phone rang immediately.

"Excuse me," I said firmly, leaning over the desk toward
her. "I'm Dr. Morgan." She hesitated between me and the
phone. I looked her squarely in the eye. "My mother may

be having a heart attack!" I didn't think she was, but it certainly got attention. The phone went unanswered as the volunteer hastily rang for a nurse, and one soon appeared with a wheelchair.

"A patient?" she asked, and then: "Oh, Dr. Morgan, it's your mother? I'm sorry." She wheeled Mother quickly to a cubicle and I helped her lift her onto a stretcher.

"She suddenly had trouble breathing at home, but I don't think it's a heart attack," I told her.

"We'll have you lie down, Mrs. Morgan," said the nurse calmly, looking at my mother's white and sweating face, "and we'll check your heart." She attached the heart monitor wire to Mother's chest. "Any chest pain?" she asked.

"No," I answered, and I could have kicked myself. She was asking my mother, not me. Doctors are a nuisance when someone in their family is sick.

"Just trouble breathing," said my mother faintly. The nurse put an oxygen mask over her face.

Frank Carter, a friend of mine, was the doctor working in the emergency room. I explained my mother's illness to him and left him to examine her.

When I came back, the nurse was rechecking my mother's blood pressure. "Dr. Carter wants to see what your pressure is standing up," she said, helping my mother off the stretcher. Mother stood up, turned blue-black, and crumpled to the floor. I was too horrified to react at first. We picked her up and put her back on the stretcher, and I felt for her pulse. She didn't have one.

I heard the emergency siren start on the central monitoring system in the hall. Frank Carter, another nurse, and a cardiologist resident rushed into the room.

"Get the crash cart," my mother's nurse shouted to them. I left the room. I was useless as a doctor. I was simply a daughter whose mother might be dead in a few minutes. I walked up and down the tiled corridor outside the emergency room and told myself that it would be worse if I cried.

"Dr. Morgan, go and have some coffee." It was Sally, an ER nurse who had worked with me through my first on-call weekend at Highcliff. "The lounge is empty. You'll feel better. Really." She steered me into the lounge, her arm on my shoulder. I was grateful indeed to be told what to do. "Pour yourself some coffee and drink it," Sally ordered before she left.

I drank the coffee slowly and returned to my mother's cubicle. She was a mass of wires and tubes — oxygen, a cardiac monitor, an intravenous line — but to my immense relief she was awake. She smiled and reached for my hand.

Frank Carter motioned me out into the hall. "I don't know what's going on with your mother. Her blood gases are normal, and the electrolytes are normal, and her cardiogram" — he pulled open the folded paper strip to show me — "has an occasional PVC but nothing more." He ran his eye over the cardiogram. "Nonspecific ST-T changes. Nothing diagnostic, but we had to give her atropine to keep her heart going. She may have the sick sinus syndrome, and the cardiology fellow agrees she should be in the coronary intensive-care unit."

I agreed too. Dr. Hamilton, Mother's physician, was himself sick and hospitalized, so Frank called another internist, Dr. Tane.

I followed my mother's stretcher to the CCU and left her to the nurses, who clustered around her, while I called Jim and Rob and Janice. They all came to the hospital at once. Then Jim and Rob went to meet my father, who was due home from the country, so they could break the news. As Rob suggested, we took him to dinner after seeing Mother in the hospital. My father was unable to stop crying, but at least he knew he had our support, which comforted him.

Dr. Tane called me that evening. "Dr. Morgan," he began crisply, "I'm calling about your mother. I want to outline my thinking."

"Yes."

"She has a viral syndrome and has spent too much time in bed, leading to deconditioning, but otherwise she has been in excellent physical health, barring mild hypothyroidism."

"Yes."

"She may have a sick sinus syndrome from poor cardiac adaptation to differing demands on cardiac output, and may need a pacemaker."

"Yes."

"Next, a pulmonary embolus is possible, but unlikely because the blood gases are normal. Cortisol deficiency or a sympathetic nervous-system disorder are also possible but unlikely."

"Yes."

"I shall keep you posted."

"Thank you." I was happy that my mother had a good doctor. He was intelligent, thorough, efficient, and kind, but I knew somehow that he would find nothing abnormal. Whatever my mother had, it would not be easy to diagnose.

Three days later the results of all the heart tests had proved normal and my mother was weak but looking slightly better. "Dr. Tane is losing interest in me," she remarked mildly. "I'm afraid that now he finds I don't have a nice, interesting heart illness he can treat, he's a bit bored. Do you think I'm a hypochondriac after all?"

"Impossible," I insisted. "Hypochondria doesn't cause night sweating or make people turn blue-black in the face when they try to stand up."

"He was pleasant when it seemed I might be cured by a pacemaker. I suppose it's frustrating for a doctor not to have the answers. He told me I just ought to exercise more."

"That's absurd, Mother. He doesn't know you. He doesn't know you're not neurotic. I do."

"Anyhow, I can go home tomorrow."

The hospital checkout time was eleven, so I came in at ten-thirty. Dr. Tane had not come in. At eleven I called his office and was told he wouldn't be free till five-thirty that afternoon. It was a long wait, but he had a series of patients with heart attacks who needed him in the emergency room. At last he arrived and came to my mother's bedside, looking tired and baffled by her illness.

"Well," he said haltingly. "Fortunately, this little heart episode you had in the emergency room last week turns out to be nothing. I think you've let yourself get deconditioned. Your body is out of shape."

"But I have been out of bed as much as I can," protested my mother. "And when I got ill last week I was lying down at home."

Dr. Tane frowned. "That's not what you told me." My mother started to object but there was no point. Like the many other doctors before him, he did not have any answers to what was making my mother ill. She was sick, but that was the closest he, or anyone, could get to a diagnosis.

Dr. Hamilton called me later that evening, having recently been discharged from hospital himself. "I tried to reach Dr. Tane, but I couldn't get through to him. How is your mother?" he asked anxiously.

"All her lab tests are normal, but she still looks terrible."

"We may never know what it is," said Dr. Hamilton. "It must be some strange viral infection. After Legionnaire's disease, I think we all learned there are a lot more strange infections than we'll ever be able to identify or treat. I wish we knew more about them. What did Dr. Tane say?"

"He said she's been in bed too much."

"Nonsense. Why, she went to bed because she was ill,

didn't she? It wasn't being in bed that made her ill. He's perplexed like the rest of us. Maybe if we wait it out, she'll get better on her own. I can't think of anything else to do for her."

I couldn't either. My mother stayed out of the hospital after that, but there were many mornings when she was so pale and weak and drenched in sweat that I thought she would be dead within a week. All we could do was wait. I studied for Boards in her room and made most of the meals. My father insisted on helping out by doing all the shopping and most of the laundry, for which I was grateful. Clare did her work in my parents' office except when I had patients to see.

Catherine Bennett, my lawyer and friend, negotiated tirelessly with Mr. O'Donnell to try to end my Twickenham lease. On a leave of absence, I couldn't afford such a large office. If and when I returned, I would prefer a more convenient place. This office was hard to find, had too little parking, and was too large for a small practice, too small for a large one. It all seemed academic, anyhow. If I failed Boards, I might not want to reopen my office; I would want to hide my head in the sand, instead. If my mother became chronically ill, I would have to find an academic or government salaried job to give me time to look after her. If I did go back at last to full-time medical practice, I had other problems to solve — how to have a normal personal life, for one thing, and how to find enough time for each of my patients while running a successful practice.

For the moment I once again did have the luxury of having enough time for all of my patients. I wasn't constantly busy, although I still had a lot of surgery to do. When a former patient, Nancy, came to show me her healed hand after she got out of jail, and when Mr. King asked me to meet his daughters the day I took his stitches out, I had time for both of them. The limited practice that my mother's illness forced on me was much more to my liking and better for my patients. I had made a lot of money, most of which went to pay off my debts, but now that the debts were paid, I could afford to wonder if money was worth the cost of my being frustrated as a doctor and as a woman. John Napier, my former professor, had told me I couldn't make it in private practice. I had made it — almost too easily. I had proved to myself I could succeed. My leave of absence would give me a chance to decide what I really wanted to do.

One thing was clear. If I kept on seeing Jeff, my career would have to come a distant second. He kept unpredictable hours and expected me to be free whenever he was and to stay out late at night, regardless of whether I had to work the next day. I missed him terribly and counted the days till he would return. I knew he wouldn't change his ways, but I wanted him back all the same. I was bounding around with happiness the day he called to tell me he was back.

"That man?" said my father morosely. "You're seeing that man again? I thought you had forgotten him. You told me you wouldn't see him again."

"Daddy, I didn't. We're going out to dinner tonight."

"When?"

"He'll come about ten. He has to work late."

"That's too late. I don't like it." My father glared at the carpet.

"Daddy," I explained patiently, "I am thirty-two. I'm a grown-up now. I'm not a teenager. I'm living at home to help you look after Mother, but you have to let me date whom I want and see them when I want to."

"She's not going to die is she? I always thought she was strong. I never worried about her health."

"We'll pull her through, Daddy." I put my arm around him. "I wish there was more I could do for her."

"I want her well."

"Daddy, she's had a very, very bad flu of some kind. She'll get better slowly."

He refused to be comforted.

Jeff came by at eleven — an hour late, as usual. My father had closed himself in his office to read and watch television.

"Daddy, good night. I'll be back quite late," I said, looking in before I left.

"Good night." He didn't look up.

"I'm sorry you don't like Jeff, but you do understand that I love him very much?" My father turned to look at me.

"I think a lot of things I don't say." He turned away.

Jeff was happy to see me, although not as ebullient as I was. He tucked me into his car and we started off.

"It's late. We'll have to try Cinnamon's if we want dinner," he said as though it was my fault.

He never apologized for being late. It was part of his nature and he took a certain pride in it. Cinnamon's was jammed, as always, with a self-consciously sleek crowd huddled around the bars and on the dance floor. An exchange of greetings and of a ten-dollar bill between Jeff and the headwaiter got us one of the best, fashionably noisy booths by the main bar.

"A whiskey sour for mademoiselle," said Jeff to our waitress, "and a Chivas for me." She was pretty. He studied her face with interest while he spoke, and her legs when she turned away. He scanned the women at the bar. "That's a sweet young thing over there," he said over his whiskey. "Delicious. Cheers. It's nice to see you again, my dear." We clinked glasses and his gaze drifted back to the women around the bar. "The blond is a nice piece too." He turned to me. "Have I told you the joke about the man, his wife, and his mistress?"

"No, tell me." I'd heard it before and I didn't like it. I don't care for jokes that put down women. He was upsetting me on purpose — for what purpose, I didn't know. It continued all week. He seemed determined to make me jealous and the pleasure he took in my company seemed to be in gauging how much taunting I would take before I objected. It was like teasing a puppy until it snaps.

"Mother, should I break up with Jeff?"

"I can't tell you that, Elizabeth. You have to make up your own mind."

I prowled around the room restlessly, straightening books. "Is he the right man for me?"

"You certainly seem to love him."

"Too much. I'm silly about him, like a girl in school with a crush on someone."

"It would be hard for you, or any doctor, to keep up a practice while dating him. He doesn't seem to think your being a doctor is important."

"He doesn't think about my career at all, except as a hobby that fills in my time when he's away. He didn't love his wife. He doesn't love his family. He's vain. He's materialistic. I think the only reason he dates me is because I'm a plastic surgeon, which gives me higher status than the other women he knows. If I didn't have an M.D. he wouldn't look at me twice," I said bitterly. "He leads me on and then rejects me. He's a one hundred percent jerk, Mother. How could I have fallen in love with a jerk? I should know better. Why did I fall in love with a jerk?"

"You shouldn't be so surprised," said my mother. "Education has nothing to do with it. You're not abnormal. Lots of other girls have done it before."

I went to see Jeff at his office the same night, having made up my mind.

"Here you are," he said happily, as though he had been expecting me.

"Jeff, I want to talk to you."

"So serious, my dear. Let's go and get a drink."

"I don't care where we go. Here is fine but I want to talk to you."

"Let's go to The Rum Keg."

"Jeff, I want to talk with you. We can't talk at The Rum Keg. It's a madhouse."

"Okay. We'll go to Peppermint Park."

Peppermint Park was dark, quiet, and deserted, as it always was on weekdays.

"All right. Talk," commanded Jeff once we had ordered. I knew it was going to be hard, and I didn't know how to begin.

"Then don't talk," said Jeff peacefully sipping his drink.

I pushed aside my drink, turned to him, and plunged ahead.

"You never tell me how you feel about me. You imply and you suggest but you never tell me. We've dated each other quite long enough for you to know how you feel about me."

"These things are hard to speak about," he said evasively, studying my face.

"If you don't know by now how you feel, it's long past time for me to say good-bye."

"I don't want to lose you, Elizabeth."

He put down his drink. "You know I care for you. I care for you a great deal, a great deal more than I ever expected or wanted."

"Do you really?"

"Yes," he snapped, almost testily.

I weakened, but carried on. "I want to settle down."

He nodded.

"I want someone who's serious about me."

He nodded again.

"If you want to be free, that's fine, but you've known me long enough to know how you feel."

He smiled, as though I was saying this to amuse him, but I continued.

"If you can't decide, pretty soon I'm going to be your ex-girlfriend." It was midnight exactly.

He kissed me on the forehead. "You are absolutely right, Elizabeth. You make things so much easier for me when you're logical like this. I don't want you to worry." He put his arm around me. "I think you'll have a nice surprise pretty soon."

12
Show and Tell

"How is she?" whispered Jim, coming into the bedroom on tiptoe.

"Studying," my mother whispered back.

"How are you?"

"Much better."

"I brought some pastry for you from Avignone Frères. Strawberry tarts. Shall I put one in the refrigerator for Elizabeth?"

"No!" I yelped from the far side of the room. "You are nice to bring us a treat. Please let me take a break. I can't stand this."

"Are you in a mood?" asked Jim suspiciously. "If you're going to waste time and then pretend I distracted you, you can eat this over in your corner."

"No, I'll be good."

My mother was much better, despite helping me study for the oral Boards, which meant my reciting out loud anything from contraindications for a face-lift to the embryologic cause of syndactyly.

"It's the countdown," said Jim, passing pastry around. "Seven days till Boards for Elizabeth. If we survive, it's a miracle. I called her last night and I thought I had got Hitler on a bad day."

"I was trying to label all my photographs."

"Oh, show and tell. I must say Elizabeth, for a sophisticated specialty, it seems silly to be putting together a scrapbook of 'Operations I Have Done.' Heck, I did that in seventh grade." He picked up my bound volume of cases. "I hope you've got everything you need in here. Didn't you tell me they flunk people just because they don't have all the lab reports in the right place?"

I pointed to the instruction sheet proudly.

"I have everything."

" 'Cases with pre- and postoperative pictures,' " read Jim. " 'Pertinent laboratory data, operative reports, x-rays must be as copies or prints of the originals. Originals will not be accepted.' "

"What?" I read the instructions again. I had read them hundreds of times before, but I had overlooked the requirement that X ray originals would not be accepted.

"Oh, God. I can't get prints ready in a week."

"Take the originals then. They won't fail you for that."

"Yes, they would. They would love to fail me."

"Can't you make tracings?" suggested my mother.

"Brilliant!" I spent the rest of the day making tracings of X rays onto onionskin paper. I had seven cases, as required, each fitting one of nine possible categories of plastic surgery. I had a cleft lip, a facial fracture, a nerve reconstruction, a tendon graft, a cancer reconstruction, a burn reconstruction — this was my Vietnamese lady, Mrs. Gau — and a breast reduction. I had carefully reviewed each case. I felt proud that I could do this surgery. I was good at it. I enjoyed it. I was confident in a way I would never have been if I hadn't succeeded on my own.

"It's wonderful," said my father, coming up behind me and

patting me on my shoulder. "Wonderful. I'm proud of you. That'll knock the Tarantula dead. You've really beaten him, hands down."

"I haven't passed yet, Daddy." I'm superstitious.

"You will." He had been in a good mood for a week now and I was happy leaving him to look after Mother. I would be away for a week, and he had enough filet mignon, strawberries, and champagne to last them both a month.

The day I left, I packed my clothes carelessly, put my cases in a briefcase, and discovered that I had lost my examination card, without which I could not take the exam. I found it at last — in a separate folder labeled IMPORTANT. EXAMINATION CARD.

Jim drove me to the airport, Daddy stayed home with Mother, and I was transformed from a normal, human plastic surgeon to a sheep being led to the slaughter.

"I know I'm going to fail, Jim."

"Do you?" he said cheerfully. "With that attitude you probably will."

"I don't want to fail but I know I'm going to."

"You have to pass, Elizabeth. If you fail, I'll blame Tewkesbury and fly up to his house and kill him, and you can't trade corn from jail." He parked at the airport and pulled out my bags. "Look, those guys are smart. They know better than to fail a woman. If they do, we'll have Rob sue them for discrimination, make it a landmark case; and you can go to China as a medical missionary till it blows over."

"It doesn't help, Jim. You're trying to cheer me up but I don't think it's possible."

"Don't think at all, but don't miss the plane."

He handed me my briefcase and suitcase and waved me off.

"Good luck! Elizabeth, carry on the briefcase — don't check it through and don't lose it!"

He drove away and I was on my own.

Solo Practice

The exams were to be held in a resort hotel in Palm Beach. The Examining Board stayed in the hotel, but the examinees were forbidden to stay there, for reasons known only to the Board. I stayed in a nearby Hilton, arriving at nine that night. The next day, Tuesday, we were instructed to hand in our cases. Hurdle one was having your cases accepted. If they were accepted, you were then examined Wednesday, Thursday, or Friday. On Saturday you were to be told if you passed.

At nine o'clock on Tuesday morning I walked through the resort hotel lobby and stood in line in the broiling Florida sun with two hundred other examinees, waiting to file into a dark hotel room and hand in our cases. There were four other women.

"They fail twenty-eight percent on the written Boards," the man ahead of me was saying to someone ahead of him. He sported a dark tan and a toothbrush mustache, and he sounded disgustingly confident. "And at least that many are failed on the orals. The older guys don't like the competition, so they try to keep the numbers down."

"Think you'll pass?" asked the other man in a light but slightly tremulous voice.

"Me? Oh yes. I've got fantastic cases. I'm looking forward to it. If you're prepared, you'll enjoy it. I'll pass without trouble."

"Phil, is that you sounding off again?" said a familiar voice behind me. It was Percy Peregrine, whom I had last seen at the hand course. "More of that garbage and we're going to lynch you. Liz, is that you? Are you going to pass, do you think?"

"No!" I said emphatically. I was so nervous already my hand was shaking slightly.

"That's the spirit," said Percy approvingly. "The right attitude. Phil, this is Elizabeth. Liz, meet Phil. Phil's a Chicago Gold Coaster. You know the type. Gucci loafers and a

Maserati." The line advanced. We were out of the sun now and in the dark room.

"No, Percy, please," said Phil, waving a deprecating hand. "Maseratis are the common touch."

"Are you going to talk all morning, young man, or are you going to hand in your cases?" The speaker was a thin lady behind the desk who was glaring at Phil over her glasses.

"So soon! What a delight. Permit me." He handed over his cases with a flourish. She shoved a card at him.

"Name, hotel, phone number. Put your cases in the pile under the sign with the first letter of your last name. Next."

It was my turn and I must have gone white. "I don't know my hotel phone number."

She gave me a friendly smile. "What hotel, dear?"

"The Hilton."

She wrote in the number for me and handed me the card. "Put down your room number, too."

"Hey," protested Percy, "you can't entertain the Examining Board in your room, Liz. Unfair advantage."

The lady smiled indulgently.

"It's so they can call to tell you to go home if your cases are unacceptable. We need everyone's room number." I filled out my card, turned it in, put my cases in the proper pile (checking three times to make sure that it was under *M*), and walked out into the blazing sun, where Phil was lighting a cigarette and surveying the courtyard.

"Looks like a lovely day, Liz. Time for a dip in the pool and then a leisurely lunch. Care to join me?"

"No, thank you."

"Don't tell me you plan to go to your room and study some more? It's much too late for that."

"I have to. If I fail, at least I won't feel it was because I missed my last-minute studying."

"Well, perhaps after the exam you'll let me take you out

to dinner. It's an invitation. I won't let you forget." He strolled away, and I walked back to the Hilton, rereading the exam instructions. I reread for the hundredth time the X-ray instructions — "copies or prints of the originals." Were tracings considered copies or prints? What if "copies" meant X-ray duplications, not tracings? I went back to my room and sat on the bed, slightly dizzy from the sun, as I realized that I had misinterpreted the X-ray instructions. My last-minute amateurish X-ray tracings were obviously not what the examining committee had in mind. How could I have been such a fool? "Copies" meant an X-ray-like duplication of the original, not a tracing. My studying was wasted and I had only to wait now for the call to tell me to go home. There were no planes out of Palm Beach that evening, so I made a reservation on an early morning flight the next day. At two o'clock I got up the courage to call home and tell my parents.

"Tell me what I can do to help" was the first thing my father said. "I'll fly out right now and bring you the originals. Can you get a copy made there? Shall I go to Metropolitan to get copies first? Hold on. I'll ask Clare to make my plane reservations now." I had a few moments of hope, until Clare picked up the phone.

"Elizabeth, I've called everywhere. The only way your father could get down to Florida is a night flight with a change in Atlanta, and he wouldn't arrive in Palm Beach till ten tomorrow morning. I'm sorry." My next Board session was scheduled for early the next day. Ten would be too late.

"Elizabeth!" It was my father on the line again. "I'll charter a plane."

"Daddy, you are wonderful, but it's my own stupid fault for being so dumb about this. I wouldn't dream of letting you do it. I suppose there's some chance they'll overlook it. The X rays are only a minor part of my cases."

"When do you know for sure?"

"Not until tomorrow at eight, I suppose."

"They won't call," said my father with conviction, "and if they do, just tell them this: 'If I have to leave Palm Beach now, my father will blast the bastards with a German Mauser he's kept since World War II.' You tell them! I'll call you at ten tonight to see how you are."

My father can be the nicest man in the world. I was grateful to him for being so nice to me now. I needed it. I waited all day for the fateful call, staring at my notes, but the words meant nothing. I had dinner in my room. I couldn't face seeing someone like Phil, who'd be offensively oozing confidence. I wanted to be alone.

The phone rang at ten — but it was my parents, to wish me luck. Then Rob called, then Jim, and that was all. Maybe the woman in charge of collecting the cases had gotten the Hilton's phone number wrong. Finally I went to sleep, praying for good luck.

At eight the next morning I joined my fellow examinees in the resort hotel conference room. The Examining Board chairman addressed us from the front of the room.

"Those of you who failed to follow the instructions and submitted unacceptable cases are not here. We called all those boneheads last night and sent them on their way. At least you guys can follow simple instructions." A sigh of relief was heard around the room.

"If your number starts with a one, you will be examined today, with a two, tomorrow, and with a three, on Friday." Mine was 1001, so at least the agony would be over the first day. "I know all you guys hate our guts and think we're out to fail you. We try to be fair. You'll be examined by two groups of two examiners, four in all. If two examiners fail you, that's it — you're failed." He went on to explain what happens if only one examiner fails you and the others pass you or are undecided: you have to be reexamined by two more surgeons. If they don't both pass you, you fail.

"Good luck, gentlemen." Then, as an afterthought: "And ladies."

It was 8:45. My first exam was set for 9:00 in hotel room 401; my second, at noon in room 613. The resort hotel had all its rooms in clusters around swimming pools or lush gardens. I sat waiting outside room 401, watching a sparrow pick at a palm tree while a lizard sunned itself on a rock.

"He won't eat you. They're really honey bears at heart," said a happy voice. I turned to find it was coming from a smiling woman who was leaving a nearby room. She was an elegant blond in a bright print dress and sunglasses. "My husband is examining you, but he wouldn't dare fail you. I cured him of being a male chauvinist years ago. I'm off to sightsee. Good luck!"

My examiners were her husband, Ted Rowntree — a famous academic plastic surgeon — and Stuart Yancey, from Oregon. I had met Dr. Rowntree once before and I knew he was fair and honest. If he failed me, I deserved to be failed. He was a handsome man with red hair, a freckled face, and green eyes. He ushered me into the room with a smile, shook my hand, and took the casebook I handed him. Stuart Yancey was a fit, friendly man in his fifties. He began to set up bottles on the exam table, pulling them from a cooler on the floor, while Ted Rowntree looked through my casebook.

"This exam is a lot of fraternity ritual," said Stuart Yancy. "We can tell who's good and who's not. The trouble is, Ted said I couldn't bring beer. Want a Seven-Up?"

"No, thank you."

"Oh, come on." He handed me a glass. "So, are you any good?"

"Yes, I'm a good, safe surgeon."

"Boarded in general surgery?"

"Yes."

"Good girl. So, how are her cases, Ted?"

For each of my seven cases I had chosen they asked me, in great detail, why I had done the operations, what other choices I had had, what the risks were, what long-term results I could expect. To my surprise, I enjoyed the grilling. All my operations had been well planned and well done. I liked talking about them, explaining what I had done and why.

"So how long does it take muscle to come back after this nerve graft of yours?" Stuart Yancey asked me.

"As long as two years."

"Will it work?"

"I hope so, but the operation was done for the lack of sensation in his foot and that has already returned. The intrinsic muscle function is relatively unimportant, compared to sensation in the foot."

"Good cases," said Ted Rowntree, closing my casebook. He checked his watch. "It's ten o'clock. I'm afraid we won't get to your last one. We've enjoyed this." They stood up and shook my hand. "Don't worry. You'll pass."

I floated out of the room and sat in the lobby in a happy daze till my next exam at noon. The exam had been fair after all. At a few minutes before noon I walked slowly to room 613 and was stunned by what I saw: Tewkesbury was sitting in a deck chair by the swimming pool outside the examining room. He saw me and watched without a smile as I nodded hello and walked around to the front. The door was open and I looked in.

"We're not ready for you. Wait out there!"

A burly man leaped up from a chair and slammed the door. There was no shade and I waited in the sun till twelve-thirty. The Florida sun was so hot that joggers were being warned not to run in the middle of the day. I tortured myself wondering if there was any significance in Tewkesbury's being outside the examining room. He was not supposed to be one of my examiners.

The door jerked open. "Come in." The burly man motioned me in and sat down behind the desk. His colleague had dark hair and a mild, serious face.

"Dr. McInroe," snapped the burly man, pointing to himself. "That's Dr. Thorne there. What's that?" He opened a notebook with photographs and pushed it toward me.

"That's a bilateral cleft lip."

"What would you do?"

"Well, there are various options. I could do a lip adhesion and a Millard repair as a —"

"What would you do, doctor? Don't give me a lecture. Give me an answer."

He leaned across the small table and glared at me. "You're a surgeon. What would you do, or don't you know? Have you studied?" If he meant to rattle me, he succeeded. What with seeing Tewkesbury, and roasting in the hundred-degree sun for thirty minutes, and walking into this attack, I was unnerved. I wanted to be cool and confident but I heard my voice tremble nervously, and I knew with a sinking feeling that I wasn't going to think clearly — that I would panic, give silly answers, and fail.

"Draw me a Millard repair." Dr. McInroe shoved a piece of paper at me. I sketched the operation, but badly. He sneered at it.

"What else? What else could you do? Tell me what you know," he barked.

"There's the Skoog, the Millard, Millard with a lip adhesion . . ."

"Manchester. Ever heard of Manchester? Know what that is?"

"Of course."

"What is it?"

I knew it was a straight-line repair. I could even hear the first time Dr. Villiers explained it to me. But I couldn't say it. I was afraid of being wrong, and I froze, like a mouse before a boa constrictor. Whatever his reasons, Dr. McInroe wanted me to fail, and he was making me fail myself and laughing at me all the way. I wondered irrelevantly if his wife disliked him.

"So, if you don't know clefts, try this," he snapped, shaking his head as though this was all a boring waste of his valuable time. The second case was a face-lift and the third was a burn. Somehow I got a grip on myself and gave more sensible, reasonable answers, but he harassed me all the way: "Ever done one of these? How many? Are you any good? Who taught you, anyhow? Where did you read that?"

After an hour he threw up his hands, shrugged, and looked at Dr. Thorne, who had said nothing the entire session. "Any point in going on?" Dr. McInroe asked disgustedly.

"I'll ask her a few things." Dr. Thorne turned to the next case in the book. "Here's an injured hand. Tell me what you would do, step by step." He sat back in his chair, smiled, and waited. In two minutes I had told him everything, from the initial examination in the emergency room to taking the cast off. I touched on the function of the vincula, the extensor hood, and the Chinese loop tendon sutures.

"Finished?"

"Yes."

He nodded and turned the page.

"Facial fracture. Tell me about it."

I started, but Dr. McInroe interrupted me.

"Tell me the most diagnostic sign of a zygomatic fracture, Dr. Morgan."

I named the five diagnostic signs.

"You gave me five. I told you to give me one. I said 'the most diagnostic.' Plain English."

"All five are diagnostic signs," I objected.

"Give me the most. One. Choose one. You're a surgeon. Make a decision."

I hesitated. "There's diplopia."

"At last! Don't you know that's the most important sign?"

"Yes, but it's not a sign, it's a symptom."

Dr. Thorne looked from me to Dr. McInroe.

"Finished?" he asked him, and he turned to the next case. After half an hour, he stopped.

"Thank you. That's all I have to ask."

As the door closed behind me, I heard Dr. McInroe start to laugh. I blinked in the sunshine and went in search of lunch, uncertain if I had passed or failed. Dr. Thorne was my only hope. McInroe would fail me for sure; Dr. Thorne was too impassive for me to be able to tell.

I found Percy and Phil at a poolside table. Harvey Courtauld, a medical-school friend, joined us, looking glum.

"I passed, I'm sure," said Phil. "How about everyone else?"

"Three examiners fair. One stinker. Verdict: uncertain," pronounced Percy. Harvey and I nodded in agreement.

"Who examined you?" asked Phil.

"Oh, shut up," said Percy, but Phil entertained us with a detailed description of how much more he knew than any of his examiners. He was intelligent, quick, and very glib, with the arguing ability of a trial lawyer. I was sure Phil had talked rings around his examiners, had been not at all intimidated, and had passed easily, as he so smugly assumed. He stopped me after lunch.

"Join me for a victory dinner, Liz. We'll go somewhere nice. I'll pick you up at seven." I accepted. It would at least take my mind off the exam.

But the exam was not yet over for me. Harvey and I were among the names listed for a third exam that afternoon. At least I hadn't failed. There was still hope. Dr. Thorne had given me a reprieve. Of the sixty of us that day, twenty were to be reexamined. My reexamination was not to take place till four o'clock. I passed the time sitting around the pool with Harvey and Percy, and Sarah and Polly, two women plastic surgeons from Long Island. None of us could speak or think about anything but the exam. We spent the afternoon largely in silence, drinking iced tea. No wonder we were so preoccupied. Our careers, our hospital privileges, and our personal pride depended on the outcome.

Four o'clock found me outside room 462, which had a shady alcove. The door jerked open.

"Hello, Dr. Morgan? If you're ready, we are. Come in. I'm Dr. Davis." He was a bright-eyed, brown-haired, lively man in his fifties. "My partner in crime is Dr. Robins. Now, we're here to see what you know, so you tell us. It's easier than the dentist. Have a chair. They really should have a chaperone for you young ladies. I feel it's quite indecent to have an assignation with a young woman in my hotel room. What would our wives say?"

"Sit down and stop trying to embarrass her." Dr. Robins, suntanned and in his shirt sleeves, smiled at me. "We're old friends, Dr. Morgan. If he gives you a hard time, ignore him, and talk to me. I'm a nice guy."

Dr. Davis opened the examination casebook and flipped through. "You must have seen the cleft lip and the hand already. Boring. Same cases every year. Here, try the nose."

I told him about nose surgery.

"Chin. Would you touch her chin?"

"No."

"Why not?" he leaned forward, frowning.

"You said the patient wanted nose surgery. I've always been taught it's unethical to suggest cosmetic surgery until the patient has asked about it." Dr. Davis leaned back with a smile.

"Why, that's absolutely correct. I completely agree."

We covered a burned leg, a breast reconstruction, and gangrene. Then he turned to his partner with a grin.

"You do some work, boy. Ask her something."

Dr. Robins grilled me on hand surgery, and cancer of the skin, then fixed me with a solemn stare.

"What is McGregor's patch, Dr. Morgan?"

I looked at him aghast. "I've never heard of it."

"What is Pitanguy's ligament?"

"I have no idea."

"I wouldn't worry about it, Dr. Morgan. No one knows what they are. I toss them out to make you humble. I'm through."

"A pleasure, Dr. Morgan," said Dr. Davis, rising. We shook hands. It was over at last, whether I passed or failed. They had been friendly but canny. Except for the chin, I had no idea whether they had approved of any of my answers. Dinner with Phil took my mind off the exam. Over the Châteauneuf-du-Pape he explained that he was married, but that it was an open marriage. His wife understood completely that he needed sexual freedom. With the coffee, he told me how rich he was. It seemed his family owned an oil well or two. Over brandy, he suggested we spend the night together. I declined, and it didn't bother him at all. He suggested we stroll around the pool after dinner, and I accepted.

"It's a lovely, warm, romantic night, Elizabeth," he murmured under a palm tree.

"It is nice."

"I like you."

"Thank you."

"May I ask something?"

"Certainly."

"You won't be shocked?"

"Probably not."

"I respect you for not wanting to sleep with me tonight, but why don't we go to my room to snort some cocaine?"

"What?"

"Yes, it's first-rate stuff. An actor friend of mine in New York sent it to me. A thousand dollars an ounce, but he can get it at a discount. What do you say?"

"No, thank you."

"I have some superb Turkish dope, if you're into that."

"No, thank you."

"You don't take drugs of any kind?"

"No, I don't."

"None?"

"No."

"Never?"

"I smoked part of a reefer ten years ago and I didn't like it."

"But it's wonderful, Liz. You must try cocaine. It's not what you think. It will make you feel good. It's marvelous. Very therapeutic for you. Take your mind right off your exam."

"A weak whiskey sour is plenty."

"Elizabeth, I'm shocked. I'm disappointed. Oh, well, I respect that." He took me home in a chauffered Cadillac limousine.

"We'll meet again," he said, escorting me to the door of the Hilton. "I know that. We're the same sign. Moon children. Good night."

I met Percy moping in the hotel lobby.

"The more I think about it, the more I know I failed, Elizabeth. Harvey is sure he did. He left town today. He didn't want to stay to find out. Did you hear about John? After the exam — and he did a superb job, John is smart as a tack — after it was over, the examiners called him back. They told him they didn't believe he had done the surgery. They said it was too good and that his chief must have done it. They failed him and sent him home, telling him to be honest about it next year when he's examined again. I know for a fact that every case John presented he did himself. His chief doesn't even do microscope work and the examiners know that. They're using John to settle old scores. Academic politicking makes me sick. Are you involved in a feud?"

"Sort of. Tewkesbury doesn't like me."

"You could have chosen better, kid. I wouldn't want him on my tail."

The next day I waited in Palm Beach. I visited the zoo, looked up Carol, a college friend, and worried. Saturday between nine and noon the pass-fail envelopes were passed out on the patio. I arrived at ten, one of the last to come.

"Here you are, Dr. Morgan," said Dr. Farmer with a smile as he handed me my envelope. He was a friend of Tewkesbury's and I walked out of his sight before I opened it. I didn't want to give him the satisfaction of watching my defeat. I was resigned and calm. If I failed, it would not be China, but the Middle East. Yemen needed doctors.

I opened the envelope. *"Dear Dr. Morgan. Congratulations . . ."* I had passed! I was now a Board Certified Plastic and Reconstructive Surgeon.

I stopped to read it again. I was the 2298th Board-certified plastic surgeon in the United States. I walked across the courtyard in a blissful daze, squinting in the sun. I wasn't wearing sunglasses and I almost walked right into Tewkesbury before I realized he was approaching, his eyes narrow, his lips compressed. I gave him a wide smile and wider berth. "I passed!" I said, waving the letter in the air. His expression didn't change, but I didn't care anymore. I was out of his power. I had reached the top of the mountain at last. I passed by him and went on to the hotel lobby. The most important thing was to call my parents, Jim, Rob and Janice, Clare, Jeff, and all the friends who had helped and encouraged me. Dr. Meade would be happy to hear, and so would Robert Fletcher. I could never have gotten so far without a lot of help, and a lot of luck.

"Liz, do you know where Harvey Courtauld practices in Florida?" It was Percy. "Say, did you pass?" he asked, embarrassed.

"Yes, thank God. Did you?"

"Yes! So did Phil, natch. Did you know they failed almost a third, not counting the group they sent home the first day? It makes you feel lucky. Harvey was so sure he failed that he went home, and now he won't get the written notice for weeks. I found out through the grapevine that the poor bastard passed after all, and I want to tell him before he commits hara-kiri. If the name of his hometown comes back to you, give me a yell." He dashed away.

We hadn't disappointed the surgeons who had trained us. We were now part of the brotherhood.

13
Saying
Good-bye

THE week after Boards, Robert Fletcher gave me a call.

"Elizabeth, I don't know exactly what your plans are but I thought I'd drop a word to the wise." He paused. Robert is diplomatic. "You haven't been around, but I've had my ear to the ground and I hear hoofbeats." I waited. Robert always knows what is going on behind the scenes. "This county is growing, right?"

"Right, Robert."

"But the hospital is the same size, right?"

"Right."

"And there's sooner or later going to be a limit to how many surgeons can operate in twelve operating rooms, even if they're open day and night, which they aren't. Right?"

"Right."

"And full hospital privileges are only given to men — or it may be a woman, if you follow me — who are Board-certified. Correct?"

"Correct."

"And you're Board-certified, now, right?"

"Right."

"I don't want you standing on the shore when the boat leaves, Elizabeth."

"I'll write to Meade today and ask for promotion to active, full privileges."

"Smart girl. So, how's your mother?"

"Much better, but it takes so long. I wish we had antibiotics for viruses, as well as for bacteria. Do you have your partner — or partners — yet?" Robert had been increasingly busy, and the last time we had spoken he had made arrangements for two friends to join his practice.

"I'm not going that route, Elizabeth. I'll tell you something. Private practice changes what you want out of life. I've noticed that it has for you, and I can tell you it has for me. I'm not so sure I want the biggest, busiest, richest practice, with a big group of my own. I don't want a lot of hassle. I want time for my patients and time for myself. You know, a lot of people out there hate doctors. I've had a dentist tell a patient to sue me. This was a guy whose face hit an oak tree at sixty on a motorcycle. I spent two months making him look like a human being again. His bite was good but he needed some crowns and the dentist told him I'd ruined his jaw and gave him the name of his lawyer. The patient came back to talk to me and there's no problem, but it's not worth killing yourself so a pack of jackals can go after you. And it happens in our field, too. I know plastic guys who routinely tell patients to sue other surgeons, and ENT guys who do the same. I want no part of it. I want to be left alone to be a good doctor, my way. I get the feeling you feel the same."

"Yes, I do."

"Well, nice talking to you, as always. Don't forget what I told you."

I didn't forget, and I got a pleasant reply from Ronald Meade. He said that if I was planning to resume full-time practice, he'd have my promotion to full privileges considered at the next committee meeting.

"Am I going back to private practice?" I asked Jim the next night.

"You can't be a stockbroker. You still add on your fingers, don't you?"

"I'll leave that to you. I've considered doing something different, especially if things don't work out with Jeff. There's a mission in Haiti. I would like to do some work in an underdeveloped country."

"And come back in a pinewood box."

"No, Haiti is safe. I've looked into it."

"I can see you doing it for a while." Jim studied me. "A month at most, but you never even liked Girl Scout camp. In fact, ten days in the woods at Occoquan and you refused ever to go again."

"So?"

"Haiti is like the backwoods. People invented electric lights and plumbing for a reason. They're nicer than old candles and latrines. Listen, if you go to Haiti, stop by Peru. There's a copper man down there I want to get some information from. Copper is the undiscovered metal. I've been trading copper for my own account."

"Successfully?"

"But of course. Templeton's approach is useful — he's the greatest financier in the world today — but I'm working out my own system. I want to start a commodities fund. What's going on with you and Jeff, anyhow?"

"I don't know."

"Yeah, well, I'll tell you." Jim paused and drew circles on his fingertip with a ball-point pen. "No, I won't tell you. It's your own funeral. I don't want to interfere."

"What exactly are you driving at?"

"You like the guy?"

"Yes."

"Well, there you are. That's the answer in a nutshell. He's not my type, but then I'm not the one who's dating him. Listen, I'll give you ten-to-one you get everyone all stirred up, buy a machete, pack mosquito netting, and then decide to stay in practice here. After all, you ought to. You're American. To hear you speak, we need more good doctors. Fat lot of good you'd be, ducking off into the jungle after all your training. It makes as much sense as my trading hogs from Outer Mongolia. What you need is a vacation."

"No, I'm going to Haiti."

I wrote to the Haiti mission, but only to suggest that I spend a month with them. I missed my patients, my practice, and my colleagues. My mother still needed care and I was enjoying my time off, but I was restless. My parents live in the industrial suburbs. I wanted to live in the city, where I could see my friends. Odette and Catherine seldom heard from me. I thought how much fun it would be to have a place of my own and meet a lot of new people. I was no longer sure how I felt about Jeff. He was much older than I was. His chief interest was money. I wasn't sure how much I would miss him if I stopped seeing him and I didn't like to think about it. But I was beginning to think I would have a happier life without him.

"I'll take you to the Washington Circle tonight," he said one evening. "To celebrate Boards." At dinner he was more attentive than usual, now that I was less anxious about him. He ordered champagne and lobster and the waiter looked at us with approval.

"You're looking lovely tonight, my dear. I love you in red." He watched me over the top of his wine glass, expectantly.

"Oh!" I said, suddenly remembering something. "Didn't you ask me to call you last Tuesday at eleven?"

"Yes," he smiled.

"I did, but that meeting must have gone on later than you expected."

His eyelids dropped slightly and he smiled again, but this time to himself. "How late did you call?"

"I think I tried again at one, before I went to bed."

Jeff paused before he spoke. "The meeting ended at ten. I went and had a drink with" — he looked at me slyly — "let's call it a friend."

"Fine."

"It's not someone you know," he went on. "We had a nice time." He seemed disappointed that I didn't ask him more.

"I'm glad you did. I had a nice time in Palm Beach. It was a lot of fun." I thought of Phil and the cocaine and I laughed.

"It's wonderful to see you again," said Jeff. "I missed you." It felt like an old routine. If I was nice, he was bored and rejecting. If I didn't care, suddenly he missed me.

That night I couldn't sleep. I sat up watching old movies with the sound turned off and thinking. I had realized some time ago that the Jeff I fell in love with did not exist and never had. The real Jeff was intelligent, successful, sophisticated, but also cold and conceited. What I had at first taken for gentleness and kindness was merely indifference. I now knew quite abruptly that it was over. I wondered also why I had fallen in love with him. Love at first sight does happen, but more often it turns out to be an almost juvenile infatuation. Maybe it was something I had to go through — a final growing-up, long delayed by my years of residency. Perhaps, too, I had been looking for an escape, someone to take me away from the problems of Boards, my practice, my mother's illness, my father's moods. I longed for the Jeff part of my life to be over.

"Tonight's the night, Mother," I said the next day.

"Good luck, dear. I don't know quite what to tell you."

"I think I know the way things will be, and it's long overdue."

Jeff took me to dinner at an underground jazz restaurant, and talked lightly about a clever deal he had made, about his office, about skiing, about politics. He usually did most of the talking, but tonight he did it all. I felt detached, as though he had nothing to do with me.

"Shall we go to the Fontainebleau?" he suggested. "We can dance."

We danced and had a drink at a secluded corner table. At midnight I realized that he was going to pretend everything was fine.

"Jeff," I said at last, "it's time we talked."

"Oh, Elizabeth." He set down his glass petulantly. "I thought I made it perfectly clear. I told you I want to be free. I don't want to be tied down. I want to be able to go and pick up a girl in a bar whenever I feel like it."

"Jeff, that's not true. You never said that." I wondered what I had ever seen in him. He was a plain, older man who had treated me callously. For the first time I was really angry. I had been an incredible fool.

I stood up. "Good-bye. I'm going home."

"No, don't go." He jumped to his feet. "I'll take you."

"I don't want you to take me."

"I'll take you. You're upset."

"Yes, I'm upset!" But I had come out with no money and I couldn't walk home in the dark. I put on my coat and walked away anyway while he hurried to pay the bill. He caught up with me in the lobby and came over with an apologetic smile.

"You look adorable," he said, putting his arm around me. I pulled away.

"Jeff, it's over." He looked at me in astonishment, and drove me home in silence.

"Good-bye," he said in a hurt tone. "I'm sorry you feel this way."

I walked in. "Mother, it's over."

"Are you all right?" She studied me anxiously.

"Absolutely. It's like getting over measles."

She looked at me closely. "You *are* over it. I can tell."

Two weeks later I stopped by the Metropolitan OR to say hello to the nurses. Elena, an attractive nurse from Cuba, was gesticulating vehemently. "I am going to go to this party with Greg in a fantastic dress. Real silk. Slit up the sides. My face will be beautiful. I know how to make myself up for the nighttime. Gold earrings. I will wear perfume to drive him wild. Everyone will look at Elena — and I will not speak to Greg, like poof!" She puffed away an imaginary Greg. "I will not look at him. I will make him weep."

"Elena, why?" asked a plump, silver-haired nurse, grandmother of four.

"I love him," said Elena.

"But treat him like this?" squeaked the grandmother.

"I don't want to see him again."

"Why not, if you love him?"

"You don't understand," said Elena, sitting down. "I love him very much — that I cannot help. But he is a jerk. A bastard. I am getting over it, but it takes time. I will see him some more. I am getting stronger, but getting over him completely is hard. It takes time, right, Dr. Morgan?"

"Absolutely right, but when it's over, you're glad."

"Fantastic. See, she understands. Everyone falls for a jerk sooner or later. Haven't you?" she demanded of the grand-mother.

"No, never."

"Never?"

"Well, yes, but it was so long ago."

14
Behind
the Scenes

"I'VE decided not to go to Haiti," I told Jim one day when I stopped by his office. He wanted to introduce me to Nelson Drew, the soybean czar.

"What happened?" asked Jim without turning away from his computer.

"I wrote four months ago and they haven't answered my letter."

"That's Haiti for you. I told you you wouldn't like it. It's backward. What are you going to do? Work for a living?" He frowned and fed the computer.

"Yes, I'm going back into full-time practice once I have a place to live and a new office. Mother's well enough. Boards are over. Jeff is over and Daddy has settled down."

"And in one year you'll quit because you're too busy and you don't have time to be a good doctor. I can see it now. Will she or won't she practice this year? They'll be betting on you in Vegas."

"No, I'm going to go back in practice on my terms. This time off was the best thing that could have happened. I'm through with trying to be a doctor the way everyone else is.

I have to be a good doctor my way. That means an hour for each new patient, half an hour for follow-up patients. I'm only going to take emergency call four days a month. I'm going to keep one day a week free to allow for emergencies and to keep up-to-date."

Jim put down his commodity printout and stared at me. "I don't believe it. Can you make a living?"

"Yes. I'll never be rich, but I'll be practicing medicine my way. The way I think it should be, not the way it is. Everyone knows most doctors are too busy for their patients — and it's up to the doctors to change."

"Frankly, it sounds a lot smarter than running away to Haiti. You could start a new craze."

I wasn't the only doctor to take such an approach. Dr. Eastman had cut back his practice several years ago. "I didn't want to be the busiest corpse in the cemetery," he told me at a Christmas party. "That's not for me. I was too busy to be good. That shocks a lot of people. Most people — in fact, most doctors — think 'busiest' means 'best,' but that is not the way medicine should be."

I had one problem before I started my new practice. I had to find a place to live. My mother was well enough now not to need me at home. I had wanted to leave the suburbs ever since I returned to look after her. I love the excitement of the city life and I had moved so often since medical school that I wanted to buy a place that was mine — without landlords, or rising rents, or noisy neighbors overhead. Jimmy helped me work out how much I could afford.

"With the money you've saved from your practice and with your good credit rating as a doctor, you ought to try for a nice place," he advised me. "A really nice place."

'How much will I have to spend?"

"A lot of money, more than you can comfortably afford,

but Templeton says buying your own home is the best hedge against inflation. You'll pay a lot, but for a nice place, it's worth it."

In Washington, any home can be used by a doctor as an office as well as a living quarters. I wanted to find a house that could double as an office, so that I could see patients in Washington as well as in a Virginia office. With a Washington office I could apply again to the teaching hospitals in the city, and try once more to do some teaching.

Newspaper ads are vague about real estate prices. The first really nice house that was also suitable as an office was brand-new, with an elevator, four bedrooms, a butler's pantry, a maid's suite — and a staggering price tag.

"I don't need such a big house," I told the agent, a depressed man in baggy gray trousers. "I'd prefer an older house on a quiet street at half the price."

"Let me show you Q Street," he mumbled and took me off in his car to an old Victorian brick house covered with ivy, located on a busy downtown avenue. "It's a nice area," he said, opening the door as the traffic rushed by us. "Embassies on either side of you. A nice property." We walked in and stepped around a huge support pillar that filled most of the foyer. Gray paint was peeling from the walls of the large, dark living room. "It would be fun to fix up. Go upstairs. Be careful. The first two steps have rotted away."

On the second floor, the lights didn't work, the toilet was broken, the bathtub was cracked, and the ceiling of the front bedroom had caved it. Plaster and rotten boards were strewn on the floor.

"I need a place to live," I explained for the third time, "and to use as an office."

"You can live in this," he said, looking at me in surprise. "There's a lot of room. It's a nice house. Needs a bit of work."

"What about the third floor?"

He hesitated. "The owner asked me not to show the third floor. He says it's not in good condition."

"How much is he asking for the house?"

I gasped when he told me. He looked surprised. "It's a reasonable price. You can't beat the location. You've got embassies on either side."

"I don't need embassies. I want a house to live in."

"Nobody does it that way now, Dr. Morgan. It's a valuable property, I assure you." I shook my head dubiously. "Let me show you Eighteenth Street," he offered. "You'll like Eighteenth Street."

Eighteenth Street was a huge corner house of white brick, with six bay windows and an impressive wrought-iron gate. The first floor had been partially renovated. There was a modern yellow kitchen in the midst of a combination living room–dining room that was freshly painted and paneled in oak. I opened the hall closet. A rat scurried away amid a cascade of falling plaster. The remaining seven rooms — three bathrooms and two kitchens — were "original."

"But I can't live in this," I protested, looking out the top-floor bay window. A derelict was lounging peacefully against the wrought-iron gate, an empty bottle in his hand. "I can't use it as an office. It's not a safe area."

"Dr. Morgan, in five years this will be choice. It's coming up fast and you can renovate the top two floors, rent them out for extra income, do the same to the basement, and you're sitting pretty. It's a gold mine."

"But I don't want to run a boardinghouse."

"It's a bargain," he lowered his voice to a whisper. "They're asking a lot, but they will come down. Substantially."

"Renovation alone would cost a fortune."

"Only if you did a good job. Renovate cheaply and resell. Everyone's doing it, Dr. Morgan."

"But I need a place to live."

273

"I have nothing more to show you."

He gave up. A friend of mine in real estate found a nice house for me, a bit too big but affordable. At the last minute the owner decided not to move after all, and I gave up. All Washington had to offer was decayed grandeur.

Janice and Rob had recently moved to a restored Victorian house in a fringe neighborhood. The police made weekly raids on the brothels to pick up wanted criminals a block away. I couldn't live in a fringe neighborhood. I didn't want my patients mugged. The next Saturday I wandered forlornly around the fashionable West End, looking at house for sale for extraordinary sums and wondering whether I should write to Haiti again. I strayed down a side street I hadn't noticed before. A small brick house had an OPEN FOR SALE sign, and I drifted in. The real estate agent looked up from her knitting. She was a middle-aged blond lady with a foreign accent.

"It's little. Too small, really. Look around." She went back to counting stitches. The house was in good repair and suitable for an office. Unlike almost all other houses I had seen, the first floor was not one open room but two separate rooms off a hall. They would easily be a small waiting room and a consulting-and-examining room. There were two rooms upstairs. One would be a sitting room, one my bedroom. The setup was what I needed, and I thought joyfully of how easy it would be to clean. The lavish homes I had seen so many of would need a full-time maid to keep them in order. The bathroom fixtures here were ugly, but they worked. There was a small patio, huge windows to let in light, and a tiny garden. The place needed some improvements but it was livable. I walked back to the agent in the living room.

"It is too small," she said, "and it needs fixing up to look nice."

"It's a nice neighborhood," I said.

"But everyone wants a big house." She pointed to the street. All the other houses except for four like this one were large Victorian renovations.

"How much are they asking?"

"For this? They dropped the price last week. I don't remember, but it is very reasonable."

"I think I might like to buy it."

She stopped knitting and looked at me closely. "You are going to renovate for investment?"

"No. I am going to live in this house."

"That is unusual, but yes, it can be arranged."

I moved in a month later, and I called Odette to give her my new address.

"Elizabeth. Fantastic! I have news for you, too. I am opening my own office. I am tired of working for other people. I am going to be an internist my way. I have an office — René is going to share his with me. His practice is doing well, thank heavens, or we would starve."

"You won't starve," I assured her. "In six months, you'll be too busy. There aren't enough good doctors. Wait and see. In six months you'll have to get a partner or cut back."

"I don't believe you, but it is nice to pretend. It is good to know you are coming back. I will have company. There aren't many of us women in solo practice."

It was a lucky time for me. Besides the small office in my new house, I would also need a new full-time office, since my Twickenham lease had finally expired. I could start afresh in a new place. I couldn't find an office I liked at first. Then Catherine Bennett, the lawyer who had helped me with my first office lease, called to say hello one day.

"If you know anyone who wants a great townhouse office, our firm built a new office plaza just off the expressway."

She showed me a suite that afternoon. Catherine had designed the floor layout herself, and she might have done it with me in mind. There were two huge storage rooms for files and supplies, and a conference-workroom on the ground floor. The first floor had a sunny front room that could be the waiting room, and other rooms — two on the first, three on the second — that could serve as two examining rooms, a children's waiting room, a consulting room, and an operating room for minor surgery. Above all, the rooms were light, there was plenty of parking, and the plumbing was perfect. A doctor's office needs more sinks and bathrooms than a regular office. There were two bathrooms, and sinks, originally intended as wet bars, just off the examining rooms. The suite was a little too big, but then my home was a little too small, so it worked out right. The rent was reasonable.

"Catherine, I'll take it."

"You'll take it?"

"I'll take it."

"You make snap decisions. Just like me," she said and took me back to her office to open a bottle of champagne in celebration. I couldn't wait to be back in full-time practice. Clare had me moved in at the end of ten days.

One of my new patients was actually an old one — Mrs. Mason. She was an attractive woman — a computer analyst and a mother of six — who had fallen at work over a year before and had broken her shoulder, damaging the nerves. I had helped to reconstruct them and had not seen her since her recovery. She now came to see me late one afternoon after finishing work. Clare was on vacation and the temporary secretary left as soon as Mrs. Mason arrived. I was shocked by the difference in her. Mrs. Mason was a young woman, but her face now was haggard and drawn. She sat down in a chair, crossed her legs, and looked at me with determination.

"Dr. Morgan, my face has changed. I look old. I would like to arrange a face-lift." She sat expressionless, listening while I explained the surgery, my fee, and the risks involved.

"Good. I would like one," she said promptly when I was finished — but I knew something was wrong. She looked desperate. A face-lift would not help despair.

I asked whether there were any medical problems. She had none. Her husband was healthy too, and they had been happily married for years. She had recently been promoted and was working harder, but that was just for something to do. "I like working, but we don't need the money," she explained.

"Have you lost weight?" I asked. She looked drained.

"Ten pounds."

"When?"

"Over the past few months."

"Are you on a diet?" She certainly had been thin enough before.

"No."

"Why then?"

"My oldest son, Tommy, died in a car accident last summer," she said simply.

"Oh, no!"

"He was thrown out of the car. He died instantly. I lost my taste for food after that," she went on. "I put food in my mouth and I know I should eat, but I can't swallow sometimes."

"Tommy was young, wasn't he?"

"Yes. He hadn't even turned twenty — and I miss him so, Dr. Morgan. I love all my children, but for some reason I was closest to Tommy. Maybe because he did so well in school and he was my oldest. I was proud of him. He was so good. He was such a wonderful boy." She abruptly stopped talking so that she wouldn't cry.

"Can you sleep?"

"No; maybe an hour or so — I lie there thinking of how he looked after the accident. That's why I went back to work.

I cry when I'm around the house, thinking of Tommy. Somehow I feel it was my fault."

"Have you thought about suicide?"

"No. I wouldn't think that way, but I often wish I wouldn't wake up in the morning. Life is too hard."

"You don't need a face-lift, Mrs. Mason. You need someone to talk to, to help you over this."

"I look so sad, Dr. Morgan. Won't a face-lift fix that?"

"No, but smiling will, and you won't smile till you're over Tommy's death."

She smiled briefly and for a moment looked young again. "I was fine till his birthday, but he loved a party. Getting the family together meant so much to him. It took all the heart out of me."

I asked her about her pastor. She felt she couldn't talk to him. She agreed to talk to a psychologist. She wouldn't see a psychiatrist.

"You're depressed, Mrs. Mason, and I agree you need help — but not with a surgeon's knife." She smiled again. I gave her the name of a psychologist. "When you're better, maybe in three months or in six, when things are going well and you're happy, if you still want a face-lift, come and see me again."

We had talked for over an hour. She seemed a bit more hopeful when she left. Although I had done my best to help her, I couldn't control fate: The psychologist I suggested was taken to hospital that very day with a broken leg. Then, two days after she saw me, Mrs. Mason crashed her car, breaking four ribs, an arm, and the fingers of her previously injured hand.

We called to see how she was. "I'm fine. Tell Dr. Morgan I don't need that psychologist," she told Clare with a laugh. "You won't believe it, but I'm going back to work already and I'm concentrating on healing these bones. I feel a lot better."

A psychiatrist explained to me that Mrs. Mason had expiated her guilt over her son's death by trying subconsciously to kill herself too. Whether or not this was so, I had at least spared her a face-lift she didn't need. In my busier days I might well have done the surgery because I didn't have time to talk to her or to consider what was best. My practice was back on the right track.

Being back in practice had its drawbacks, too. Meetings. I have never been good about going to meetings. There are surgery department meetings, plastic-surgery-section meetings, complications conferences, grand rounds, tumor conferences. They all take time. Surgeons must attend certain meetings, and the discipline is good, but they take up most of a Saturday morning.

My first conference back in practice was a monthly surgery meeting at Mattaponai to discuss deaths and complications. The meeting was held in an orange-carpeted conference room with a table at one end and metal chairs arranged in rows to face the table. When I arrived, ten minutes late, about twenty surgeons were already there, but the meeting had not begun.

An ENT surgeon was holding forth loudly by a coffee urn set up at the back of the room. "The only way to beat inflation is to spend money — Elizabeth, welcome back! — and that's why I have a sailboat. It's doubled in price, and it's great for taxes, too. I write the whole thing off."

There was a loud rapping on the conference table. "The chairman of the department is away and he asked me to run this meeting," said Dr. Featherwell, a gray-faced elderly surgeon smoking a cigarette. "He's at a seminar on how to manage a surgical department."

"He needs it!" called a voice from the back of the room.

Dr. Featherwell ignored the wisecrack and gave me a friendly nod, peering over the top of his glasses. "Let's get started." We all sat down.

"About those dictations," said Dr. Featherwell. "Now the JCAH [Joint Commission on Accreditation of Hospitals] says you guys are not dictating discharge summaries on your patients. If you want this hospital accredited, do them."

An orthopedic surgeon let his breath out in a wheeze. "It's ridiculous for us quarter-of-a-million-dollar boys to waste our time speaking into a goddamned tape recorder about a patient whose been in hospital one night for a broken bone."

"Don't give me a hard time, Matt," Dr. Featherwell said. "Dictate a two-sentence summary and sign it when you get around to it. If you want the hospital accredited, do the paperwork."

"We pay the JCAH thousands of dollars to send their investigators here to tell us to do paperwork. Ridiculous!" said the orthopedic surgeon.

"Everyone will dictate summaries," said Dr. Featherwell, checking it off the list. "Paperwork is part of our life. Adam, you're next."

Adam was Dr. Eastman, the general surgeon who had operated on Mrs. Spencer-Neville and who had cut back his own practice because "busiest is not the best." He stood up, jingling the change in his pockets.

"We have a problem with Cromarty Medical School. They send us residents to work here. We pay Cromarty well over a million dollars for the privilege. That's over forty thousand dollars each. Half of the money we pay goes into the retirement fund for surgical professors."

There was a shocked silence, then various obscene protests. The orthopedic surgeon raised his hand. "The medical schools are bankrupt. It's a slave trade in surgical residents if we're paying forty thousand dollars for their bodies. Tell the medical schools to screw themselves."

Dr. Eastman shook his head. "We need some sort of assistants to help look after our patients nights and weekends, and to hold retractors during surgery so we can operate. I'm suggesting we pay for the Cromarty residents this year, but start our own program to train surgical assistants to do the mindless work anyone can do. Then we tell the medical school we will teach their residents, but we don't pay to do it."

There was a murmur of approval and the suggestion was passed. Next, a cocky young man with slicked-back hair and a blue suit stood up to tell us that the cramped hospital medical library would not be expanded for two years.

"We need a bigger library now!" exploded Dr. Eastman.

"Put the library in the administrative offices," called the ENT surgeon "and put administrators in the library."

"Impossible!" snapped the administrator, alarmed. "It won't fit as subunits."

Dr. Featherwell thanked him and the administrator left. "Let's move on to the deaths." Dr. Featherwell passed out printed summaries. "We have three deaths, and the surgeons involved are here."

The first patient was an old man who died from cancer of the prostate. There were no errors in management. The death was inevitable. The second death was a child born severely deformed. The surgeon had done an emergency tracheostomy in a desperate but unsuccessful attempt to keep the infant alive. Again, there was little discussion. The child's death, though sad, had been inevitable. Autopsy showed the lungs had not developed.

I looked down at the summary of the third and last death. The dead man had been in a car accident and had suffered a laceration of the aorta, the main artery out of the heart. Aorta lacerations are a rare injury, usually the result of high-speed accidents. If the aorta is torn, death is inevitable without emergency surgery, preferably performed by a heart surgeon, who can put the patient on the heart pump. Dr. Cushoff, a well-known heart surgeon, had come to Mattaponai just the year before.

The man's surgeon the night of the accident had been Dr. Otler, a chest surgeon who usually treated lung cancers, chest abscesses, and rib tumors but did no heart surgery. Dr. Otler read aloud the summary about his patient, a thirty-one-year-old man involved in a head-on collision with a truck. On arrival in the emergency room he was in shock. He received six units of blood and was taken to the operating room. The aorta had been torn off the subclavian artery. At first clamps were not placed for fear of blocking blood to the brain. The laceration was repaired, but massive bleeding continued. Clamps were then placed on the aorta, but the reinforcing sutures tore out. Bleeding was uncontrollable. The chest was closed. The patient died in the recovery room.

The accident victim probably was a good as dead before he arrived in the hospital, but a heart surgeon might possibly have saved him. Even if he had lived, he might have been permanently brain-damaged, but miraculous "saves" do occur. Everyone present knew it.

While Dr. Otler read out loud, I saw in my peripheral vision a pair of legs clad in green scrub-suit trousers impatiently cross, uncross, and recross themselves. It was Dr. Cushoff, the heart surgeon, a fiery, impatient man. He stared gloomily at his feet. He was never happy unless he was operating on a heart. And his surgery had superb results — to the embarrassment of the medical-school heart surgery professors, who liked to think they were better than private surgeons. When Dr. Otler finished reading, Dr. Cushoff glared at him.

"Comments?" said Dr. Featherwell nervously. "A very

difficult case. Tragic. These crazy drivers. What were your feelings at the time, Dr. Otler?"

"I made a desperate attempt to save him, but the man was dead when I operated. The chest was a sea of blood and I couldn't see a thing. It was a tragedy."

"Comments?" said Dr. Featherwell again, looking around the room at everyone but Dr. Cushoff.

"Yes. If no one else is going to speak up, I have a comment," said Dr. Cushoff in an angry voice. "This man ought to be alive today. He should have been put on the pump, the aorta repaired, and in the intensive care unit. Like that." He snapped his fingers disdainfully. "It's not the kind of case you meditate on for an afternoon."

"With all due respect," said Dr. Otler, flaring up. "You weren't there. I had this man in the OR as fast as I could. It takes your pump team half an hour to get here. He was dead long before then."

Dr. Cushoff sank back in his chair, his arms folded on his chest. "I looked at the record. A surgeon arrived an hour after the man came to the emergency room. After two hours, a chest surgeon arrived. After four, he was on the operating-room table" — Dr. Cushoff raised his head, his voice becoming passionate — "and after five, he was pronounced dead. I was in the hospital. I wasn't even notified. My pump team is ten minutes away. I know, because they're my team. This is what happens when you sit around with a torn aorta. I understand that for two hours there was a discussion as to whether he should have an angiogram." He uncrossed his legs and stood up. "Angiogram! You can do an angiogram on the operating table with the chest open and the patient on the heart pump if you need an angiogram. I do it all the time. This man should not be dead, and if people in this room don't admit that, it's going to happen again."

283

"Now look," said Dr. Otler in a reasonable voice. "The mortality rate with this injury is over eighty percent."

Dr. Cushoff stalked out of the room with a look of frozen disgust.

There was an embarrassed silence.

"It's easy to criticize in retrospect," said Dr. Feartherwell. "We all do our best. Dr. Otler tried to save a life as best he could." He cleared his throat. "Dr. Cushoff is a dogmatic man — but having a heart surgeon around, we should use him. There's no place for professional jealousy at such a time."

There was a snort from the back of the conference room. "You try getting Cushoff out of bed in the middle of the night."

Dr. Featherwell got up with a smile. "We all do our best. These conferences remind us that we all make mistakes. Even Cushoff." The conference was over.

"Don't go yet, Elizabeth." Ronald Meade touched my arm. "We've got a plastic-surgery meeting next." I joined him and the other plastic surgeons at the conference table.

"The trouble," said Ronald, "is oral surgeons. Some of these dentists are telling patients to sue us. Now they want us to let them take care of all face and jaw fractures in the emergency room."

Robert Fletcher nodded gloomily and mentioned his litigious patient, the motorcyclist who had crashed and smashed up his face. The patient's dentist had advised him to sue Robert, who had done a tedious but successful reconstruction that had changed the bite a fraction.

Dr. Taylor, a well-established plastic surgeon, spread out his hands in a deprecating manner. "There are too many oral surgeons here since the oral-surgery residency began at Friendship Affiliated. One told a patient of mine I had ruined her mouth, after I fixed her broken jaw with a good result. I sent her to four other oral surgeons and they all agreed she was fine.

The younger boys want business though, and some of them fight to get it."

"I wouldn't mind," I said, "if oral surgeons fixed broken jaws better than I can and if they were available, but they don't do the emergency work we do. They think being available means Tuesday through Friday from ten to four in the office. Once, at another hospital, the oral surgeon on emergency call couldn't be found for twenty-four hours. Another time I spent eight days trying to get an oral surgeon to see a patient before surgery. The fourth one I called agreed to come to the operation but didn't show up till two days after the surgery. I know that's unusual, and I know there are doctors who are hard to track down, but I think they shouldn't have emergency call unless they're available for emergency work the way we are. We take emergency call seriously and half the time we come in to reassure patients as much as to treat them. I don't think a busy oral surgeon is prepared to do that."

"So we agree we should do the facial fractures even if we have to give up sleep," said Dr. Meade. "We can always call in an oral surgeon if we want. Everyone should realize that medicine is changing. Chiropractors want to be GP's, podiatrists want to do orthopedic surgery, oral surgeons want to be plastic surgeons, and in California osteopaths are given M.D. degrees, all because medical care is too expensive."

"Let's call this quits, Ronald," said Dr. Ohlsen. "We all know the problem. We don't know the solution. The lines are blurred. No one knows who anyone is."

We were a small group and we all tried to do our best. Doctors in private practice are forced to think too much about money. Few are really greedy. Perhaps half of them think of money first and patients second, but for the most part they still do their best. There are no easy answers.

Solo Practice

I loved my new practice. I took emergency call only four days a month. These four busy emergency days were enough to keep me up-to-date on trauma without taking excessive time from scheduled patients — and without costing me a whole lot of sleep. Clare scheduled my office patients far apart. Because the waiting room was never filled to overflowing with worried patients lined up to see me, I was never forced to cut short a patient's questions or hurry my explanations or surgical planning.

My new system paid off, almost immediately, when Dr. Eastman referred a young patient to me — Richard Vanveer, a computer salesman in his thirties who had been born with a cleft lip and a cleft palate, both of which had been repaired when he was an infant. His palate had healed perfectly, and his speech was fine, but his nose and lip were still abnormal. He had had over ten separate operations as a child, and had been told by his plastic surgeon to return when he was sixteen for further surgery on his lip and nose. All children born with cleft lips have misshapen noses to some degree, and Richard was no exception, but the unpleasant memories of his childhood operations had prevented him from returning for further surgery at sixteen. He didn't want any more surgery as a teenager. In the years since then, his plastic surgeon had retired. Suddenly, at thirty, Richard decided to have his long-delayed surgery and found his way to me through Dr. Eastman.

He was a tall, good-looking young man, but when I ushered him into the consulting room, he had a generally discouraged air. His shoulders drooped. He didn't have the confidence I expected from a successful salesman. I examined his nose and lip and we sat down to talk about surgery. He was by no means seriously deformed, but his right nostril was higher than the left and was unduly wide. His nose had the characteristic curve on the top and drooping tip of a cleft-lip patient. At rest, his lip was virtually normal, but when he smiled there was a noticeable notch on one side of the lip. I explained the nose surgery he needed. I needed to operate on the bones and cartilage, to shift tissue in his nose and thus bring the nostril into a better place, and to shift lip tissue to improve the lip notch. I explained the possible complications —infection and bleeding, and poor wound healing. He listened attentively.

"Fine," he said when I finished. "I'd like to have the surgery as soon as I can."

In the "old days" my next step would have been to ask Clare to book the operation, and then to move on hastily to the next patient. In my new practice I had set aside time, for a purpose. There must be a reason why Richard Vanveer decided to have the surgery he had postponed for fifteen years. I asked him why.

"I never got around to it before," he said. "I should have."

"What happened to make you get around to it now?" I persisted. "I agree surgery can help you, I agree the surgery should be done; but tell me more about yourself. What about your job?"

He hesitated before he answered. "Actually, I quit about four months ago. I didn't get fired. My boss wanted me to stay but I felt self-conscious and depressed about the way I looked. I think the surgery will turn my life around."

"It won't," I said firmly. "You are handsome to begin with. The surgery will improve things, but it won't radically alter your life. Where are you living?"

"I had my own place, but when I got to feeling depressed and quit my job my brother had me come to stay with him. The fact is, Dr. Morgan, I get so depressed I can't even go out of the house. I want to get a job. I'm good at my work, but I get ready to go to a job interview and I can't get past the front door."

"Have you tried to kill yourself?" I asked matter-of-factly.

"Last week I took a sleeping-pill overdose. I know it was silly, but I feel so down about myself. I'm pinning my hopes on this operation to help me out."

"Do you have a psychiatrist or a psychologist helping you? I know you're not crazy, Mr. Vanveer, but you're depressed. Everyone has down times, but when you're down far enough you need help getting up again. What I'm afraid of is that you have the surgery, everything goes well from my point of view, but you don't look exactly the way you imagined, or maybe you get an infection that slows down your healing. If you're depressed, that could be enough to tip the scales and make you kill yourself. If you kill yourself, even if the operation was a surgical success, have I helped you?"

He smiled ruefully. "No. I see your point — I expect too much from the surgery. But I do want it done."

We worked out a plan. I agreed to book the surgery two months ahead, and he, in turn, agreed to see a psychologist for evaluation and counseling in those two months. He would come back to see me before surgery. If he was still depressed, we would postpone the operation. Discussing his depression took twice as long as talking about the surgery, because it was inherently more complicated and more difficult to talk about, but the time was well spent.

Richard came in six weeks later, a changed man. He was anxious to get the surgery behind him, because he was going to work. He talked about his fiancée, his plans for the summer, softball, movies he had seen. The psychologist had not needed to do much more than talk with him; they had several sessions, during which Richard focused on himself, his worries, and his long-range plans. With a little help, and a lot of his own inner resilience, Richard had pulled himself out of what had threatened to be a severe depression.

I went ahead with surgery. Richard had a happy time in the hospital. Recalling his past operations, he had expected a lot of pain. He had remarkably little and never once complained. He was a stalwart young man. He teased the nurses. They loved him, and he stopped by the hospital after his release to bring them a box of candy. That same day he came to my office so I could take the dressing off his nose. It was still swollen, of course, but that didn't bother him. Two weeks later I came in early to the office and found Richard waiting to see me.

I almost didn't recognize him. The swelling was gone and his nose looked excellent, but most of all it was his manner that had changed. His head was high, his shoulders were straight, and he was explaining to Clare with ebullient charm the intricate workings of a new computer. He was eager to get back to work.

"The surgery worked a lot better than I expected," he told me. "I knew all along it couldn't make a huge difference, but I'm really pleased."

"I'm glad we waited," I said. "The surgery didn't cure the depression. You did it yourself."

"I know," he admitted. "When I was down, I don't think anything would have pleased me. I know this scar on my nostril doesn't show too much and that it will fade, but if I'd had to wake up in the morning with that when I was depressed, it would have made life unbearable."

That was the beauty of my new practice. I could really help my patients. A year ago I could have automatically done the identical operation, overlooking Richard's depression and doing him immeasurable harm. It was wonderful having time for my patients, and it made me a much better doctor. In the old days I was often so busy I didn't have time to do complete physical exams on my patients. I made sure surgery would be safe for them, but I didn't have time to look for hidden diseases or to solve difficult diagnostic problems, which is the most challenging part of medicine.

Now that I could devote more time to my patients, a number of women came to see me because their own doctors were too busy or had ignored their symptoms, dismissing the complaints of "one more neurotic female." One such patient was Mrs. Lloyd-Jones, an attractive, elegantly dressed widow who came to see me because of pain in her hands. She had increasing difficulty doing such simple chores as ironing, driving her car, and typing at work. The symptoms — weakness in her grip, numbness and tingling in her fingers — were diagnostic of the carpal tunnel syndrome, in which a nerve in the wrist malfunctions because of pressure from a nearby ligament. It can be easy to treat. A nerve test confirms the diagnosis and surgery is done to cut the ligament and take pressure off the nerve. I explained this to Mrs. Lloyd-Jones. She smiled at me kindly, but looked disappointed.

"I know that, doctor. I saw another hand surgeon for this, and he told me the same thing. Unfortunately, the nerve test was normal. He wanted to wait three months and repeat the test. Apparently the symptoms sometimes begin before it shows up on the nerve test. Is that right?"

"Yes. The other hand surgeon probably ordered a neck X ray to be sure the nerve malfunction wasn't caused by a bone pressing on it high up in the neck."

"Oh yes, I had that too, and it was normal." She looked down at her hands. "That doctor thought I was neurotic and imagining things. You may think I am too. I'm not, but when everyone tells you you are, you begin to wonder. My family doctor told me I needed a vacation. I don't need a vacation. I'm not depressed. I need my hands to work right. I support myself. Maybe it'll get better by itself. Sorry to have wasted your time."

I knew she wasn't imagining her symptoms and I knew also I had missed something important, but I wasn't sure exactly what. The "medical history" — what a patient can tell you about symptoms and past illnesses — is the most important part of diagnosis. Mrs. Lloyd-Jones and I sat down like two detectives on a criminal's trail as I tried to track down the disease afflicting her.

"How long have you had your symptoms. The very first twinge you remember?"

"Maybe several years ago, but it wasn't a problem then."

"What else has happened to you — the things you notice but don't think are important."

She frowned. "I've been tired, naturally, with so much to look after since my husband's death. I tend to gain weight much more easily now than I used to. I guess I've put on ten pounds over the past two years, which won't come off. I don't think I'm eating more than I used to, but your metabolism changes after your teens. You slow down a bit."

I doodled on my memo pad, thinking. She must have thought I looked unbelieving. "Maybe I am imagining my hand symptoms. I can live with them, at any rate." Low thyroid can produce mild carpal tunnel symptoms, because the thyroid-deficient body tends to collect protein-rich fluid that may be deposited under the ligament and put pressure on the nerve. The symptoms can be discouragingly vague — fatigue, and a tendency to gain weight: typical "neurotic female" complaints.

"Have your outer eyebrows thinned?" I asked abruptly. She sat up in surprise.

"Yes. Is that important?"

"Your hands look puffy?"

"Yes. They always swelled with my period, but now they're a tiny bit puffy all the time."

"You're tired all day? Not only at the end of the day?"

"Yes. I can push myself, but it feels like an effort."

She had the classic, textbook symptoms of low thyroid. She didn't have the slow reflexes or enlarged thyroid neck gland that can occur, but her "history" made the diagnosis easy. Given the symptoms, a medical student could diagnose Mrs. Lloyd-Jones correctly. It was a matter of asking the right questions. Her hand pain had nothing to do with her hands, but rather with a gland in her neck. Her problem was not surgical.

I referred her to an internist. His blood tests showed Mrs. Lloyd-Jones's thyroid levels were a third of normal. She didn't need surgery, because all her symptoms improved after a few weeks of thyroid pills and they disappeared completely after eight weeks of treatment. There's a famous surgical maxim — "A chance to cut is a chance to cure." A chance for me to think was what cured Mrs. Lloyd-Jones. She was one of many examples. The human body is infinitely complex. Every person has something abnormal. The challenge of medicine is detecting the abnormal. I wouldn't be a good doctor and I would be wasting seven years of training if all I did was cut.

Even the simplest plastic-surgery problems arise in patients with far more serious undetected diseases. A middle-aged man, Mr. Gordon, came to see me two years after a terrible accident in which his neck and nose had been broken. I had originally fixed his broken nose and his neurosurgeon had treated his neck. Miraculously, there had been no spinal-cord injury. Now, two years later, the cartilage inside his nose had curved and Mr. Gordon was having trouble breathing. This is not uncommon after a badly broken nose. I would be able to reoperate on his nose under local anesthesia and send him home the same day. Apart from the accident, Mr. Gordon had never been sick in his life, although he was a smoker. I examined his heart and lungs before booking surgery. With the slower pace of my new practice I could afford to be thorough. When I checked his abdomen I discovered an abnormality lurking there: an aneurysm, in this case an enlargement of the aorta — the two-inch-wide main artery — from atherosclerosis. Mr. Gordon had had no idea there was a problem. I did the minor nose surgery and sent him to a vascular surgeon the same week. He could breathe with ease now, after my operation — and my finding the aneurysm may have saved his life. A dilated aorta has a tendency to rupture after a few years, requiring emergency surgery. Mortality from this emergency surgery can be as high as thirty percent. Early diagnosis, on the other hand, allows elective aneurysm correction, which has a low mortality rate.

I was a good doctor now. It took time, though it was inefficient from a business viewpoint. Diagnosing Mr. Gordon's aneurysm and Mrs. Lloyd-Jones' hypothyroidism was not cost-effective. I didn't get paid any more for doing it. But I didn't care. I went to medical school to be the best kind of doctor I could be. The business aspects would have to take second place.

Odette called me one evening. "Elizabeth, I can't meet you tomorrow for dinner. I'm too busy tomorrow. I'm so popular, ever since the flu epidemic. People come to me because of the flu. I say fine, though they will not come again — but they come back! Suddenly I have no time. It's only a few months, and I'm a success!"

"Odette, you're a first-rate doctor. Didn't I tell you not to worry?"

"Yes, yes, and why should I believe you? You're a friend — you would say that anyhow. But soon I will have problems. I may have to get a partner."

"Take a vacation first."

She laughed. "Take a vacation? I thought I would never be able to take a vacation again, but you're right. In six months I could afford one. I think I have arrived!"

We had both arrived. It had been a long and rocky road, but it was worth it all.